MW00812458

COURT REPORTING

Grammar and Punctuation

2d Edition

Diane Castilaw B.A.,M.A.

SOUTH-WESTERN PUBLISHING CO.

Acquisitions Editor: Betty Schechter
Development Editor: Inell Bolls-Gaither
Production Editor: Susan Freeman
Designer: Jim DeSollar
Production Artist: Sophia Renieris

Library of Congress Cataloging-in-Publication Data

Castilaw-Palliser, Diane
Court reporting: grammar and punctuation/Diane Castilaw. — 2nd ed.
p. cm.
Includes index.
ISBN 0-538-70577-9
1. English language—Grammar—1950- 2. Law reporting—United States. 3. Law—United States—Language. I. Title.
PE1116.L3C37 1993
428'.008834—dc20 91-41344
CIP

3 4 5 6 7 8 D 99 98

Printed in the United States of America

PREFACE

A court reporter's reputation as a skilled professional depends entirely on the accuracy and readability of the end product: the transcript. Obviously, it can be neither accurate nor readable without effective punctuation, which depends in large part on applying grammatical principles. Without these two elements, a transcript would be confusing and a mass of meaningless words, without structure, shape, or value.

Court Reporting Grammar & Punctuation, second edition, provides the basics necessary to fulfill the court reporter's goal of an excellent transcript. Grammatical rules are presented in a clear, uncomplicated format, as are the guidelines for correct punctuation. This information is supported by examples, tests, and situations that are specific to the court reporter's job. All units have been expanded and new examples added; in addition, new exams have been presented and existing tests expanded.

Objectives

This text seeks to serve as a guide to both students of court reporting and professionals who are already on the job. Recording accurately the exchanges of attorneys and witnesses is an impressive achievement in itself; however, fine-tuning the recorded words is perhaps an equally challenging aspect of the job. Many questions arise when attempts are made to impose grammatical order on an oral dictation; this book can serve as a guide to finding the answers to those inevitable questions. The lengthy debates over hyphenation, commas, rambling run-ons, and other such time-consuming issues can be resolved with a quick reference to this book. A student or reporter who masters the principles of both grammar and punctuation, and then goes on to become a skilled proofreader, will have a distinct advantage. As much pertinent information as possible has been compacted between the covers of this book with this goal in mind.

Approach

The approach is purely practical, excluding information that is not useful to the working reporter, either directly or in terms of foundational knowledge. Much of the material in traditional grammar texts, such as those used in college English courses, is not included because some of the more esoteric aspects of grammar would not be useful to a court reporter (although it might not hurt). Whereas the practicality of certain sections that have been included may not be immediately apparent, the reader can be assured that such sections were included always with the end result in mind of producing good, clear transcripts.

Organization

The text is divided into 12 units, with the sections numbered sequentially for quick and easy reference. Unit 1 is a glossary of grammatical and other specialized terms. This unit was placed at the beginning of the book, rather than in its usual location at the back of the book, to stress the importance of knowing these terms. It also makes defining terms as they occur unnecessary.

Unit 2 covers all of the grammatical principles that a court reporter needs to know. This unit is particularly important because no one could go on to Unit 3, covering punctuation, and understand it without knowing grammar first. Unit 2 is the foundation upon which Unit 3 rests and builds. The two units are interdependent. First impulse might lead the reader to want to skip Unit 2 and go straight to the seemingly more practical Unit 3, but this would be a mistake unless the reader has a very sound understanding of grammar.

Units 4 through 8 cover capitalization, numbers, abbreviations, word division, and compounds. Unit 9 discusses homonyms and other confusing words, shows how to distinguish between confused pairs, and gives examples of their use. Noting that a lack of uniformity in formatting transcripts exists in the court reporting industry, basic suggestions for setting up a transcript are presented in Unit 10. A section on proofreading included in this unit lists the standard symbols, gives suggestions for effective proofreading, and presents examples of how to use the proofreading symbols.

Unit 11 is devoted to exercises that test for understanding Units 1-10.

Unit 12 is an updated reference list of valuable resources to which either a student or a court reporting professional can turn for information. Both general and specialized resources are listed. This listing has been expanded considerably from the list in the first edition.

Features

Exercises are interspersed within and at the end of units. Those at the end of the units cover that entire unit. Throughout the units are abundant examples, including not only "correct" and "incorrect" but often also "preferred" and "acceptable" uses. Attention has also been given to exceptions to the rules, as these can be particularly troublesome situations. Because the court reporter's requirements often differ from those of other language practitioners, such circumstances have received special attention, with advice on how these special situations can be effectively handled.

Instructor's Manual

The instructor's manual makes suggestions for handling the material in the text. It contains a midterm and final exam and gives correct answers to the tests and two examinations. It also presents guidelines for other activities that might be helpful to the court reporting student.

Acknowledgments

This work has been greatly enhanced by professionals who reviewed the manuscript and suggested improvements. We thank the following persons who served as reviewers: Dianne Thomason of the Court Reporting Institute of Dallas and Terri Hayes of Broward Community College, Pembroke Pine, FL. A special thanks to Elizabeth Waggoner, formerly of Sparks College, Shelbyville, IL, who served as a contributing author.

CONTENTS

1
GLOSSARY

Unlike the usual glossary, this glossary is at the front rather than the back of the book. The reason for this departure from tradition is to encourage the reader to become familiar with these basic terms before proceeding to subsequent sections. Understanding these terms before embarking on the units that follow will make the reader's path much smoother. For example, the statement in a later unit that acronyms do not employ periods will not stop the reader who already knows what an acronym is. Of course, the glossary is always available for quick reference.

Whereas this glossary is by no means a complete glossary of grammatical terms (and does not attempt to be), it will provide the court reporter (CR) with a vocabulary quite sufficient for the purposes of this profession. The CR generally does not wish to know grammar for its own sake, but rather for the purpose of *applying* it to the craft of court reporting. Therefore, the terms have been selected with the CR in mind as an aid in improving the accuracy and clarity of transcripts.

As you go through this glossary, see how many of the terms you know already. Study the ones you do not know, and then go on to the other units with that knowledge in hand. Refer to the glossary whenever you need to.

1 **Academic Degrees**

Degrees earned from colleges and universities. If the degree is abbreviated, periods should be used. Consult an abbreviations dictionary for specialized and foreign degrees.

Ph.D. (doctor of philosophy)
J.D. (juris doctor/doctor of jurisprudence)
D.D.S. (doctor of dental surgery)
B.A. (bachelor of arts)
L.L.M. (master of laws)
M.B.A. (master of business administration)
Ed.D. (doctor of education)

2 **Academic Titles**

Positions within academia. Capitals are used when academic titles are accompanied by the person's name but lowercased otherwise. Do not abbreviate academic titles within a transcript.

> I had an appointment to see *Professor Winston* that afternoon, but I ran into *Dean of Sciences Perez* and talked to her at length.
>
> The *department head's* office was next to mine.
>
> I did not particularly like my mathematics professor. Mary Wentworth, my English professor, studied under Chairman Ebert at Rutgers.

3 **Accent** *See* **Diacritical Marks**

4 **Acronym**

An abbreviation formed from taking the first letter or two of a series of words that together form a term. Acronyms are often pronounced and used as a "word" to the point that some people are familiar with the acronym and its meaning without realizing that they are actually abbreviations. Periods are not used after the letters. Some acronyms are written in all capitals and others are not. Consult your dictionary.

Amtrak	(American travel by track)
ASCII	(American Standard Code for Information Interchange)
BASIC	(Beginner's All-Purpose Symbolic Instruction Code)
ELISA	(enzyme-linked immunosorbent assay)
HUD	(Housing and Urban Development)
NASA	(National Aeronautics and Space Administration)
NATO	(North Atlantic Treaty Organization)
OSHA	(Occupational Safety and Health Administration)
radar	(radio detecting and ranging)
scuba	(self-contained underwater breathing apparatus)
snafu	(situation normal, all fouled up)
WHO	(World Health Organization)

5 **Adjective**

One of the eight parts of speech. An adjective modifies, qualifies, limits, defines, or describes a noun or a pronoun. There are several types of adjectives (proper, descriptive, possessive, demonstrative, and articles) and three degrees of comparison (positive, comparative, and superlative).

> The *American* girl was a student in an *Egyptian* university. (proper nouns)
> It was a *clear, starry* night. (descriptive)
> It was the *worst* accident I'd ever seen. (superlative)
> *Horace's* opinion was the same as *Jim's* stance. (possessive)
> The *better* job was the one at the factory. (comparative)

6 Adverb

One of the eight parts of speech. Like an adjective, an adverb modifies, but it modifies a verb, an adjective, or another adverb. It may also modify an entire sentence, clause, or phrase. Adverbs tell how, when, where, to what extent, etc., something was done. Many adverbs, though not all, are formed by adding the suffix *ly* to an adjective.

> *Obviously,* we were not anxious to see him.
> Speak *clearly* and stand *tall.*
> He was *very* quiet that night.

7 Ampersand (&)

A character that stands for the word *and.* The CR should use the ampersand only for company names in which it is normally used. Do not ever use the ampersand to mean *and* except in those cases.

> We decided to name our business "Green *and* Clean."
> Crest toothpaste is made by Proctor & Gamble.

8 Antecedent

Literally, that which precedes or goes before; specifically, the word or words to which a pronoun refers. A pronoun and its antecedent must agree in number and person.

> When Jim called, he asked my parents if they would be going to his party next week. (*Jim* is the antecedent of *he; parents* is the antecedent of *they.*)
> I just asked if either of the boys had lost his book. (*Either* is the antecedent of *his.*)

9 Antithetical Elements

Parallel words, phrases, or clauses in a sentence that are in opposition to each other.

Money, *not fame*, was his goal. (*fame* is "in opposition" to *money*)

He gave us *not more attention*, but *more respect*, which was what we wanted. (*more respect* is "in opposition" to *more attention*)

10 **Antonyms**

Words with opposite meanings.

lazy	•	industrious	attractive	•	repellent
kind	•	cruel	healthy	•	sick
dark	•	light	cruel	•	kind

11 **Appositive**

A substitute name or "renamer" that follows a noun or a pronoun to explain or identify it. An appositive may be either restrictive, and therefore not set off by commas, or it may be nonrestrictive and set off by commas.

My husband, *Edgar*, filed for divorce from me last autumn.
My sister, *Dorothy*, works with me.
My favorite author, *Victoria Holt*, is a prolific writer.
Author *Mary Higgins Clark* spoke at a writers' conference.
One of my cousins, *Richard Davis*, was in the car also.

12 **Article**

A word used as an adjective to indicate the degree of definiteness. The definite article is *the;* the indefinite articles are *a* and *an.*

I wanted to see a movie with *an* ending that was happy.
The secretary closed *the* door to *the* office and picked up *a* file folder from *the* desk.

13 **Auxiliary Verb**

A verb used along with the main verb to show person, number, mood, tense, or voice. The 23 most common auxiliary verbs are *is, am, are, was, were, have, has, had, be, been, being, do, did, shall, will, can, may, might, must, could, should, would,* and *does.* They are also called *helping verbs.*

I *have* seen these reports already.
I *should* speak with Mimi today.

14 **Case**

The form of a noun or pronoun that indicates its relationship to other words in the sentence. Case depends on its function in the sentence. There are three cases: nominative, objective, and possessive. *See individual entries* for nominative, objective, and possessive nouns.

15 **Clause**

A group of related words that contains both a subject and a verb. A clause can be independent or dependent (subordinate). *See individual entries.*

We studied the transcripts closely. (independent)
The doors were locked. (independent)
As we studied the transcripts closely, we discussed a course missing. (dependent)
Although the doors were locked, we never knew it. (dependent)

16 **Clipped Form**

A shortened version of a word used in conversational or informal language. No periods are used with clipped forms.

ad (advertisement)	gym (gymnasium)
con (convict)	lab (laboratory)
flu (influenza)	typo (typographical error)

17 **Colloquial**

An on-the-record dialogue, usually between attorneys but sometimes involving the judge and witnesses, often on the subject of the discovery process. The format of colloquy is identifiable from Q & A (question and answer).

Q: Did you know about Darcy's plan?
Witness: Your Honor, I don't know how to answer this question.
The Court: Answer yes or no.
Witness: It isn't that simple.

18 **Comma Splice**

The punctuation error of using a comma between two independent clauses that are not connected by a coordinating conjunction. *See also* **Run-on Sentence**

Mrs. Miller came to the front door, Mr. Johnston stormed into the house.
We were looking for the money, Jason found it.

19 **Comparative Degree**

The form of a descriptive adjective used to express a comparison between two persons or things. It is usually formed by adding *er* to the adjective or using the word *more.*

more difficult	worse (an irregular form)
more careful	sweeter
hotter	better (an irregular form)
bigger	clearer

20 **Complex Sentence**

A sentence having one independent clause and one or more dependent clauses.

If I couldn't do the job, I would tell my supervisor and he would help me.

Annie told me that she was frightened when James got home, and I understood why.

21 **Compound Sentence**

A sentence having at least two independent clauses.

We planned to meet that night, but he didn't show up.

Maria sat down at the table, she began to stare at him, and then she suddenly started screaming and ranting.

22 **Compound Word**

A combination of two or more closely associated words that constitute a single entity. Some compound words are written open, some are hyphenated, and some are written solid (or closed). *See also* **Suspended Compound** *and* **Temporary Compound**

high school (open)	notebook (solid)
self-confidence (hyphenated)	masterpiece (solid)
attorney general (open)	

23 **Compound-Complex Sentence**

A sentence having two or more independent and one or more dependent clauses.

Whenever we saw Mr. Malone, he refused to speak to us, but we just figured he was an eccentric, a loner; and we didn't get angry about it.

24 Conjunction

One of the eight parts of speech. The word comes from the Latin word for "joining together." Conjunctions act as connectives. There are three types of conjunctions: coordinating, subordinating, and correlatives. *See individual entries.*

I sent Grant *and* Gary a gift and a letter. (coordinating)
Harry will sell his house *if* he can find a buyer. (subordinating)
Not only do we have too many bills, *but* we also have a poor cash flow. (correlative)

25 Conjunctive Adverb

An adverb that acts as both adverb and conjunction. It is followed by a comma and usually occurs between two related independent clauses that are separated by a semicolon or a period. Examples: *also, anyway, besides, consequently, finally, futhermore, hence, however, incidentally, indeed, instead, likewise, meanwhile, moreover, nevertheless, next, nonetheless, otherwise, still, then, therefore, thus.*

We read the case history; *therefore,* we have an understanding of the situation.
The position of the president was clear. *Indeed,* he sent out several memos stating his viewpoint; *however,* he is a fair man.

26 Coordinating Adjectives

Two or more adjectives that modify the same noun and are separated by commas.

We bought a playful, fluffy, funny kitten.
The sealed, signed, delivered contract was in his file.

27 Coordinating Conjunction

A conjunction that connects parts of equal rank. These include *and, or, but, nor, yet,* and *for.*

Across the river *and* over the hill we ran. (connects two phrases)
Neither Alex *nor* Erica attended. (connects two nouns)
Tell me what he said *or* get out of my house. (connects two clauses)
Neither she *nor* we want this trial. (connects two pronouns)

28 **Correlatives**

Connectives or conjunctions that are used in pairs but are not adjacent to one another. Some of the most common correlatives are *either...or, neither...nor, not only...but also, both...and,* and *whether...or.*

> *Either* get off the phone *or* put her on hold.
> *Neither* Jane *nor* Tom know of their deal.
> *Not only* the students in Mr. Smith's class *but also* those in Mrs. Thom's class will participate.
> *Whether* we remain here or move, we will remain together.

29 **Declarative Sentence**

A sentence that makes a statement and ends with a period.

> I will train with Leonard Gold.
> The dog was old and sick.

30 **Definitive Article.** *See* **Article**

31 **Demonstrative Pronoun**

A pronoun that acts as a "pointer": *this, that, these, or those.* Demonstrative pronouns act as adjectives when paired with a noun (*this house, these children*).

> *This* was my idea, not yours.
> *These* are not his pants.
> I'd never seen *that* happen.

32 **Dependent Clause**

A clause that cannot stand alone as a sentence (even though it has a subject and a verb) because it begins with a subordinating conjunction. Also called a subordinate clause. *See also* **Independent Clause**

> While he was away...
> Before we left town...
> Because of all the problems the family had...
> If the package arrives today...

33 **Descriptive Adjective**

An adjective that describes a noun or pronoun. A descriptive adjective will be in one of three degrees: positive, comparative, or superlative. *See individual entries for degrees.*

pretty	clever
violet	more selfish
worst	but
clean	multiple

34 **Designators**

An identifying title or term, usually followed by a number. Designators generally are not capitalized. A few examples of designator include *case, factor, group, page, paragraph, part, phase, section, stage, subsection,* and *volume.*

I will read from page 23, paragraph 1.
Patients in group 1 were given a placebo.

35 **Diacritical Marks**

Accents that show pronunciation. Very few English words employ diacritical marks, and those that once did (e.g., resume, role, facade) have for the most part dropped diacritical marks from common use. Exceptions are proper names and foreign terms that have not been adopted into common use in English.

Acute accent: café au lait
Cedilla: garçon
Circumflex: crêpe de Chine
Danish O: Hans Christian Ørsted
Grave accent: après ski party
Tilde: mañana
Umlaut: führer
Wedge: Leopold Ružička

36 **Direct Address**

Word(s) representing the person, thing, or group to whom one is speaking.

Call your assistant, *sir.*
Jan and Mary, you are both exaggerating.
Members of the jury, you have received your instructions.
Your Honor, I cannot answer that question.

37 **Direct Object**

The word or words denoting the thing or person that receives the action of the verb. To find the direct object, first find the subject and the verb and then ask "whom?" or "what?" The verb must be in the active voice to have a direct object. *See also* **Indirect Object**

> Jose watched the *game* with us.
> I gave Timothy a *gift* because he was leaving the next day.
> The child hit the *cat.*

38 **Direct Quotation**

Quotation of words exactly as they were spoken or written. A direct quotation is set off with quotation marks.

> John Samuels said to me, and I quote, "Mrs. Alvarez, you must leave the house immediately."
> He wrote in his letter of June 30, and I read from that letter, "You will regret these actions, and I will make sure that you do."

39 **Divided Quotations**

A quotation that is interrupted by other words, i.e., words that are not being quoted.

> "Mrs. Wilfred," he said in a whisper, "I am warning you."
> Corky lied to me when he said, "Carol, I never went to Atwater's Cafe on December 12th" — he couldn't look me straight in the eyes — "and furthermore I have never been there in my entire life," he added.

40 **Ellipsis Mark**

A mark (...) indicating the omission of words, sentences, or even paragraphs within quoted material. The CR will not need to use an ellipsis mark unless, while reading quoted matter, the reader says, "Dot dot dot" to indicate an ellipsis. Do not use this mark to show an interruption, pause, or dropping off of speech.

41 **Elliptical Construction**

An omission of a word or words that does not obscure the meaning of the sentence.

> His sister was living in Indiana; my mother, Illinois. (*was living in* has been omitted after *mother*)
> His appearance was normal but his voice strange. (*was* has been omitted after *voice*)
> I am a faster and better typist than she. (*is* has been omitted after *she*)

However accomplished, the job must be complete by tomorrow. (*it is* has been omitted after *however*)

42 **Enumeration**

A list, set up formally and indented from the body of the text. Do not use periods after the items in a list unless they are complete sentences.

The following have been proved today:
1. The defendant was present when Mr. McRae died.
2. The defendant did nothing to help Mr. McRae.
3. The defendant could have assisted Mr. McRae and possibly saved his life.

We requested the following items:
1. a complete inventory of their stock
2. five years' income taxes
3. outstanding debts
4. collectibles
5. copies of all correspondence between that company and Jal-Tech.

43 **Expletive**

- An exclamatory word or phrase, often a "four-letter word" or obscenity, usually followed by an exclamation mark. *See also* **Interjection**

Glory be! I am so happy to see you.
Help! The house is on fire!

- A filler, usually "it" or "there," that fills some kind of space but does not add to or change the meaning of the sentence.

Try harder to make *it* understood what you mean.
There were several boys standing around on the corner that night.

44 **Extract**

A direct quotation. If it is long, it is set off by indenting a few extra spaces on the left, at the top, and below the extract. Extracts are set off by quotation marks.

45 **Fragment**

A phrase or clause written as a complete sentence although it is not complete.

Working early in the morning, trying to get the task done.
To joke with the woman in the lobby.
While the plane landed.
Stella's brother, who lives in Ohio.

46 **Function**

The "role" a word plays in a sentence; for example, whether it is the subject of the sentence, the direct object, the object of the preposition, and so on.

47 **Generic Name**

A general, nonproprietary name. *See* **Trade Name**

camera
automobile
cereal
photocopier

48 **Genitive Case.** *See* **Possessive Case**

49 **Gerund**

A verbal that acts as a noun and is an *ing* form of a verb.

Talking too much always got her into trouble.
Thank you for *calling* us.

50 **Homographs**

Words with the same spelling but different meaning and pronunciation. Sometimes confusion between homographs can be avoided by using hyphens.

bow and arrow • *bow* your head in prayer
conduct the orchestra • poor grades in *conduct*
reform (to change) • *re-form* (form again)

51 **Homonyms**

Words that have the same pronunciation but differ in origin, meaning, and spelling. Homonyms can be particularly troublesome to the CR.

bear/bare
hair/hare
imminent/eminent
meet/meat
isle/aisle
mail/male
flair/flare
wear/where

52 **Idiomatic Language**

A way of using words that is peculiar to a specific language and cannot be translated literally, or word for word, into another language and produce the same meaning.

We tried to *break the ice* with a joke.
Neville *carried out* his plan with great determination.

53 **Imperative**

A command or request. Even when expressed in question form, an imperative ends with a period.

Would you please take a seat.
Come here, John.
Listen.

54 **Indefinite Article.** *See* **Article**

55 **Indefinite Pronoun**

A pronoun used to replace a nonspecific group. The indefinite pronouns include *all, each, several, most, many, few, someone, anybody, some, another, neither,* and *either.*

56 **Independent Clause**

A clause that can stand alone as a complete sentence. It contains both subject and verb. *See also* **Sentence**

Warren delivers our newspaper.
Selling automobiles was a job he never enjoyed.

57 **Indirect Object**

The word or words denoting the person or thing to which something is given or for which something is done. It is found in a sentence by using this formula: subject + verb + direct object; then ask "to whom?" or "to what?" The answer will be the indirect object.

I gave *Donald* a book for Christmas.
Ms. Adamson told *Janice* the truth that day.

58 **Infinitive**

A verbal that usually (though not always) functions as a noun. An infinitive comprises the word *to* and a verb in its present tense.

To graduate was my immediate goal.
We expected *to move* in December.
I wanted only *to talk* to him.

59 **Intensive Pronoun**

A "self" pronoun used for emphasis. *See also* **Reflexive Pronoun**

I *myself* handled the travel arrangements.
Mrs. Ellis *herself* appeared at the door, not the butler.

60 **Interjection**

One of the eight parts of speech used to express emotion. An interjection is followed by a comma if mild in tone or by an exclamation point if expressing strong feeling. Because the CR records and does not interpret, exclamation marks are seldom used. *See also* **Expletive**

Oh, I think I understand now.
Wow! This is fantastic!
Gee, this is awkward.

61 **Interrogative Phrase**

A phrase that is added to the end of a statement that then transforms it into a question rather than a statement.

He was happy in the marriage, *wasn't he?*
You have the book, *don't you?*

62 **Interrogative Pronoun**

A pronoun used to ask a question: *who, whom, which, what, whose.*

Whose ring did you find on the floor?
Which desk belongs to you?
Who broke the radio?
Whom did you ask?
What film did he see?

63 **Interrogative Sentence**

A question.

How did he do it?
Do you remember what he said to you?

64 **Introductory Element**

A word, phrase, or clause that comes before the main clause. Unless it is short (usually shorter than four words), it is followed by a comma. Sometimes a single word is followed by a comma.

In my opinion, there is no issue.
In 1988, we moved to Seattle.
Hence, we voted against the proposal.
If you disagree with us, you must say so.

65 **Inversion**

A change in normal word order, usually the placement of a verb before its subject.

Round and round goes the carousel. (The carousel goes round and round.)
Down Lake Road and hidden among the trees stands our cabin. (Our cabin stands down Lake Road and hidden among the trees.)

66 **Irregular Plural**

A plural form that does not follow the usual pattern. When in doubt, consult the dictionary.

child/children	tooth/teeth
deer/deer	ox/oxen

67 **Jargon**

(1) Highly technical terminology of a certain profession or group or (2) confused language that does not make sense.

CCDs are not random access; instead, they are serial storage and cycle data through read points to access stored information.
The releasee, releasee's heirs, executors, administrators, successors, and assigns from all actions, causes of action, suits, debts, dues, sums of money, specialties, covenants, variances, promises, judgments, extents, executions, claims, and demands whatsoever in law, admiralty, or equity which against the releasee...
In case of a formulating incident profusing our sense, we can obfuscate reworking or rejuvenation by preventing the termination—conceivably.

68 **Jury Charge**

Judge's instructions to the jury regarding the laws applicable to the case at hand.

69 **Lowercase**

Small letters as opposed to capitals (uppercase).

70 **Main Clause**

An independent clause. It can stand alone as a complete sentence, but it may have attached to it other main clauses, dependent clauses, phrases, or parentheticals.

> Although we were exhausted, *we climbed* to the top of the mountain by using all the strength we had and by refusing to give in to our fatigue, believe it or not.

71 **Modifier.** *See* **Adjective; Adverb**

72 **Modifier, Sentence**

A word that modifies the entire sentence.

> Unfortunately, we couldn't help her.
> Certainly, we tried our best.

73 **Nominative Case**

The form of a pronoun that is used for a subject, a predicative nominative, or an appositive of the subject. Also known as the *subjective case. See also* **Case**

> I thought that *she* was the best candidate. (subject)
> It was *he* James wanted to speak to that day. (predicate nominative)
> The most productive team, Josef and *I*, should be in charge. (appositive)

74 **Nonrestrictive Element**

A sentence element that is not essential to the meaning. It adds information to the sentence but does not change its meaning. A nonrestrictive element should be set off with commas or dashes. *See also* **Parenthetical Element; Restrictive Element**

Timothy O'Mara, *a man I met only twice in my entire life,* was known to me by reputation.

The teacher of the course, *who was hired last month,* is doing an excellent job.

75 **Noun**

The name of a person, place, thing, idea, or concept. Nouns can be proper (Ohio, Miss Parker, Union High School) or common (state, teacher, school); collective (team, choir, orchestra); abstract (hatred, envy) or concrete (floor, coins, door).

76 **Object of a Preposition**

A word or group of words that the preposition is relating to another part of the sentence. *See also* **Prepositional Phrase**

In my *opinion*, the estimates of the land's *value* were too low.
After *today* Mr. Carpenter will speak for *us*.
I'm sure that I put it on the *table*, but I found it under the *sofa*.

77 **Objective Case**

The form of a word that is used for a direct object, object of a preposition, appositive of a direct object, object of a verbal, or indirect object.

Will you go to the movie with *us*? (object of preposition)
Give *him* your report when it is finished. (indirect object)

78 **Ordinal**

A number designating place or sequence—first, second, third, etc.

Rent is due on the *15th* of each month.
The *second* child was a girl.
For the *hundredth* time, I tell you I don't know.

79 **Paragraphing**

The dividing of groups of sentences when there is a change in subject or some kind of discernible shift.

80 **Parallel Structure**

Using the same kind of word or phrase in a sentence for words or phrases that are being used in the same way.

The group was *leaving* on Sunday, *arriving* late on Monday, and *returning* the following week. (gerunds)

He learned *to lay* carpet, *to install* electric wiring, *to put up* wallpaper, and *to install* windows. (infinitives)

81 **Parenthetical Element**

A nonessential word, phrase, or clause set off by commas or dashes or a combination of the two. CRs should never set off parentheticals in parenthesis. *See also* **Nonrestrictive Element**

What you are saying, *in other words,* is that you aren't sure.

I know he was there—*you can't convince me otherwise*—that night and saw everything that happened.

The conference on medical ethics—*the one I did not attend, although my partner did go because of Peter's funeral*—resulted in several resolutions.

82 **Parenthetical Remarks**

Notations by the CR of some action or movement that is other than the spoken words during a proceeding. These are always in the CR's own words, in parentheses, and should be used sparingly and only when helpful to the reader.

Q Mr. Johnson, did you see Timothy Reynolds enter Fifth National Bank on April 28, 1988?

A (Witness nodded affirmatively.)

83 **Participle**

A word that has the characteristics of both an adjective and a verb.

The contract *being* of five years' duration, we were anxious to do a good job.

84 **Parts of Speech**

The classification of words according to the function they perform in a sentence. The eight parts of speech are nouns, pronouns, verbs, adjectives, adverbs, prepositions, conjunctions, and interjections. *See individual entries.*

85 **Person**

A term used to indicate whether one is the speaker (first person), is being spoken to (second person), or is being spoken about (third person). "Person" affects the form of verbs and of personal pronouns.

I hope things will improve. (first person)
You are the first to arrive. (second person)
Mrs. Tell and she left on their trip last night. (third person)

86 **Personal Pronoun**

A pronoun used to replace a specific noun: I, my, mine, me, we, our, ours, us, you, your, yours, he, his, him, she, her, hers, they, their, theirs, them, it, its.

87 **Phrase**

A group of related words that may contain either a verb or a subject, but not both. A phrase cannot stand alone as a sentence. There are several kinds of phrases. The CR need not learn to label all the kinds of phrases but should know the difference between phrases and clauses.

On the side of the road (prepositional phrase)
Having finished his report (gerund phrase)
To understand him fully (infinitive phrase)

88 **Positive Degree**

The form of a descriptive adjective that involves no comparison; the basic form that has no characteristic ending. *See also* **Comparative Degree; Superlative Degree**

rusty kind
soft easy

89 **Possessive Case**

The form of a pronoun used to show ownership or a similar relationship.

Your car is new, but *mine* isn't.
Our case, though strong, may not seem valid to the judge.

90 **Predicate Adjective**

A complement that acts to modify or describe the subject of the sentence.

Carlos felt *tired* all day.
Sheila seemed *bored* by the discussion.
I am *certain* he told the truth.

91 **Predicate Nominative**

A complement that renames the subject, usually after a form of the verb *to be*, and not placed beside the subject as an appositive is.

> Miss Peterson will be the organization's next *president.*
> That boy is a real *scoundrel.*

92 **Prefix**

One or more letters placed in front of a root word or stem to change the meaning of the root.

*ante*room	*pseudo*intellectual
*bi*weekly	*super*human
*re*organization	*non*partisan
*semi*monthly	*un*do

93 **Preposition**

One of the eight parts of speech. A preposition shows the relationship between a noun or pronoun (the object of the preposition) and another element in the sentence. *See also* **Object of a Preposition; Prepositional Phrase**

> We worked *around* the house *for* a few hours.
> Jean discovered the money *under* a brick *in* the cellar.
> His actions were *beneath* contempt.
> *In* my opinion, he was headed *toward* disaster.

94 **Prepositional Phrase**

A preposition, its object, and any modifiers.

> around the house
> for a long time
> under the kitchen table
> after the second traffic light

95 **Pronoun**

One of the eight parts of speech. A pronoun is a word that takes the place of a noun. Pronouns may be classified as personal, indefinite, relative, interrogative, intensive, reflexive, or demonstrative. *See individual entries.*

96 **Proper Noun.** *See* **Noun**

97 **Quotation.** *See* **Direct Quotation** *and* **Indirect Quotation**

98 **Reflexive Pronoun**

A "self" pronoun that refers to its antecedent. It is used when the performer and receiver of the action are the same. *See also* **Intensive Pronoun**

Joe hurt *himself* with that knife.
We did *ourselves* an injustice.
I convinced *myself* to go alone.

99 **Relative Pronoun**

A pronoun that introduces a dependent clause.

The boy *who* spoke to you was my cousin.
Whoever comes to my house first will help me prepare.
The house *that* we bought had a swimming pool.

100 **Restrictive Element**

An element that is essential to the meaning of a sentence. Omitting it would alter or obscure the meaning of the sentence. *See also* **Nonrestrictive Element**

The money *that I lost* was Mary's savings.
The child *who wins the contest* will appear on television.

101 **Root**

The base of a word to which prefixes and suffixes may be added to change or qualify the meaning of the original root.

rephrase	imperfect
overestimate	bimonthly
hurting	mailed

102 **Run-on Sentence**

Two sentences improperly written as one. Run-on sentences are of two kinds: fused or comma splice. A fused sentence is one without any punctuation between the two sentences. A comma splice uses a comma instead of a period or semicolon to separate two independent clauses.

Mr. Warner ran toward me he was furious. (fused)
Maria fought the change, however, she could not win. (comma splice)

103 **Salutation**

A greeting.

Ladies and Gentlemen of the Jury:
Your Honor,
Madam,

104 **Sentence**

A complete thought that contains both a subject and a verb and can stand alone (an independent clause). Sentences can be grouped according to their structure (simple, compound, complex, compound-complex) or by their "tone" or content (declarative, imperative, interrogative, exclamatory). *See individual entries.*

105 **Serial Comma**

The final comma before the conjunction in a series or list. The CR should not omit this comma unless the final items constitute a unit.

We purchased nails, boards, and a hammer.
The lunch consisted of salad, bread, and red beans and rice.
(red beans and rice is one dish: no comma)
She wanted to decorate the room in beige, pine green, rust, and dark brown.

106 **Series**

Three or more words, phrases, or clauses listed and separated by commas, semicolons, or conjunctions. *See also* **Enumeration**

Nonetheless, I consulted my attorney, Ms. Perkins; had her look over the plans, advise me, and make changes; and I then embarked, though carefully.
We searched in the office, under all the desks, in the drawers, and on the shelves.
I invited Sara and Jamie and Marta and you.
I bought a radio, a toaster, a blender, and a microwave oven.

107 **Simple Sentence**

A sentence consisting of one independent clause; either the subject or the verb may be compound, however.

His team won the meet that night.
Joyce was supposed to buy the hot dogs and take them to the picnic.

Susan and David plotted and printed the route.

108 **Slang**

Nonstandard, informal language.

He ain't a bum.
I busted my leg all up.

109 **Slash.** ***See*** **Virgule**

110 **Subject**

The person or thing talked about in a sentence or clause.

John called last night.
A good *impression* is important to me.

111 **Subjective Case.** ***See*** **Nominative Case**

112 **Subordinate Clause.** ***See*** **Dependent Clause**

113 **Subordinating Conjunction**

A conjunction that connects a subordinate clause with the main clause. When a subordinating conjunction is placed at the beginning of an independent clause, the clause is rendered dependent, or subordinate. Subordinating conjunctions include the following words: although, after, unless, until, while, where, whereas, when, whenever, if, before, as, as if, as though, because, before, and whenever.

Wherever I went, I kept in touch with Jorge.
I will tell you about that *after* I explain one essential matter.

114 **Suffix**

Syllable(s) added to the end of a root or root word to change or qualify the meaning of the root.

play*ing* care*less*
jump*ed* careful*ly*
work*able* child*like*
instruct*or* five*fold*

115 **Superlative Degree**

The form of a descriptive adjective used to compare three or more persons or things or objects. The superlative is usually formed by adding *est* to the end of the word or using the the word *most.*

rudest	most disagreeable
kindest	most considerate
worst (an irregular form)	most unsatisfactory

116 Suspended Compounds

Compound adjectives that have one element that is exactly the same in both or all. This common element can be omitted in all except the final compound adjective. The common element cannot be omitted in compound words that do not contain a hyphen.

Would you describe her injuries as first-, second-, or third-degree burns?
His hypersensitivity and hyperactivity were both problems that he tried to work on.

117 Synonyms

Words that have the same or nearly the same meaning.

insane • mad		lukewarm • tepid
jovial • cheerful		baby • infant
sluggish • lethargic		smell • scent
luxurious • plush		

118 Temporary Compounds

Unlike terms that are always compound (e.g., newspaper, self-imposed, notebook), two or more words may be connected by a hyphen to modify another word simply because of the way they are used in that specific sentence.

Mother had one of those don't-say-anther-word expressions on her face.
The fair-haired child seemed never to smile.

119 Tense

The form of a verb that indicates the time of the action. The tenses are the present, past, future, present perfect, past perfect, and future perfect.

Beatrice *sings* beautifully. (present)
They *are planning* a long trip. (present)
They *asked* Miss Tephra to telephone their home that night. (past)
He *will investigate* your complaint. (future)

He *will have completed* the report by Monday morning. (future perfect)
Since September of 1987 I *have worked* in the lab. (present perfect)
She has been so sick that I *was forced* to call in the doctor. (past perfect)

120 **Terminal Punctuation**

A period, question mark, or exclamation point used to end a sentence.

121 **Trade Name**

Also called a brand name. The proprietary name given to a product by the company that produces it. *See also* **Generic Name**

Kodak camera	Saran Wrap
Xerox machine	Kleenex tissue
Scotch tape	Buick

122 **Uppercase**

Capital letters as opposed to small (lowercase) letters.

123 **Verb**

One of the eight parts of speech and one of the two basic, essential elements that make up a sentence. Verbs show action, state of being, or occurrence.

Cassie *screamed* at her mother.
Sharon *believed* every word Jeff said.

124 **Verbal**

A form derived from a verb that functions as a noun, adjective, or adverb. There are three types of verbals: gerunds, infinitives, and participles. *See also individual entries.*

The *playing* children heard nothing but their own laughter. (functions as adjective)
To play cards bored me, so I left the room. (functions as subject)
I liked *waking* at 5 a.m. (direct object)

125 **Virgule** (/)

A short diagonal line used between two equivalent words, in dates or fractions, to express "per," etc. A virgule is also used to separate lines of poetry when they are written paragraph style rather than line for line.

and/or
feet/second
5/18/82

126 **Voice**

A characteristic of verbs indicating whether the subject does the action (active voice) or the action is done to the subject (passive voice).

> Mrs. Simmons asked Greg Mendes to recite the poem. (active)
> Greg Mendes was asked by Mrs. Simmons to recite the poem. (passive)

Exercises

A. Match the example in Column I with a term from Column II that best describes the example.

Column I	Column II
1. myself, himself, ourselves	a. trade name
2. acute, cedilla, tilde, umlaut	b. homographs
3. page, subsection, case, column	c. articles
4. pair/pare, pen/pin	d. salutation
5. toilet paper, painkiller, steel	e. clipped forms
6. to do, to drive, to become	f. adjectives
7. eating, sleeping, waking	g. ampersand
8. B.A., J.D., Ed.D.	h. conjunctions
9. pup, lab, ad	i. auxiliary verb
10. neat/tidy, hard/difficult	j. conjunctive verb
11. have, has, had, do, did	k. correlatives
12. declarative, imperative, interrogative	l. designators
13. bright, foolish, low, black	m. eponyms
14. jargon or technical terms	n. comparative adjectives
15. Hansen disease, Alzheimer's	o. acronyms
16. &	p. diacritical marks
17. moreover, however, likewise	q. byte, macro, bit, binary
18. recreate/re-create	r. gerunds
19. WHO, OSHA, BASIC	s. ordinals
20. widely, constantly, very	t. types of sentences
21. a, an, the	u. academic pronouns
22. either/or, neither/nor	v. case

23.	Tide, Tylenol, Panasonic	w.	reflexive pronouns
24.	sweet/bitter, smooth/lumpy	x.	adverbs
25.	and, or, but, nor, for	y.	generic names
26.	nominative, objective, possessive	z.	antonyms
27.	nicer, calmer, more significant	aa.	homonyms
28.	11th, second, 103rd	bb.	prefixes
29.	non, un, semi, bi, sub	cc.	infinitives
30.	hello, good morning, howdy	dd.	synonyms

B. In looking through newspapers, magazines, and other written matter, collect at least five examples of each of the following.

1. temporary compounds
2. slang
3. parenthetical elements
4. trade names
5. idiomatic language
6. jargon
7. extracts
8. words with diacritical marks
9. direct address
10. designators

C. Think of five examples of each of the following:

1. generic and trade names of the same product
2. correlatives
3. acronyms
4. homographs
5. homonyms
6. declarative sentences
7. complex sentences
8. imperative sentences
9. appositives
10. comparative and superlative forms of adjectives

2
GRAMMAR

This unit examines the rules and concepts of grammar. Although a grammarian might find this treatment somewhat incomplete, at least from a theoretical viewpoint, it *is* complete for the CR's needs. Any material not of practical value to a CR has not been included here. The aim of this unit is to present sufficient information so the CR will produce excellent transcripts with increased ease and decreased investment of time. We shall begin with the most basic concept of grammar: the sentence.

The Sentence

127 A group of words becomes a sentence only if a complete thought is conveyed or a complete statement made. Because people do not always speak in complete sentences, the CR will not be able to eliminate all nonsentences from transcripts. Nonetheless, the CR should avoid nonsentences *whenever possible* in the witnesses' words and *always* in the judges' and attorneys' words.

Groups of words that are written as a sentence can be classified as one of the following: correct sentence, fragment, or run-on. A fragment can be thought of as "not enough" and a run-on as "too much" to be a single correct sentence.

The minimum requirement for a group of words to be classed as a correct sentence is that it contain at least one subject and one verb. To ensure that this requirement is met, first search for the verb, which can show action, state of being, or occurrence. Remember to watch for auxiliary (or helping) verbs.

My car **runs** well most of the time.
Janet **felt** sorry for Russ.
I **remained** calm despite the general panic around me.
Alvin **tried** to telephone you on Monday.
Mr. Swathmore **has informed** his class of his decision.

In the first example, the verb is *runs*. To find the subject of the sentence, ask who or what runs? The answer is *car*. The subjects of the other sentences are *Janet, I, Alvin, and Mr. Swathmore.*

Sometimes the subject is understood *(see section on* **Imperative Sentences**).

Find his address quickly.
Don't forget about the seminar next month.

In both of these examples, the subject is *you*, even though the word *you* does not appear in the sentence.

128 Phrases and Clauses

To gain a clear comprehension of what constitutes a complete sentence, one must be able to distinguish between phrases and clauses. Both can be defined, at least in part, as a group of related words; but there is a crucial difference: a clause has both a subject and a verb, whereas a phrase may have one or the other, but not both; or it may contain neither.

Clauses

If we were still friends
The dog chased me.
Maria said so.
Because there were no objections
Whenever he cries

Phrases

inside my pocket
to give freely
for heaven's sake
with hope and love
giving us time

Because a clause contains both subject and verb, one might readily assume that a clause is always a sentence. Actually, a clause may or may not be a complete sentence.

129 Types of Clauses

There are two types of clauses: independent and dependent. An independent clause is a complete sentence; a dependent clause, also called a subordinate clause, is not. A dependent clause that is written as though it were a complete sentence is what is commonly called a sentence fragment. The difference between the two types of clauses is that a dependent clause has at its beginning a subordinating conjunction, that is, a word or group of words that actually causes that clause to become less than a whole sentence. Without that subordinating conjunction, the same clause would then be transformed from dependent to independent; but with it the clause cannot stand alone. Table 2-1 lists common subordinating conjunctions.

The following are dependent clauses:

If the doorbell rings
As soon as my sister makes her travel plans
While Juan was outside looking for the child
Unless Cory can show us some proof
Whenever I spend money

Take away the subordinating conjunctions, and you have whole sentences:

The doorbell rings.
My sister makes her travel plans.
Juan was outside looking for the child.
Cory can show us some proof.
I spend money.

Table 2-1

Subordinating Conjunctions

after	in order that	what
although	in order	whatever
as	no matter how	when
as if	once	whenever
as soon as	since	where
as though	so that	whereas
because	that	wherever
before	though	while
even if	till	who
for	unless	whoever
if	until	

130 **Fragments**

A sentence fragment is a group of words that do not constitute a whole, complete sentence, although they are written as though they do.

Sometimes the CR is able to avoid using fragments, but not always. The examples below show fragments (in the Answers) that could not be avoided but do not negatively affect the quality of the transcript.

Q. When did you learn of Noelle's absence?
A. When I got home Tuesday evening.
Q. Did you regularly converse with your neighbors?
A. If I felt like talking.
Q. Carmen was asked to serve as president; is that correct?
A. Instead of me, yes.

Sometimes the CR can avoid using fragments by joining them to the subsequent sentence or group of words.

Q. Where did you see Anthony?
A. Near Danio's Pizza Parlor, at least I think that's where I saw him.

There are, however, situations in which the fragment cannot be joined to the sentence it precedes because to do so would alter the meaning.

Q. Did Saul know about the trade?
A. Maybe. He was close to Jonathon.

If the answer were written as "Maybe he was close to Jonathon," the meaning would be completely different from that conveyed by separating the two elements.

Acceptable

A. Maybe he was close to Jonathon.

OR

A. Maybe—he was close to Jonathon.

Avoid

A. Maybe, he was close to Jonathon.

131 Run-Ons

A run-on is at least two sentences that are incorrectly written as though they constitute a single sentence. They must be separated by a period, semicolon, question mark, or exclamation mark to correct the error. Run-on constructions are also called comma splices, but in this text they will be referred to as run-ons. Unlike the fragment, the CR can—and absolutely must—avoid run-ons entirely by inserting the proper punctuation. The following are examples of run-ons and how they can be corrected.

Run-On Sentences

The trip is cancelled, we will get a refund of our deposits within a month.

If I needed him, I would telephone he's at home most of the time.

He promised to return the money, however, I had my doubts.

I couldn't find my receipts, I was frantic to find them.

Corrected Sentences

The trip is cancelled; we will get a refund of our deposits within a month.

OR

The trip is cancelled. We will get a refund of our deposits within a month.

If I needed him, I would telephone; he's at home most of the time.

OR

If I needed him, I would telephone. He's at home most of the time.

He promised to return the money; however, I had my doubts.

OR (but not generally as acceptable)

He promised to return the money. However, I had my doubts.

I couldn't find my receipts. I was frantic to find them.

OR

I couldn't find my receipts; I was frantic to find them.

The CR cannot add words at will; otherwise, the problem of run-ons could be managed by adding a coordinating conjunction between independent clauses:

EXAMPLE: I couldn't find my receipts, but I was frantic to find them.

One of the most common problems with run-ons involves conjunctive adverbs (CA) (Table 2-2) and transitional phrases (TP) (Table 2-3). There seems to be a tendency to use a comma before CAs and TPs, but this can often result in a run-on sentence when two independent clauses are joined by either a CA plus a comma or a TP plus a comma.

He has cooperated with the investigation, moreover, he has led us to some surprising information.

Mr. Reiger was to return the child by 6:00 p.m., otherwise he would be in violation of the agreement.

She was going to school as a full-time graduate student, at the same time, she was working for us as well as for Morton and Case.

In both examples, a comma is used incorrectly: preceding *moreover, otherwise,* and *at the same time* because the clauses on either side of the CA or TP are independent clauses. Either a semicolon or a period should be used in place of each of these commas. A semicolon is the preferred punctuation, although a period would not be considered incorrect.

Remember: Both clauses on either side of the conjunctive adverb must be complete, independent clauses. Also, if the subject is understood, a comma may suffice. The CR must make an effort to examine the sentence carefully before inserting a semicolon at the sight of a CA or TP.

Warren called out for Nora, then sat down and wept.

Mr. Bickford was an obstinate man, yet a kind and gentle one.

In these two sentences, what follows *then* and *yet* is in neither case an independent clause.

Correct

He returned at 2:00 a.m.; incidentally, it wasn't the first time he was so late.

Acceptable

He returned at 2:00 a.m. Incidentally, it wasn't the first time he was so late.

Wrong

He returned at 2:00 a.m., incidentally, it wasn't the first time he was so late.

Correct

Juanita was an ambitious young woman; in other words, she was determined to get ahead.

Acceptable

Juanita was an ambitious young woman. In other words, she was determined to get ahead.

Wrong

Juanita was an ambitious young woman, in other words, she was determined to get ahead.

Table 2-2
Conjunctive Adverbs

accordingly	incidentally	nonetheless
also	indeed	otherwise
anyway	instead	so
besides	likewise	still
consequently	meanwhile	then
finally	moreover	therefore
furthermore	nevertheless	thus
hence	next	yet
however		

Table 2-3
Transitional Phrases

after all	by the way	in fact
as a result	for example	in other words
at any rate	in addition	on the other hand
at the same time		

Classifying Sentences

132 **By Content**

Sentences may be classified by either their content or their structure. The content of a sentence determines its end punctuation. The following are the types of sentences classified by content:

1. **Declarative Sentence.** This type makes a statement. It declares something to be so or not so. Declarative sentences end with a period.

   The students left the gymnasium quietly.
   We talked all night.

2. **Imperative Sentence.** This type is a command or a request. It ends with either a period or an exclamation point. Imperatives do not end with question marks.

Would you please answer the question.
Tell us your name and address, sir.
Go home!

3. **Interrogative Sentence.** This is simply a question; and, of course, it ends with a question mark.

Did you hear the question?
Shall I explain?
Where did you hide the letters?

4. **Exclamatory Sentence.** This is a sentence that expresses strong emotion. It ends with an exclamation point.

I can't believe this!
I refuse, I tell you!
He hit that child twice!

133 **By Structure**

Sentences can be classified according to the way they are set up or written.

1. **Simple Sentence.** A simple sentence is made up of a single independent clause. It may have a compound subject, a compound verb, or both a compound subject and a compound verb; but it contains only one clause.

Tim walked to school. (single subject, single verb)
Tim and Lena walked to school together. (compound subject, single verb)
Tim walked to school and arrived late. (single subject, compound verb)
Tim and Lena walked to school together and talked the entire way. (compound subject, compound verb)

2. **Compound Sentence.** A compound sentence is composed of more independent clauses.

The ledgers were locked in his desk drawer, but I had a key.
The family reunion was planned for May, and I bought my airline tickets in March.

3. **Complex Sentence.** A complex sentence is made up of one *independent clause* and at least one *dependent clause.*

[dependent] [independent
Because of my obligations, I decided to work that day

]
after the funeral ended.

[dependent] [independent
Whenever that happened, he was sullen for several days

]
afterward.

4. **Compound-Complex Sentence.** A compound-complex sentence comprises two or more independent clauses and one or more dependent clauses.

[dependent][independent]
If he searches my closet, he will find the jewelry, and then

[independent
I will have to explain everything to my husband when he hears

]
about it.

[independent] [independent
My friend arrived at midnight, and we went directly to

] [dependent]
Piero's cottage because they needed to settle things.

Exercises

A. Find the subject and the verb of each of the following sentences.

1. The Johns Hopkins University is famous for its excellent medical school.
2. Would Cordelia deliver the manuscript on time and in good order?
3. My father-in-law urged me to apply and defended me to my family.
4. Mrs. Lawton and Miss Genessee favor the first proposal, but the Committee on Development is inclined to vote for the third proposal.

5. There were several hundred students camped out in front of the administrative building.
6. Must I greet him?
7. In the mist, I could see a small boat but recognized neither of the two men aboard.
8. He picked up the glass, then drank.
9. "The Sound of Glass" meets with our criteria for poetry, and we will consider it for publication.
10. Neal, Bryant, Carl, and Will comprise the study group.
11. Did Phyllicia sing at the affair and make a big splash, as usual?
12. Under these unusual and trying circumstances, the staff will be required to remain on call.
13. Do not let me see you here again, not ever.
14. Certainly little information is distributed through that newsletter.
15. Will there be a meeting to discuss the terms of the settlement?
16. Tell me about his running career.
17. Where did the children find those pieces of junk?
18. We cried all night and then gathered ourselves together; moreover, we found ourselves determined to get past those horrible events, and we proceeded to begin a new life.
19. Harriet told Marissa that Benjamin and Elton, among others, were trying to sabotage her efforts.
20. The governments of those states, not the people, can be said to have made these decisions, and the two are not one in the same.

B. Identify the following as fragments (F), run-ons (R), or complete sentences (C).

1. So that I can better understand what you are trying to say and also so that the members of the jury will have a clear idea about what you are saying.
2. Go.
3. Under the table, on the shelf, around the whole room, as we searched but never found the missing item that Claire needed so desperately to find.
4. We had planned to be there to state our opinion on the matter, however, Jan's accident prevented our attending.
5. We knew where Dad was staying, we had no way of finding Uncle Jonas if we needed him.

6. Everything I knew about his finances and all I could find out.
7. When we were vacationing in Ontario, driving around in our camper, we realized we were lost.
8. To understand how difficult it was for her and to figure out a solution to the problem, knowing that I could never really make things right again.
9. I should have known the minute Ms. Cummings sent you here, although I didn't suspect any underhanded plot myself.
10. We weren't surprised to learn of his demise, moreover, we had been expecting it.
11. Since the time I attended that school, unfortunately, never having graduated.
12. Neither the first nor the last time nor any of the incidents in between-none of them.
13. Unless you come with me.
14. The preference being clear, I made my selection.
15. Because I knew better.
16. We needed the money, therefore, I accepted the offer.
17. Will Jenny purchase the car from Mr. Harper, can she afford it?
18. After we had moved from Seattle to Omerville and he had gotten started on his new job.
19. We didn't know where he was, and we didn't really care too much, but we were concerned about our legal responsibility.
20. Under the circumstances, Bertha could not agree to sell the house to him or to anyone else, not at that time.
21. She was an excellent student, nevertheless, she did not win a scholarship to the university as everyone expected she would.
22. As soon as we received the telegram from Simone and Phillippe, not knowing what else to do.
23. Raphael, thinking that he was safe.
24. Margo cried.
25. I assumed that Jason knew, did he?
26. Ellie was an early riser, whereas her husband had a hard time getting up in the morning, and they both had trouble adjusting to each other's schedules.

27. Did he or didn't he?
28. He was a good friend, indeed, the best.
29. Matthew sent his regards, he seemed quite concerned.
30. Where the roof was leaking.
31. Consider this.
32. Going around in that outfit, getting plenty of attention.
33. My typewriter, my dictionary, my pens and pencils, all setting on the desk.
34. After all, didn't you know exactly what was going to occur?
35. To believe your story.

C. Mark each sentence in two ways: by its content (D=declarative, I=interrogative, IMP=imperative); and by its structure (S=simple, C=compound, CX=complex, CC=compound-complex).

1. I didn't know if he was coming or not.
2. Think.
3. She wasn't there, but I was.
4. Would you describe his state of mind.
5. He stabbed her repeatedly, and it was horrible!
6. Unless we made the payment, we would lose our car, and then how would Matthew get to work?
7. Until he came to New York, had he done any acting at all, either on stage or in TV or in the movies?
8. My mother asked me to do it, not my brother.
9. Don't tell me the rest of the story just yet.
10. Sit here and talk to me.
11. When we left, the room was filled with people.
12. Are you certain you didn't talk with Mr. Moore that night, and are you sure you didn't see him the next day?
13. Sometimes when she sang, she messed up but kept on singing regardless of the humiliation.
14. I returned the wallet without taking anything from it.
15. My husband spent about 15 days a month on the road driving a truck and earning a living.

16. Martha and Janet argued and they parted ways.
17. I telephoned his house every 10 minutes that day and never got him.
18. Whenever I met him on the street, he was friendly and cheerful.
19. Both of them were confused by his inability to communicate.
20. I don't know why I bother, why I stay here, why I don't get out.

Parts of Speech

Nearly all words in the English language can be classified as one of the eight parts of speech: nouns, pronouns, verbs, adjectives, adverbs, prepositions, conjunctions, and interjections. These divisions are made according to a word's function within a sentence as well as the idea or concept it represents. Why does a court reporter need to be able to distinguish among the eight parts of speech? They are the fundamentals of grammar and of proper handling of the English language. An understanding of the eight parts of speech is like fitting together all the pieces in a jigsaw puzzle. Suddenly the whole picture becomes clear. Handling the English language in transcripts becomes a far simpler task when the CR understands this fundamental concept.

Some of the information that follows, you may have heard since grammar school. Other parts may be unfamiliar. Go through the entire section, concentrating on those areas where you are weakest.

Nouns

134 The most common definition of a noun is that it names a person, place, or thing. This definition, which many of us first heard in grammar school, is still a good one; but it may be helpful to go further with this definition. Nouns also name someone or something, concepts, ideas, feelings, qualities, animals, establishments.

135 Classifying Nouns

Nouns are either common or proper. Common nouns name an individual or a specific group, but they do not name a particular member of a group; this function belongs to proper nouns. Proper nouns are specific, whereas common nouns are general. Common nouns are lowercased, proper nouns capitalized. Table 2-4 shows some differences between common and proper nouns.

Table 2-4
Common and Proper Nouns

Common	Proper
woman	Mrs. Jensen, Cora B. Smith, Ms. W.A. Muntz
man	Mr. Timmons, Roberto J. Juarez
store	Macy's, Sak's, Bloomingdale's, Sally's Five and Dime, Willie's Meat Market
book	*Jane Eyre, Crime and Punishment*
magazine	*Time, Life, National Geographic*
pet	Rex, Tweety, Minnie, Fido, Benji
road, street, highway	Route 112, Greene Avenue, Apple Lane, Jackman Road, Westway Highway
school, college	University of New Hampshire, Martin Luther King High School, Shelburne Middle School, Bates College
city, town	San Francisco, Miami, Rome, Copenhagen, St. Hubert, Covington, Hot Springs
mountain ranges	Blue Ridge Mountains, Alps, Rockies, Adirondacks, Southern Alps
pain reliever	Bayer, Tylenol, Bufferin, Advil, Nuprin
car	Subaru, Audi, Cadillac, Honda Civic

136 **Collective Nouns**

Collective nouns name a group of words or things that are considered a unit. Table 2-5 lists common collective nouns. Collective nouns often present a problem to the CR because it is not always clear whether they take a singular or plural verb.

Our **herd** of sheep comprises about 225 animals.
The **crew** is on strike.
The **congregation** is opposed to his nomination.

All the examples above use a singular verb because the group acted as a single entity. Thus, the collective noun was treated grammatically as a singular subject. Most collective nouns take singular nouns because the group is acting as a unit; however, there are instances when collective nouns take plural verbs, specifically, when it is clear that the members of the group are acting individually rather than as a unit.

The **staff** were filling out their job descriptions.
The **team** are trying on the new uniforms they just received.
Half of Janna's books are missing.

Although sometimes it is obvious that the members of a group must be acting individually —team members would have to try on their uniforms individually—this issue can be quite confusing. The plural verb is used less frequently than the singular, and this is usually only in cases where the activity under discussion is clearly done individually rather than as a group. When in doubt, use the singular verb.

Table 2-5
Common Collective Nouns

army	crowd	herd
audience	delegation	jury
band	duo	majority
cast	family	membership
choir	flock	number
chorus	fractions:	orchestra
class	one-fourth	panel
coalition	one-half	percent
committee	seven-eighths	platoon
company	two-thirds	staff
congregation	gang	team
crew	group	trio

137 **Concrete and Abstract Nouns**

Another way to classify nouns is according to whether they represent a tangible (concrete) or an intangible (abstract). Concrete nouns name something that can be perceived by any one of the senses, whereas abstract nouns represent ideas, concepts, or qualities. Table 2-6 lists some concrete and abstract nouns.

Table 2-6
Concrete and Abstract Nouns

Concrete	Abstract
window, nail, fence, tablet,	strangeness, fear, hatred,
root, pencil, photograph,	malice, envy, courtesy
shoes, child, lipstick, snow,	sickness, anger, happiness,
ink, necklace, eyeball,	taste, clarity, wisdom,
grandmother, bed, roof, tomato,	beauty, love, malice,
telegram, ponytail, skin, water,	significance, ambition
rubber, ship, tongue, handball,	peace, death, life,
plant, rag, clouds, detergent,	humility, pomposity
lake, blanket, dictionary,	greatness, intelligence,
gun, jacket, toilet, owl,	stringency, tranquility,
freckle, machine, baby, library	apathy, confidence, nosiness

138 Verbal Nouns

Verbal nouns look like verbs but behave within a sentence as nouns. Verbal nouns can be a little confusing, but once recognized should cause little or no problem. Gerunds and infinitives are verbals that can act as nouns.

1. **Gerunds**. Gerunds are verbals that end in *ing* and act as nouns within a sentence. Not all words that end with *ing* are gerunds, although they may be nouns, for example, *awning, evening, gelding.*

   Writing a good novel is my dream. (The gerund acts as the subject of the sentence.)

   Working 20 years in the same job is not exciting, but it is secure. (The gerund acts as the subject of the sentence.)

   It was his third arrest for **drinking** and **driving**. (The gerund act as object of the preposition.)

   His hobby is **sailing**. (The gerund acts as a predicate nominative.)

2. **Infinitives**. Another verbal that can act as a noun within a sentence is the infinitive, which consists of the word *to* combined with a verb. However, not every phrase that begins with the word *to* is an infinitive phrase, as *to* can behave as a preposition as well.

   To listen is not always easy. (The infinitive acts as the subject of the sentence.)

   We liked **to sing**. (The infinitive acts as a direct object.)

   Hannah's ambition was **to dance** on Broadway. (The infinitive acts as predicate nominative.)

139 Nouns and Number

The term number refers to whether a word is singular or plural. The plurals of most nouns are formed by adding the letter *s.*

table/tables
person/persons
pen/pens
tape/tapes
cottage/cottages

- Plurals of words that end in *ch, s, sh, j, x,* or *z* are usually formed by added *es.*

church/churches
bunch/bunches
dish/dishes
lass/lasses
boss/bosses
ax/axes
box/boxes

- To form the plurals of words ending in *f, ff,* or *fe,* usually change the *f, ff,* or *fe* to *ves.*

loaf/loaves
shelf/shelves
life/lives
knife/knives
wolf/wolves
thief/thieves

BUT:

cuff/cuffs
proof/proofs
gaff/gaffs
giraffe/giraffes
skiff/skiffs
boff/boffs
tiff/tiffs

OPTIONAL:

scarf/scarves or scarfs
staff/staffs or staves

- Plurals of nouns that end in the letter *i* are usually formed by adding just *s.*

rabbi/rabbis
kiwi/kiwis
khaki/khakis
alibi/alibis
ski/skis
martini/martinis

- Nouns that end in *o,* if the *o* is preceded by a consonant, usually employ *es* to form the plurals.

heros/heroes

motto/mottoes
veto/vetoes
tomato/tomatoes
mosquito/mosquitoes

There are exceptions to this rule:

halo/halos
gringo/gringos
zero/zeros
commando/commandos

Musical terms use only the *s* to form plurals, not *es*.

banjo/banjos
piano/pianos
octavo/octavos
solo/solos

- Plurals of words ending in *o*, if the *o* is preceded by a vowel, are formed by adding just *s*.

cameo/cameos
ratio/ratios

- Plurals of nouns that end with *y* are usually formed by changing the *y* to *i* and adding *es*.

lady/ladies
baby/babies
spy/spies
cry/cries
city/cities

EXCEPTIONS:

monkey/monkeys
toy/toys
bay/bays
turkey/turkeys

- Some nouns, many of them names of animals, remain the same, whether in singular or plural form.

deer/deer
moose/moose
swine/swine
aircraft

chassis
corps
goods
proceeds
series
scissors
sperm

- Some nouns that are taken from other languages use their original plurals, that is, from the original language.

alumnus/alumni
ovum/ova
phylum/phyla
monsieur/messieurs
larva/larvae

Others have optional plurals, one from the original language and one from English usage.

dogma/dogmas, dogmata
vortex/vortexes, vortices
fungus/fungi, funguses
femur/femurs, femora

- A few plurals are formed by changing the vowels within the noun.

foot/feet
goose/geese
tooth/teeth
woman/women
man/men
mouse/mice

Remember that some words that appear to be plurals are actually singular:

news
whereabouts
checkers

- Plurals of compound words that are not hyphenated, but rather written solid as a single word, make the last part of the compound plural.

workman/workmen
handful/handfuls
chairwoman/chairwomen

- Compounds comprised of several words (either hyphenated or open) are made plural by making the primary or most important part of the compound plural.

  member at large/members at large
  mother-in-law/mothers-in-law
  commander in chief/commanders in chief

- Plurals of proper names are formed as though the names were "regular" nouns usually by adding *s* or *es;* do not, however, change the *y* in a name ending in *y* to *i* and add *es.*

  Harry/Harrys
  Peter/Peters
  Williams/Williamses
  Burger/Burgers
  Johnston/Johnstons
  Carvey/Carveys
  Mary/Marys
  Carolina/Carolinas

Mention should be made here of one of the most common errors involving plurals: Confusing plurals with possessives (see the following section on possessives). For example, family names are frequently written incorrectly, as in the example below.

Wrong

The Black's travel extensively.

Correct

The Blacks travel extensively.

The error of using the possessive form instead of the plural form is a common one. We often see signs on mailboxes or front doors that read: The Miller's, The Willis's, etc. They should be written: The Millers, The Willises.

Remember that plural refers to number; possessive refers to ownership.

- Plurals of abbreviated titles of respect are formed as follows:

  Miss/Misses   Mrs./Mmes.
  Mr./Messrs.   Ms./Mses.

- Plurals of letters or symbols are formed with *'s* if omitting the apostrophe would cause confusion.

  a's   o's   x's

If there is no possibility of confusion, plurals of numbers, letters, and symbols may be formed without the apostrophe.

1970s (1970's is acceptable, though not the preferred style)
ABCs (ABC's is acceptable)
Ps and Qs (P's and Q's is acceptable)

Note: Use the apostrophe to form the plurals of *A, E, I, O,* and *U. As, Es, Is, Os,* and *Us* are words, or look like words, not like plurals of letters.

- The above does not claim to be a complete analysis of plural formation. Every rule has exceptions, sometimes many. It is, however, a general guideline that covers many plurals. As usual, when in doubt, consult the dictionary.

140 Nouns and Ownership

The possessive form of nouns demonstrates ownership or a similar relationship. Most singular possessives are formed by adding *'s* to the singular noun.

The **teacher's** relationship with his students was good, but the principal wanted the **board's** evaluation.

Plural possessives usually are formed by adding an apostrophe after the *s.*

Several **officers'** assignments remained the same, but their **secretaries'** assignment changed dramatically.

There are exceptions. If a singular word already ends with *s,* use just the apostrophe or the *'s.* Some texts advise that the *'s* should be added *if* it is pronounced.

Miles' car

If a plural noun does not end with *s,* treat it as though it were a singular noun by adding *'s.*

children's playground
chairmen's meeting

141 Joint/Individual Ownership

Probably the most troublesome aspect of the possessive nouns is when two or more are used together. The rule is this: for joint ownership, make only the second (or last) noun possessive; for individual ownership, both (or all) should be made possessive.

Mary's and Fran's dresses (unlikely that Mary and Fran would own a single dress jointly)

Mary and Fran's car (if they owned a single car together)

Chung and Kim's restaurants (if they owned a restaurant jointly)

Chung's and Kim's restaurants (if they each owned separate restaurants)

Sometimes *logic* will tell you whether ownership is joint or individual.

Toma's and Mel's toothbrushes (not something anyone would want to share)

In less obvious cases, the content of the transcript hopefully will reveal whether the object or objects are owned individually or jointly.

A relationship similar to ownership, though not exactly the same, employs the possessive form. Examples include such relationships as three months' pay, money's worth, and car's cost.

Exercises

A. Underline all nouns in the following paragraph.

Usually Janet did not take the subway so late at night. Her mother lived about 45 minutes away in an old neighborhood of varied ethnic groups, small groceries, odd shops, cluttered sidewalks. Janet always did the laundry for her elderly mother and aunt. It was a difficult task, primarily because of the hauling involved. Getting the laundry done was not the hard part of the job. To get the clean clothes back to her relatives was a form of torture. Pushing and shoving were necessary to enter the train. To stand there with her baggage in her arms was a strain. The young woman wanted to scream. Her urge was to drop the basket and take off. Exasperation and fatigue, frustration, and annoyance were her constant companions. Standing, walking, enduring all were trials. Janet would refuse to look at the faces of the other riders. Holding tight with one hand to the pole, Janet stared at the floor. The other passengers probably felt annoyance at her for taking so much space. Winter was the worst time because Janet had to wear so much clothing herself, but in some ways summer brought special problems. For example, the heat was nearly unbearable, and the crowds had a restlessness, perhaps an anger. Janet let out a sigh. Is this a privilege? Or is it a burden? Her smile was an involuntary reaction.

B. Which nouns in the paragraph are abstract?

C. Which are verbal nouns?

D. List 10 common nouns and a proper counterpart for each.

E. Collective nouns. Underline or circle the correct verb in each sentence.

1. The committee (is, are) meeting all morning.
2. Our family (has, have) financial difficulties right now.
3. Two-thirds of the students (is, are) attending their special activity meetings.
4. The chorus (has, have) not learned their parts.
5. The orchestra (is, are) picking up their instruments and preparing to play.
6. The flock (is, are) migrating south.
7. The staff (was, were) satisfied with the new CEO.
8. The trio (is, are) performing tonight.
9. The jury (has, have) made its decision.
10. Fifty milliliters (is, are) a sufficient amount.

F. Write first the plural and then the possessive of each of the following nouns.

1. Mr. Loomis
2. baby
3. workman
4. clutch
5. box
6. lord
7. crew
8. Jennifer
9. inch
10. half

11. bench
12. life
13. year
14. library
15. commotion
16. year
17. act
18. boss
19. click
20. editor-in-chief
21. century
22. charm
23. herd
24. crime
25. fox

G. Select the correct form of the plural and/or possessive for each blank.

1. My _______ cars are both wrecked and in the repair shop.
   a. sister and brother's
   b. sisters' and brothers'
   c. sister's and brother's
   d. sisters and brothers
2. Every Saturday we shopped at our favorite general merchandise shop, _______ General Store in Concord.
   a. Santigo, Marco & Garena's
   b. Santigo, Marco's & Garena's
   c. Santigo's, Marco's & Garena's
3. Mary searched all over the building for the _______ room.
   a. lady's
   b. ladies
   c. ladys'
   d. ladies'

4. Every _______ budget is approved by its mayor.

   a. cities

   b. cities'

   c. city's

5. The _______ playground is in unsafe condition.

   a. children's

   b. childrens'

   c. childrens

6. Every employee is entitled to three _______ vacation.

   a. week's

   b. weeks

   c. weeks'

7. The organization for city bus _______ met last night.

   a. drivers

   b. drivers'

   c. driver's

8. The police found several fingerprints left by the _______.

   a. thieves

   b. thiefs

   c. thief's

9. Several _______ complaints were heard by the manager.

   a. customer's

   b. customers

   c. customers'

10. Do you feel that you got your five _______ worth?

    a. dollars

    b. dollars'

    c. dollar's

11. My _______ phone number has been changed recently.

    a. sister-in-law's

    b. sister's-in-law

    c. sister's-in-law's

12. I was having lunch with _______ Black, Thomasie, and Cruz.

   a. Misters'

   b. Mister

   c. Messrs.

   d. Mr.'s

13. His ______ health was checked by the veterinarian, who proclaimed it to be very fit.

   a. dogs

   b. dogs'

   c. dog's

14. ______ reward is more than just physical.

   a. Runnings

   b. Running

   c. Runnings'

   d. Running's

15. Three _______ is too much to then go drive.

   a. drinks

   b. drink's

   c. drinks'

16. His _______ were never important to him.

   a. job's

   b. jobs

   c. jobs'

17. The _______ assignments had become far too time consuming and difficult.

   a. class's

   b. class'

   c. classes

18. Whenever I couldn't find Tony, I checked with the _______.

   a. Jacksons

   b. Jacksons'

   c. Jackson's

19. _______ quality, in my opinion, is improving, albeit only slightly.

a. Televisions

b. Television's

c. Televisions'

d. Television

20. The _______ safety was questionable, particularly in light of recent events.

a. campus's

b. campuses

c. campus

H. Correct any errors in plural or possessive nouns in the following paragraph.

My brothers wife was having problem's with the Clifton's. The Cliftons were her neighbors' in the seaside town where she had lived for five year's. Janeen, was just one of my three sister-in-laws, and she had no kid's. The Cliftons children lived with Janeen and her dog, Rufus Jone's. Rufus Jones' size was an amazement—135 pounds of thick cream-colored hair and huge black eye's. He loved to go over to the Cliftons' to play with the boy's and girl's next door. Rufus Jones was docile animal whose greatest fault was his clumsiness. Rufuses' bark, however, was loud. The Clifton childrens love of the dog could not overcome their parents objections to the dogs' visitations.

Functions of Nouns

142 We know the definitions of nouns, and we know that they can be singular or plural; they can also be possessive. We now take a look at the ways nouns function within a sentence. Nouns are extremely versatile and can put on many "faces" within a sentence. Except for pronouns, nouns have more functions than any of the other parts of speech.

The following is a list of noun functions:

1. subject of a clause
2. direct object

3. indirect object
4. predicative nominative (also called predicate noun)
5. appositive
6. direct address
7. object of a preposition

These are the primary ways in which nouns can be used, and each will be discussed in some detail.

143 Subject of a Clause

When we talk about subjects, we usually mean the subject of a sentence, that is, who or what is doing the action or experiencing the "state of being." Not only sentences have subjects, however. Dependent clauses also have subjects.

Subject of a Complete Sentence:

My **friends** seemed to have abandoned me then.
Opinions and **objections** can be raised after we return from recess.

Subject of a Dependent Clause:

If **Mrs. Fobbes** returns tomorrow, we shall see her.
Benjamin ran away from home because his **parents** were divorcing.

144 Direct Object

The direct object is easily found in sentences that have an active verb. Formula: Find the verb, find the subject of the verb; then say subject + verb, and ask "who" or "what."

Jimmy caught the **cat** by the tail.
We found **ashes** in the fireplace.
Kochi handed Sue the **box**.

Direct objects are found not only in main clauses, but also in dependent clauses.

I knew that Paul had hit **Sarah**.
Unless the doctor treated **James**, the boy would continue to suffer.

Direct objects can be verbals.

I have tried **to learn.**
The children love **swimming.**

145 Indirect Object

The indirect object usually can be found between the verb and the direct object. Not every sentence that contains a direct object will have an indirect object, but there can never be an indirect object unless there is a direct object. The formula is: Say subject + verb + direct object, and then ask "to whom"or "to what."

Maurice gave **Nelson** the answers to the examination.
Did Mr. Frasier tell **Kate** the truth?

146 Predicative Nominative

The predicative nominative, sometimes called the predicate noun, renames the subject. The verb will be a "state of being" verb (am, is, are, was, were, shall be, will be, has been, was named, was elected) rather than an action verb.

Mr. Brown was named **chairman** last night.
Jeremy is her **hero.**
Terrence Hardin is a **fool** and a **clown**, but he is also my **friend** and **confidante.**
Harriet hoped to be elected **president** of the senior class.
My brother may seem adventurous, but he is really a **whimp.**

Note: Remember that the predicate nominative renames; for example, in the first example above, *Jeremy* and *hero* are the same person. It is easy to confuse the predicate nominative with the predicate adjective, which does not rename, but rather describes. In the third example, *adventurous* is a predicate adjective, not a predicate nominative, because it describes rather than renames.

147 Appositive

An appositive, like a predicate nominative, renames; however, it is in apposition to, or next to, the word it renames. Position, then, is the difference between an appositive and a predicate nominative. Appositives are usually, though not always set off by commas. (See the section on commas in Unit 3, Punctuation.)

My supervisor at work, **Mrs. Dominick,** allowed me to work flexible hours.
Cecilia, my close **friend,** will be moving to another country by the end of the year.

Of my three brothers, my brother **Joseph** was the least likely to become involved in that sort of activity.

148 Direct Address

Direct address names the person or thing being talked to in a sentence. It is followed by a comma if it occurs at the beginning of a sentence, set off with commas if in midsentence, and preceded by a comma if it occurs at the end of a sentence. Direct address can be a proper name or other term for the person or thing being spoken to.

Certainly, **Mother**, I will inform you of his progress.
Don't you remember, **Mr. Reynolds**, whom you called?
No, **sir**, I do not have that information.

149 Object of a Preposition

The object of a preposition completes the meaning of the preposition. The preposition and its object, and often a word or words that modify the object, constitute a prepositional phrase. (See the section on prepositions in this unit.)

I saw him hiding beneath the dining room **table**.
We couldn't grasp the meaning of his **lecture**.

Exercises

A. Indicate the function of each underlined noun (SC = subject of a clause, DO = direct object, IO = indirect object, PN = predicate nominate, AP = appositive, DA = direct address, OP = object of the preposition.

I was planning a <u>meeting</u> with <u>Mr. Thornton</u> and Mrs. Willoughby, but I must tell you, <u>Caroline</u>, I was dreading the <u>discussion</u> with those <u>people</u>. I couldn't make <u>contact</u> with <u>Harrold Bensen</u>, my attorney and general <u>advisor</u> in all of life's <u>challenges</u>, because his <u>sister</u>, <u>Beatrice Bensen McLevy</u>, was experiencing some <u>problems</u>. He had gone to visit her. Anyway, my <u>friend</u>, I had planned the <u>encounter</u> in every <u>detail</u>. <u>Mrs. Willoughby</u> is a <u>stormtrooper</u> of a <u>woman</u>, not an agreeable sort by any <u>means</u>. I give <u>Mr. Thornton</u> <u>credit</u>, however, because he has charm and good sense. The table, a large oak <u>beauty</u>, was cleared of all of my <u>paperwork</u>, and I thought that my <u>planning</u> was complete. An unexpected <u>visitor</u>, however, my <u>father</u>, changed everything. He entered my <u>house</u> like a <u>hurricane</u> presents itself to the coastline of <u>Florida</u>.

B. Write five sentences using an appositive and then rewrite those same sentences to employ a predicate nominative.

C. Write two sentences for each of the following words. In the first sentence use the word as a direct object, and in the second use *it* as an indirect object.

1. Tommy
2. the prosecutor
3. my sister-in-law
4. child
5. professor
6. Mrs. Millet
7. Dad
8. Davis P. Donnat
9. the fireman
10. classmates

Pronouns

150 At first glance, pronouns might seem to be simpler to manage than other parts of speech because there are a limited number of them. Yet this is far from being the case; indeed, pronouns are perhaps the most troublesome of all the parts of speech. Pronouns are complicated by factors such as case and pronoun-antecedent agreement. To learn to use pronouns correctly requires considerable effort, but once mastered, the skill will be yours for life.

An understanding of pronouns is important to the CR for the same reason that the CR needs to know grammar in general. The CR must produce correct English as spoken by the attorneys and judges. For example, the sentence below contains a pronoun error:

> **Whoever** I asked to do the work for me, I knew I would have to assist that person greatly.

Did you find it? The pronoun **whoever** should be **whomever**. We shall examine why later in this section.

151 The definition of pronouns is a familiar one: they take the place of nouns.

Simon met Simon's wife while Simon and Simon's wife served on a committee in Simon's favorite charity.

Using pronouns can make the above sentence read much better:

Simon met **his** wife while **he** and **his** wife served on a committee in **his** favorite charity.

152 **Personal Pronouns**

Personal pronouns may be first-person, second-person, or third-person. First-person pronouns refer to the person(s) or being(s) *doing* the speaking. Second-person pronouns refer to the person(s) or being(s) that are being spoken *to*. Third-person pronouns refer to the person(s) or being(s) that are being spoken *about*. Table 2-7 lists the personal pronouns.

FIRST-PERSON PRONOUNS:

I told Maria about **my** hopes, but she didn't encourage **me** at all.

We found **our** home had been broken into, and someone had robbed **us**.

SECOND-PERSON PRONOUNS:

You saw that work was appreciated, I assume.

Your wardrobe enhances **your** appearance, but **you** know that his admiration is already **yours**.

THIRD-PERSON PRONOUNS:

She expected **him** to do **his** part in planning **their** seminar.

He hoped that **their** children would improve **their** grades.

Her garden was small, but **it** was becoming a real showplace.

I expected **them** by 8:00, but **they** never arrived.

Table 2-7
Personal Pronouns

	Singular	Plural
First Person	I, my, mine, me	we, our, ours, us
Second Person	you, your, yours	you, your, yours
Third Person	he, his, him, she, her, hers, it, its	they, their, theirs, them

153 Case

Pronouns change in form according to their case. Case refers to the way in which a pronoun is used in a sentence—as a subject or as an object, for example. This is perhaps the most important aspect of pronouns. The issue of case is the one that the CR faces when he or she is unsure whether to use who or whom, I or me, he or him.

There are three cases: nominative, objective, and possessive (genitive).

1. **Nominative Case.** Also known as the subjective case. Pronouns in the nominative case usually function as subjects or predicate nominatives. Pronouns that can be used in the nominative case are as follows:

   FIRST PERSON: I, we
   SECOND PERSON: you
   THIRD PERSON: he, she, it, they
   INTERROGATIVE/RELATIVE PRONOUN: who, whoever
   They sought the truth. (subject)
   I heard that **he** was sick, but **who** told me. (subjects)
   The only players receiving awards were Adam and **I**. (predicate nominative)

2. **Objective Case.** Pronouns in the objective case are used as the direct object, indirect object, or object of a preposition. Pronouns that can be used in the objective case are as follows:

   FIRST PERSON: me, us
   SECOND PERSON: you
   THIRD PERSON: him, her, it, them
   INTERROGATIVE/RELATIVE PRONOUN: whom, whomever
   Mona gave **me** an unusually expensive gift. (indirect object)
   The Williams family was suing **us**. (direct object)
   He doesn't believe **you**. (direct object)
   I did it all for **him**, for **us**. (objects of the preposition)
   I told **them** the truth. (indirect object)
   Whom can I trust? (direct object)
   Ralph grabbed **her** and held on to her arm. (direct object)
   Whomever Miss Luce, promotes, I know it will be a change for the better. (direct object)

   Note: The last two sentences contain pronouns that are not used in the objective case: **her** arm (possessive pronoun) and **it** (subject of clause).

3. **Possessive (Genitive) Case.** The genitive case is the possessive form of pronouns:

FIRST PERSON: my, mine, our, ours
SECOND PERSON: your, yours
THIRD PERSON: his, her, hers, its, their, theirs
INTERROGATIVE/RELATIVE PRONOUN: whose

If a possessive pronoun is used with a noun, it acts as an adjective.

My money has been taken.
The animal ate **its** food.
His viewpoint is not as clear as **her** opinion.

Do not confuse possessive pronouns with contractions.

Correct

That blame was ours, not yours.

Wrong

That blame was our's, not your's.

154 Confusion over when to use the nominative case of the pronoun and when to use the objective case is a common problem, especially with *who* and *whom.* Because pronouns are noun substitutes, they are used in the same ways that nouns are used. Unlike nouns, however, pronouns have *case,* which depends solely on the function of the word in the sentence. For example, pronouns that function as the subject of the sentence are in nominative case, as is the predicate nominative. A pronoun that shows possession is possessive case, obviously, and pronouns that function as objects take the objective case. The following sentences demonstrate common errors and explain why they are incorrect.

Who did Mr. Harris see in his office?
You made those photocopies for **who**?

The subject of the first sentence is *Mr. Harris*; the verb is *see.* That makes *who* a direct object; therefore it must be in the objective case. The subject of the second sentence is *you,* the verb *made.* You made what? *Photocopies* (direct object). So what is the function of *who?* It is the object of the preposition *for* and therefore must be in the objective case. The sentences, corrected, would read as:

Whom did Mr. Harris see in his office?
You made those photocopies for **whom**?

OTHER EXAMPLES:

Janette and **me** are confused about our roles in this department.
Ben Reiger invited Joe, Carmen, and **I** to the theater.

The subject of the first sentence is *Janette* and *me,* which must be in the nominative case. Thus the subject must be *I,* not *me.* The subject of the second sentence is *Ben Reiger,* the verb is *invited;* the direct object is *Joe, Carmen,* and *I.* The *I* is incorrect because a direct object must be in the objective case, which is *me.* The corrected sentences read as follows:

Janette and **I** are confused about our roles in this department.
Ben Reiger invited Joe, Carmen, and **me** to the theater.

When confronted with sentences like those above, taking an extra moment to ask yourself how the pronoun functions in the sentence will clear up any confusion about correct usage.

155 Interrogative Pronouns

These are the pronouns that ask a question: who, whose, which, what, whom.

Who is the best player?
Whom did you ask?
What do you think he wanted?
Which was the clearest of the three?

Interrogative pronouns can function as adjectives when they are next to the noun they modify.

Whose coat was warmer?
What dress did you buy?
Whose account had the most money in it?

Interrogative pronouns can act as the subject of a verb.

Who was going to the seminar?
Which is the better bargain?

Interrogative pronouns can function as the direct object.

Whom did he see?
What did the minister say?

Interrogative pronouns can act as the object of a preposition.

With **whom** had you discussed the strategy?

For **what** did you seek?

Interrogative pronouns can act as the indirect object.

You loaned **whom** $5,000?

156 Relative Pronouns

Relative pronouns act as subordinators; that is, they join a clause to a noun or pronoun. Relative pronouns include *that, whoever, whomever, who, whom,* and *which.* Note that some relative pronouns are the same as some of the interrogative pronouns. The difference is in the way they are used in the sentence. Relative pronouns can also act as the subject of a clause, as in the second example below.

The students **who** played sports often did very well scholastically.
Whoever runs the show, I will offer my support.
Mr. Trask was the only associate **who** had no ambition to become a partner.
I thought **that** he had returned the report to her for input.

157 Demonstrative Pronouns

These serve to point: *this, that, these, those.* The demonstrative pronouns can serve as adjectives when they are placed next to a noun, but they often stand alone without a noun.

These issues have been raised before. (with noun)
These are for you. (without noun)
That idea is ridiculous, Samuel. (with noun)
That is truly harsh. (without noun)

158 Indefinite Pronouns

These pronouns refer to no specific person or thing and set no limitations. Some of the most common indefinite pronouns are:

all	either	neither	some
anybody	everybody	nobody	somebody
anyone	everyone	none	someone
both	everything	no one	something
each	many	several	

Most indefinite pronouns take a singular verb.

No one is going to confront David.
None of the pie **is** missing.

Everybody has seen his temper flare.
Someone has come forward in his defense.
Each is acceptable, but **neither is** excellent.

Both, few, many, several, and *others* take a plural verb.

Both young men **are** overachievers.
Many were the insecurities that contributed to his fear.
Others were considered, but **few were** accepted.

Some indefinite pronouns can be singular or plural, depending on the content of the sentence, including the pronouns *all, none,* and *some.*

Some were eager but **none** were really thrilled.
Some of the truth was told.
None of your hope need be dashed.

159 Reflexive and Intensive Pronouns

Reflexive and intensive pronouns are the self pronouns: myself, yourself, himself, herself, ourselves, themselves, yourselves, itself. These pronouns are reflexive when the performer and the receiver of the action are the same.

I told **myself** it couldn't be true.
He saw **himself** as a failure.
You torment **yourself** by thinking about it so much.

Intensive pronouns, on the other hand, are used for emphasis. They emphasize the noun or pronouns they follow.

I **myself** saw the robbery
The doctor **himself** prescribed this.
You **yourself** know the truth.

One of the most common errors involving reflexive pronouns is using them where an objective case pronoun should be used.

He talked it over with Jim and **myself.** (**Me** is the correct form.)

160 Pronoun-Antecedent Agreement

A pronoun and its antecedent must agree in person, number, and gender.

I will see **my** son next month. (first-person singular)
The **singers** have performed **their** songs for us. (third-person plural)

Third-person singular pronouns must also agree in gender (masculine, feminine, or neuter) with the nouns they refer to. Most nouns are neuter *(rug, desk, newspaper, street)* and replaced by a form of the neuter pronoun *it.* Some are clearly masculine *(man, waiter, actor)* or clearly feminine *(woman, waitress, actress).*

The cleaning **woman** left **her** purse in our kitchen.
The **book** has lost **its** appeal for me.
Lee and Russell lost **their** savings to an unethical business endeavor.
Sheila sent **her** best regards.

Some nouns can be either masculine or feminine *(student, child, person, employee).* Whereas it was once considered "correct" to use the masculine pronoun for a noun that could be either feminine or masculine, the preferred style now is to present both alternatives.

Outdated

Each employee should clear **his** desk at day's end.

Current

Each employee should clear **his or her** desk at day's end.

- Pronoun-antecedent agreement can become a source of confusion when the antecedent is an indefinite pronoun.

  1. The following take a singular pronoun: *each, either, neither, one, everyone, everybody, no one, nobody, anyone, anybody, someone, somebody.* If the gender is unclear or undetermined, use *he* or *she, his* or *her, him* or *her.*

Each applicant is required to list three references on *his or her* resume.
Someone will have to give up *his or her* computer.
Neither George nor Mr. Farris drove *his* car. (clearly masculine)

  2. Depending on the meaning of the sentence, use either singular or plural pronouns with the following: *none, most, all.*

     Most of the girls in my class did their best.
     All of our dogs have their own beds and bowls.

- Collective nouns take singular or plural verbs, usually singular (see section 136 on collective nouns), *unless* the members of the group are clearly acting as individuals.

  The **commission** is united in **its** decision.

The **team** is hoping to win **its** last game.
The **team** are putting on **their** new uniforms.
My **family** is having **its** reunion on Thanksgiving Day.
My **family** have **their** own ideas about their careers.
The **mob** was led by **its** furor.
The **mob** went to **their** homes.

Exercises

A. Find any errors in the use of pronouns and correct them.

Either my cousin or my brother will help by giving his advice. Of course, Miss Bethune and Jack will be willing to accompany Holly and I to the act of sale. My brother will help whomever does the paperwork. None of my family members are envious of me purchasing the family estate. It is me who feels a bit odd about it. The house has it's sentimental value, of course, but its also a beauty of a home. I came up with the idea of buying it, not Holly or him. All of my cousins, including Alan and Hilary, have had his doubts about my moving into the old place, but their concerns are not the same as your's. Neither Alan nor Hilary knows who's house it is at present, but him and her will know soon enough.

B. Select and underline the proper word for each sentence.

1. Do you want to go to the theater with Jim and (I, me)?
2. It is (I, me) who needed the dictionary.
3. The chairmen is (he, him).
4. Just between (we, us) members, I think that nonmembers should not be allowed to attend.
5. He did it for Eva and (I, me).
6. (We, Us) students are planning a protest tomorrow morning.
7. (Who, Whom) did you work with at Miller & Ornette?
8. I thought that jacket was (yours, your's).
9. The best candidate is (her, she).
10. (Ours, Our's) is the smallest house on the block, I think.
11. (Who, Whom) do you think will be selected?

12. The woman I saw in the back of the building was (her, she).

13. The only employees who had to stay late were Maria, Timothy, and (I, me).

14. The house was lovely, but (its, it's) price was just too high for us.

15. We received several letters from Patricia Dell and (her, she).

16. Last month our class gave (its, their) end-of-the-year program.

17. If anyone wants to leave now, (he, she, they, he or she) may depart at intermission.

18. Either of my sisters could have left (her, their) coat here.

19. Catherine is in trouble, not (I, me).

20. Neither Sam nor Michael has (his, their) summer job yet.

21. Each of their children (has, have) a car.

22. Neither of my brothers (feel, feels) sure about (his, their) future in the family company.

23. Both of my brothers will have (his, their) education paid by grants.

24. The company is looking to hire three persons for (its, their) publicity department.

25. Everyone in my classes (is, are) aware of my struggle.

Verbs

161 The *verb* is one of the two main parts of a sentence, the other being the subject of the verb. Without a verb, a group of words cannot be a complete sentence. The *complete verb* includes all the words in a sentence that, combined, tell what was done or describe a condition or state of being. The *complete subject* includes all the words that, combined, tell about whom or what the sentence is speaking. Thus, simple sentences can be divided into two distinct parts—complete subject and complete verb. (For purposes of this book, the term *predicate* will not be discussed or distinguished from the term *verb.*)

Tomas, Sven, and Marijo / have entered the training program
(complete subject) (complete verb)

The simple subject and simple verb are the main or primary word(s) in the complete subject and verb, without modifiers or phrases or parentheticals. For example, in the example above, the simple subject and simple verb are :

Tomas, Sven, Marijo / have entered

Henceforth in this text the term *verb* will refer to the simple verb, and the term *subject* will refer to the simple subject.

162 Inverted Order

Usually the verb follows the subject, but inverted sentences reverse this order.

NORMAL: Several stipulations are attached to the document.
INVERTED: To the document are attached several stipulations

Inversion does not change the form of the verb or the meaning of the sentence. When dealing with an inverted sentence, if confusion occurs about the form of the verb that should be employed, turn the sentence around in your head to normal order. Whatever verb seems correct in normal order will be correct in the inverted form as well.

INVERTED: Carried unanimously were the three environmental bills.
NORMAL: The three environmental bills were carried unanimously.
INVERTED: Burdened by his responsibilities is my son.
NORMAL: My son is burdened by his responsibilities.

163 Auxiliary Verbs

Auxiliary verbs, or helping verbs, are used along with other verbs to help in forming the various tenses, moods, etc. A list of the 23 common auxiliary verbs can be found in the Glossary. An auxiliary verb is part of the simple verb, and a main verb can have more than one auxiliary verb.

The police officer **was** issuing a warning.
He **could have** said more, but he was exhausted.
You really **must** depart soon.
Melanie **would** become an excellent nurse.

Some of the verbs used as auxiliaries can serve as verbs in their own right or can be used alone, not as "helpers."

She **is** the best supervisor.
They **were** friends for many years.

164 Subject-Verb Agreement

Subjects and verbs within a sentence must agree in person and in number. In other words, a singular subject takes a singular verb, and a plural subject takes a plural verb. This sounds simple—and it generally is.

> **Matthew is** studying in the library.
> **Matthew** and **Victor are** studying in the library.

The second sentence above is a compound subject, which will always take a plural verb.

- Sentences that begin with "There" often cause confusion. To remedy this situation, the CR should consider the sentence as it would read "turned around."

  There is a problem with those pieces of correspondence.
  THINK: A problem is there with the pieces of correspondence.
  There were no greater confusions in my mind than what he intended.
  THINK: No greater confusions were there in my mind than what he intended.

- Another source of confusion in subject-verb agreement is in the use of collective nouns. Most collective nouns take a singular verb, but a few take plural verbs. The test is to decide whether the members act as a group or as individuals. The distinction is not always perfectly clear, but the CR should give the matter some thought and try to come to a conclusion; if no clear conclusion can be made, use the singular verb. (See the section on collective nouns in this unit.)

  1. The **board** of directors **is** scheduled to meet next month.
  2. The **orchestra were putting** on their uniforms.
  3. The **committee is voting** next month to resolve those issues.

- Subject-verb agreement can be clouded by correlatives. If both subjects are singular, then use a singular verb. (See the section on conjunctions in this unit.)

  Neither **Peter** nor **Bernard is** in favor of the move.
  Either my **sister** or my **secretary was** to pick up my briefcase.

- If both subjects are plural, use a plural verb.

  Neither my past **hopes** nor my future **aspirations were** inspirational.

Either the **plumbers** or the **carpenters have** overcharged.

- If one of the subjects is singular and the other one is plural, the verb should agree with the one that is *closer* to the verb in the sentence.

  Neither the **agent** nor the **clients have an** understanding of the contract.

  Neither the **clients** nor the **agent has** an understanding of the contract.

  Either the **bookkeeper** or the **accountants do** the job.

  Either the **accountants** or the **bookkeeper does** the job.

- Considerable confusion in subject-verb agreement is caused by intervening words—that is, words that occur between the subject and verb. These are usually phrases. If intervening words cause a problem, just imagine the sentence without those words. Find the subject and the verb of the main clause, ignoring for the moment the elements that fall between, and check to see if the subject and verb agree.

  The **book** of photographs of my family—including my grandparents and dozens of cousins—**was setting** on the coffee table when I last saw it.

In the example above, the subject is *book*, so the verb must be singular: *was sitting.*

  That rickety old **shelf** holding up the hundreds of books that we inherited **is** just about to fall down.

  A parking **lot** full of cars **was** the scene of the robbery.

  Mario's **friends**, including Peter, **become** rowdy when they drink.

  Mr. **Johnson**, accompanied by his bodyguards, **was trying** to enter the church after the wedding was in progress.

- Compound subjects that speak of a single person or entity, and not of plural persons or things, should be considered a singular subject and thus take a singular verb.

  The group's founder and current president **is** Olivia Marshall.

  Note: In the example above, the founder and president are the same individual—Olivia Marshall. If two different individuals were the subject, the verb would be plural.

  The group's founder and the current president **are** Olivia Marshall and Teri Langlois, respectively.

  Ham and eggs **is** my favorite breakfast.

My friend and confidante, Sylvia Jean, **has brought** me through many catastrophes.

- Titles of books, movies, songs, magazines, newspapers, or other similar titles may be plural in form, but they take a singular verb because they represent a single entity.

"Children of the Corn" **was** a frightening movie.

"The Northwest Counties" **is distributed** weekly at local stores.

"The Big Cats" **was** an excellent television program and of interest to animal lovers of any age.

Note: Titles are traditionally underlined or italicized in print, but CRs use quotation marks. (See the section on quotation marks in Unit 3, Punctuation.)

- Relative pronouns often are used as the subject of a dependent clause. Deciding what verb is correct is sometimes not easy. Use the verb that would be appropriate to the antecedent of the relative pronoun.

The man who **is sitting** next to Mr. Veriana accosted my brother.

In the example above, the antecedent of *who* is *man;* thus, the verb should be singular.

I, who **am** an only child, have always envied people from large families.

In the example above, the antecedent of *who* is *I;* thus, the first-person singular verb is used.

Subject-verb agreement can be tricky after the expression *one of.*

Correct

He is one of those men who always **have** something to say.

(The relative pronoun *who* refers to *men,* not *one,* so the plural verb *have* is used.)

Wrong

He is one of those men who always **has** something to say.

BUT:

Gil behaves as though he is the only man in the United States who **is going** through a divorce.

She is the only one of my friends who never **forgets** my birthday.

Another tricky construction involves "the only one who." The singular verb is used.

Jaspar thinks he's the only one of the workers who **is** competent.

- A predicate nominative that does not agree in number with its subject can cause confusion. The verb should agree in number with the subject, not with the predicate nominative.

His proudest **moment was** his feats on the playground.
The **mosquitos** in the area **were** his biggest complaint.
The **impediment was** the security measurements.

- Sometimes plural subjects are used to mean a single unit. In such cases, use a singular verb.

A **hundred centimeters** is the correct amount.
Ten dollars is all I have.
Five hours is the duration of the film.

- Fractions are handled by looking at the word to which they refer.

One-fourth of my **savings** is gone. (singular)
One-half of the **students** are failing. (plural)

165 Tense

Tense refers to time of the action. Every verb has three principal parts used to form its various tenses: the present, past, and past participle. The past participle is used with an auxiliary (helping) verb.

Regular verbs usually form the past and past participle by adding *ed* to the present form:

Present	Past	Past Participle
look	looked	looked
work	worked	worked
wish	wished	wished
clean	cleaned	cleaned
seem	seemed	seemed

This list could go on and on, but there would be little point in that. In sentences, they are used as follows:

Marvin and I **work** every Saturday night. (present)
Marvin and I **worked** last Saturday night. (past)

Marvin and I have **worked** every Saturday night this year. (past participle with auxiliary verb)

Things **seem** better now. (present)

Things **seemed** to get better. (past)

Things had **seemed** to improve. (past participle with auxiliary verb)

The problem with tense occurs with verbs whose principal parts do not follow this regular pattern. There are more than two hundred such verbs in English. Table 2-8 gives a sampling of irregular verbs. The dictionary lists the forms with the present-tense entry of a verb. For example, if you look up *eat,* the dictionary entry will give *ate* and *eaten,* the past and past participle forms of that verb. Doubt about troublesome verbs can be resolved by checking the dictionary.

The six tenses are: present, past, future, present perfect, past perfect, and future perfect. The **present tense** is used to express an action that is occurring at the present time or one that is ongoing. The **past tense** is used to express an action that occurred before the statements or that did exist at some point in the past. The **future tense**, obviously, discusses something that will occur in the future. The **future perfect** tense indicates an action that will have occurred before a specific time in the future. The **present perfect** tense describes an action that was initiated at some point in the past and continued into the present *or* that has already been completed at the time the statement is made. The **past perfect** tense indicates something that has already happened before another action that also occurred in the past. There is no need for the CR to spend a lot of time on tenses, but listed below are examples of each tense:

Present: Mr. Roberts sings well.

Past: Mr. Roberts once sang well.

Future: Mr. Roberts will sing a solo tonight.

Present Perfect: Mr. Roberts has sung many times previously.

Past Perfect: Mr. Roberts had sung many times previously.

Future Perfect: Mr. Roberts will have sung more than any other guest performer.

Present: Janna is happy.

Past: Janna was happy.

Future: Janna will be happy.

Present Perfect: Janna has been happy.

Past Perfect: Janna had been happy.

Future Perfect: Janna will have been happy.

Table 2-8
Irregular Verbs

Present	Past	Past Participle
am	was	been
are	were	been
become	became	become
begin	began	begun
break	broke	broken
bring	brought	brought
burst	burst	burst
buy	bought	bought
choose	chose	chosen
come	came	come
do	did	done
draw	drew	drawn
drink	drank	drunk
drive	drove	driven
eat	ate	eaten
fall	fell	fallen
freeze	froze	frozen
give	gave	given
go	went	gone
grow	grew	grown
know	knew	known
lay	laid	laid
leave	left	left
lie	lay	lain
make	made	made
pay	paid	paid
ride	rode	ridden
ring	rang	rung
run	ran	run
see	saw	seen
send	sent	sent
set	set	set
shine	shone	shone
sing	sang	sung
speak	spoke	spoken
spring	sprang	sprung
steal	stole	stolen
swim	swam	swum
take	took	taken
wear	wore	worn
write	wrote	written

166 Voice

Verbs can be active or passive. A subject with an active verb is performing the action. A subject with a passive verb is having the action done to him, her, or it.

> **Active:** Juan mowed five lawns today.
> **Passive:** Our lawn was mowed by Juan.
> **Active:** The typewriter fell from the desk.
> **Passive:** The typewriter was dropped by Paula.

Exercise

A. Select and underline the correct verb for each sentence.

1. There (is, are) a lot of boys in our yard.
2. There (is, are) a lot of soup in the pot.
3. There (is, are) a dollar bill in your wallet.
4. There (is, are) five one-dollar bills in your wallet.
5. My brother, and the pest that drives me crazy, (is, are) named Jason.
6. The team (is, are) putting on their shoes.
7. Each boy and girl (is, are) going to be questioned individually.
8. A pair of scissors (is, are) sitting in your sewing basket.
9. Alan's toys, including his basketball, (is, are) scattered throughout the kitchen.
10. Economics (is, are) my worst course.
11. The left tire, not to mention the brakes and shocks, (has, have) to be replaced.
12. Neither the president nor the members (has, have) any ideas about how to raise money for the club.
13. Television, even Saturday cartoons, (becomes, become) tiresome after a couple of hours.
14. The owner of that house and a millionaire in his own right (is, are) my cousin Winston Perron.
15. Either the watch or the bracelets (is, are) going to have to be removed.
16. Many children, including my son, (does, do) poor work if the radio is on.

17. May is one of those workers who (has, have) a genuinely positive attitude towards the job.
18. You, who (knows, know) the truth, cannot remain silent.
19. That's only one of the five books which (is, are) to be read for the novels course this semester.
20. A shelf stacked with encyclopedia volumes (is, are) about to fall.
21. "The Williams Boys" (is, are) a new TV program.
22. My problem (is, are) those bugs.
23. That bunch of roses (has, have) fallen onto the floor.
24. The men who are running for chairman (is, are) speaking tonight.
25. "Just One of the Girls" (has, have) run a long time.

B. The present tense of the verb is listed to the left of each sentence. Fill in the blank with the correct form of that verb.

lie	1.	He has ________ on the bed staring at the ceiling for most of the day.
burst	2.	She has ________ my bubble with her lack of enthusiasm.
begin	3.	I had ________ to like the job until my supervisor resigned.
lay	4.	That old newspaper has ________ on the dining room table since Sunday.
break	5.	You will have ________ every rule in the book if you do that.
pay	6.	Ellen has ________ for everything, and she cannot afford it.
steal	7.	Andy has ________ all of my ideas.
swim	8.	I had never ________ that far or long before.
drive	9.	After we have ________ around the block a couple of times, can we take the car out on the highway?
go	10.	David has ________ to all of his concerts.
wear	11.	I've ________ this dress to every formal function at the university for the past five years.
ride	12.	The horses were ________ too hard by those boys, so refuse to rent to them.
choose	13.	Rodriguez has been ________ to lead the neighborhood meeting.

shine	14. The sun Shone brightly every morning last week, but there were showers every afternoon.
slay	15. The criminal admits to having Slain the three students.
set	16. I set my purse down and now it's gone.
rise	17. The water rose three feet during the night.
leave	18. Candy had left her pets with me for three weeks.
raise	19. Nell's salary was raised by 8 percent.
is	20. Carl has been married three times.
speak	21. Ellis has spoken of you many times.
seek	22. We Sought to find a solution to this controversy.
become	23. Harrison had become a constant thorn in my side.
sort	24. The clerical worker has sorted through the files, but to no avail.
withhold	25. My supervisor had withheld vital information from her own boss.

C. Transform the following inverted sentences to sentences in normal order.

1. Under the chest of drawers is my wallet.
2. Within the realm of possibility are such hopes and dreams.
3. Beneath all of the chaos is an underlying sound idea.
4. To the barn we shall go.
5. Within his company can be found many fine analysts.

D. Change the following sentences written in present tense to future perfect.

1. The tree is growing tall.
2. The dentist works only four days per week.
3. The typewriter breaks each week.
4. He is speaking to his father about a loan.
5. The book rests on the top shelf.
6. My paperwork and my file cabinet are in the office.
7. He pumps gas at his uncle's station.

8. Our savings grow.
9. The car drives roughly.
10. Triumph is at hand.

Adjectives

167 Adjectives serve to modify, describe, limit, or define nouns and pronouns. They and adverbs behave as modifiers. There are five basic classifications of adjectives: descriptive, proper, articles, possessive, and demonstrative.

168 **Descriptive Adjectives**

Because adjectives describe qualities that can vary from one person or thing to another, most adjectives are descriptive: *heavy, pretty, bright, brief, cool, sweet, expensive, small, gigantic, unbelievable, silly, favorite, well-qualified, oily, rocky, old, young, torrid, dry, difficult, tough, insane, brief.* There are hundreds more. Nouns can be transformed into adjectives.

The **green** is too bright. (noun)
The **green** paint is too bright. (adjective)
Old is a state of mind, not a number of years. (noun)
Old age is a state of mind, not a number of years. (adjective)

Verbs also can become adjectives:

I am **jogging** daily. (verb)
My **jogging** suit is full of holes. (adjective)
Janis **described** the scene vividly. (verb)
The **described** scene gave me nightmares. (adjective)

- Descriptive adjectives come in three forms, or degrees: positive, comparative, and superlative. See Table 2-9 for examples. The comparative form compares two people or objects; the superlative is preferred when examining three or more. To form the comparative, the suffix *er* is added to words with one or two syllables. There are exceptions, notably two-syllable words that end with *ful* or *less (careful, faithful, hapless, loveless).* The comparative of these words is formed by adding *more.* For words of more than two syllables, the word *more* is combined with the positive form of the adjective. Other words seem to follow no rule *(little, less, least; bad, worse, worst);* some adjectives are simply irregular in form in much the way that some verbs are irregular.

Table 2-9
Degrees of Adjectives

Positive	Comparative	Superlative
bad	worse	worst
belligerent	more belligerent	most belligerent
bold	bolder	boldest
busy	busier	busiest
careless	more careless	most careless
difficult	more difficult	most difficult
excited	more excited	most excited
faithful	more faithful	most faithful
fine	finer	finest
good	better	best
hot	hotter	hottest
intelligent	more intelligent	most intelligent
large	larger	largest
late	later	latest
little	less	least
lovely	lovelier	loveliest
much	more	most
nice	nicer	nicest
old	older	oldest
painful	more painful	most painful
pleasant	more pleasant	most pleasant
quick	quicker	quickest
selfish	more selfish	most selfish
slim	slimmer	slimmest
small	smaller	smallest
strong	stronger	strongest
confident	more confident	most confident
bright	brighter	brightest
anxious	more anxious	most anxious
icy	icier	iciest
appealing	more appealing	most appealing
tiny	tinier	tiniest
loving	more loving	most loving
fast	faster	fastest
smooth	smoother	smoothest
long	longer	longest
complete	more complete	most complete

The superlative form of adjectives, which examines three or more persons or things, often is formed by adding the *est* suffix to the positive form. For words of more than two syllables, employ the word *most* with the positive form. The same exceptions apply as for the comparative.

She is the **prettier** of the two contestants.

She is the **prettiest** of the nine contestants.

This situation is a **peculiar** dilemma.

This situation is a **more peculiar** dilemma than I have seen before.

This situation is the **most peculiar** dilemma I have ever seen.

Some adjectives cannot have a superlative or comparative form, adjectives such as *perfect, unique, dead, invisible, single, infinite,* and *universal.* These are "absolutes" and thus cannot be compared. Something cannot be more perfect than something else or more dead.

- Although adjectives usually precede the word they modify, they sometimes follow it.

The little children, **giggling** and **running**, almost knocked Allison down.

The crime victim, **trembling** and **weeping**, attempted to relate the incident.

If several adjectives precede a noun, they may need to be separated by commas. If an adjective modifies both a noun and an adjective, no comma is used. (See the section on commas in Unit 3, Punctuation, for detailed discussion.) If the adjectives are of "equal" weight, as in sentences 2 and 4 below, commas are used to separate them; if not, the comma is not used, as in sentence 1 and 3. Another "test" is to change the order of the adjectives to see if the sentence reads as well and the meaning is unchanged; if this is the case, commas are used. For example, to change the order of the adjectives in sentence 1, we would have "A black huge dog was..." This is awkward and does not read the same way as the sentence did before the reversal. Therefore, a comma is not used between huge and black. The reason, really, is that huge modifies black dog, not just dog. On the other hand, reversing the order of the adjectives in sentence 4 does not change the meaning: "Our spacious, opulent, expensive house is..." This is because the three adjectives all modify house. Commas are thus used to separated the adjectives.

1. A huge black dog was chasing the child down the lane.
2. The huge, growling, ferocious dog was chasing the boy.
3. We purchased an expensive brick house in Connecticut.
4. Our expensive, opulent, spacious house is located in Connecticut.

169 **Proper Adjectives**

Proper adjectives are formed from proper nouns; most are uppercased. There are some exceptions, such as *biblical* (from *Bible)* and *congressional* (from *Congress).* Some proper adjectives have become so commonly used that they are lowercased—*china* plates, *oriental* rugs.

Do you enjoy **French** food?
I think it was a **New England** accent.
She looked like a **California** girl to me.

170 **Articles**

There are only three adjectives that are articles: *the, a, an.* The definite article is *the,* the indefinite articles are *a* and *an.*

A ray of hope was all **the** child needed to go from being **a** nuisance to seeming like **an** asset.
An effect of tranquility was **the** result of **a** great effort.

171 **Possessive Adjectives**

These are the forms of pronouns that show possession when attached to a noun.

My concerns were not voiced to **our** parents.
His feelings did not reflect **their** standards.

172 **Demonstrative Adjectives**

Demonstrative pronouns used before the noun they modify act as adjectives.

These papers are confidential.
This project is dying.
That hope has been dashed.
Those notions are outdated.

173 Predicate Adjectives

Predicate adjectives can be defined as adjectives connected to a noun by a linking verb. When adjectives do not precede a noun, but rather complete the verb, they are predicate adjectives. Often confused with the predicate nominative, which renames the subject, the predicate adjective *describes* the subject. They follow state of being verbs.

You seem quite **baffled**?
Because the editor was **conscientious**, she discovered several errors in the manuscript.

COMPARE:

You are **lovely**. (predicate adjective)
You are our **chairman**. (predicate nominative)
Miss Beavers is **difficult** but **honest**. (predicate adjectives)
Miss Beavers is our **supervisor** and our **mentor**. (predicate nominatives)

Predicate Adjectives:

The restaurant was **crowded**, but we were **determined** to eat there.
Corinne looked **depressed, angry,** and **confused**.
The children had become **wild** and **unruly**.

174 Numbers

Numbers can act as adjectives.

Twenty-five years had passed since we had seen one another.
The **two-year-old** child was sitting in the window sill alone.

Note the difference in the sentence below. In the first, three acts as an adjective; in the second, it acts as a noun—the subject of the sentence.

Three plans were discussed by the board of directors.
Three were discussed by the board of directors.

175 Compound Adjectives

A compound adjective is formed by combining two or more words to form a single modifier that expresses a single characteristic. Compound adjectives are usually hyphenated unless they follow the noun they modify (i.e., act as a predicate adjective).

They signed a **long-term** agreement on June 3, 1990.

It was a **self-fulfilling** prophesy.

The two examples above are compound adjectives. **Long-term** modifies **agreement**; **self-fulfilling** modifies **prophesy**. Note the difference in the sentences above and those below:

The paper was **well written.** (Well written is not hyphenated because it follows the noun it modifies—paper—and acts as a predicate adjective.)

BUT:

Jennifer turned in a **well-written** paper.
The thief was a **light-skinned** boy with blonde hair.

BUT:

The thief was **light skinned** and blonde.

176 **Adjectives After Linking Verbs**

Linking verbs are verbs of being and verbs that pertain to the senses: be, become, seem, remain, look, appear, smell, feel, taste, sound. It is important to remember that linking verbs are followed by adjectives (predicate adjectives), not adverbs.

Correct

I feel **bad** that she resigned.

Wrong

I feel **badly** that she resigned.

More Rules About Adjectives

177 Don't confuse adjectives and adverbs.

He plays tennis **well**. (adverb)
The pie tastes **good**. (adjective)
I feel **bad**. (adjective)
He sang **badly** today. (adverb)

178 When two compound adjectives with the same second element modify the same word, the second element may be used only once, but the hyphen is used twice. The first hyphen in the following sentences is called a suspension hyphen. Compound words that are not hyphenated cannot be written this way.

The short- and long-term predictions for the economy are positive.

The profits increased 30- and 44-fold.

Both inpatient and outpatient services will continue. (not in- and outpatient)

179 Compound adjectives sometimes can comprise several words.

We had **round-the-clock** nurses for grandfather.

Marcus read a lot of **not-of-this-world** stories.

180 Do not use *a* or *an* after *of* in the expressions *kind of* or *sort of*.

Correct

What kind of employee is he?

Wrong

What kind of an employee is he?

Correct

What sort of chemical was used?

Wrong

What sort of a chemical was used?

181 The words first and last are sometimes used with numerical adjectives. They should always be written before, not after, the numerical adjective.

Correct

Read the first 25 pages.

Wrong

Read the 25 first pages.

Correct

John and Dina were the last two people in line.

Wrong

John and Dina were the two last people in line.

182 Do not confuse possessive adjectives with contractions.

I couldn't find out **whose** wallet it was, nor was I able to determine **who's** responsible for lost objects.

You're so certain that **your** report will be applauded.

It's true that the coalition could not support **its** claims.

Exercises

A. Select and underline the correct word for each of the following sentences.

1. Do you think that Martha's or Yuri's report is (best, better)?
2. Of these three shirts, which do you think is the (nicest, nicer)?
3. I was hoping to be (more slim, slimmer) by the beginning of summer.
4. Those (kind, kinds) of dogs are notorious for their fierce dispositions.
5. He grows (bolder, more bold) with each successful venture.
6. I found the atmosphere there (pleasanter, more pleasant) than in our previous corporate headquarters.
7. We own two cars, but the red one is the (worst, worse) when it comes to reliability.
8. She used some kind of conditioning lotion on her hair to make it look (more silky, silkier, silkiest).
9. That (kind of, kind of a) report should not be published, in my opinion.
10. Which of your three brothers is (older, oldest)?
11. (Who's, Whose) telephone number were you dialing when Warren walked into the room?
12. Didn't you tear out the (last five, five last) pages of Joanna's diary and burn them?
13. We both know that (its, it's) just a matter of time before his deception is uncovered.
14. Those (types of, type of) books are too difficult for a child of his age.
15. I resent getting stuck with this (hard to start, hard-to-start) automobile, especially as the weather becomes (more cold, colder).
16. The demonstrators made (their, they're) feelings about the war clear indeed.
17. We felt (more safe, safer) in the cellar than in the house during the storm.

18. William volunteered to decorate the room, but he did it (bad, badly).
19. It was the (hungriest, most hungry) I had ever felt in my entire life!
20. Yanni's performance was (poor, poorly).
21. That is the (kind of, kind of a) mentality we are dealing with.
22. I said to him, "(Your, you're) becoming a nuisance."
23. You look (bad, badly) today.
24. I have finally become (self sufficient, selfsufficient, self-sufficient).
25. Of my daughters, Alexandra is the (young, youngest, younger).

B. Identify the predicate adjectives and predicate nominatives in the following sentences by writing PA or PN above the word.

1. Uncle Joe looked tired and worried after he talked to his son.
2. The infant was sleeping quietly.
3. The fur felt soft, warm, and expensive!
4. Langston was elected chairman of the committee, but she did not accept the office.
5. You are a scoundrel and a liar, and I refuse to believe you.
6. The trip to San Francisco was hectic, but it was enjoyable.
7. Cigarette smoking is my worst habit.
8. Rae's dog is a little monster, but she loves it.
9. The sky is growing darker and more threatening with each hour.
10. Bailey's replies were unfathomable mutterings.
11. The new rules for the office are strict and unhealthy for our morale.
12. Pepe is the best trainer in the group.
13. Maddie is friendly, but reserved at the same time.
14. I became too excited to notice that the boy was injured.
15. The song was a haunting melody that entranced all of us.
16. My husband is an excellent tennis player, but I'm a champion.
17. The new partner in the firm is Miss Armen, a young woman whose career is a brilliant example.

18. I don't know if I am capable of this assignment.
19. One student group was courteous, but the other group was overly boisterous, so they were asked to leave.
20. The apartment was vacant, but it was a wreck nonetheless.
21. Gloria was a real professional.
22. Warm milk is an excellent sleep aid.
23. Our maid had become irritable and insolent.
24. Those children were a bunch of bandits.
25. I'm uncertain.

C. Find and underline all the adjectives in the passage below.

> We parked our new car in the lot, where a bright light shone down on it. The children, exhausted and dozing, were anxious to get to the clean beds inside. The ancient night watchman smiled faintly at us as we dragged into the orange-colored hallway. Our haggard faces told the story. We were weary. As he pulled back the crisp sheets, a worried expression crossed Bill's face. He wondered if the car was safe. I walked over to the tinted window and peered into the dark night, but I couldn't see the car. We decided that we were being silly and somewhat fanatical. The needed sleep made us eager to get outside the next morning. I felt excited and anxious to get out into the warm, clear morning sunshine. Then I saw my shiny new car with its side window broken and smashed. A pitiful groan somehow came out of my gasping mouth. Villainous, hateful, monstrous thieves!

D. Insert adjectives in the blanks.

1. Mr. Ralston appeared _______ and _______ before the speech.
2. We felt _______ and _______ , but we looked _______ .
3. There was only one _______ vote.
4. He was the only one to do a solo in a _______ boat.
5. The ______ situation caused my _______ neighbor to be _______ .
6. Everyone needs a _______ word now and then in order to feel _______ .
7. This _______ book was the most _______ I had ever read.

8. I watched the movie to its end, but I considered it _______ and _______ and a bit _______ .
9. The _______ flight ended with a _______ landing.
10. _______ Susan Bitterman, _______ Tom Morton, and _______ Emma Pulaski all looked _______ .
11. The _______ house held many _______ and _______ items.
12. His _______ face made me feel _______ .
13. The _______ music became _______ .
14. His _______ aspirations had made his life seem _______ .
15. Her _______ needs made her look _______ .

183 Adverbs

Adverbs, like adjectives, are modifiers. The difference between the two lies in what they modify. Whereas adjectives modify nouns and pronouns, adverbs modify verbs, adjectives, or other adverbs. Confusion between adjectives and adverbs often leads to errors. When an adverb modifies a verb, it usually answers one of these questions: how, when, where, or to what degree.

The band played **loudly**, but the audience just was not listening. (how)
I left New York **yesterday**. (when)
Put it **there**. (where)
We were **barely** ready. (to what degree)

When an adverb modifies an adjective, it limits the adjective.

Incredibly rich men are often eccentric.
She is a **genuinely** kind woman.

Adverbs also modify other adverbs.

Selina skated **so** poorly that she increased her practice time.
We **almost** never awaken that early.

184 Forming Adverbs

Adverbs usually can be formed from descriptive adjectives by adding the suffix *ly* to the adjective form.

Miss Ewan became a **bitter** spinster. (adjective)
She laughed **bitterly** at his words. (adverb)

I always thought of Tom as a **loud** boor. (adjective)
He shouted **loudly**, but no one heard him. (adverb)

Other Examples:

Adjective	**Adverb**
pretty girl	waltzing prettily
sweet child	smiling sweetly
courteous guest	speaking courteously
frugal spender	spending frugally
poor choice	chose poorly
bright lights	shone brightly
warm greeting	greeted warmly
noisy streets	moving noisily
descriptive words	spoke descriptively
quiet room	played quietly

More Rules About Adverbs

185 The adverb *not* is sometimes mistakenly thought of as part of a verb. Its actual function is to modify the verb.

We have **not** heard from Elsa in about two weeks.
Cindy should **not** have said those things to Kirk.

186 Adverbs, like adjectives, can be compared. The degrees of adverbs are the same as those of adjectives: positive, comparative, and superlative.

POSITIVE: We will work **quietly** in my office.
COMPARATIVE: We will work **more quietly** today than we did last night.
SUPERLATIVE: Sheila can work the **most quietly** of the four of us.

Remember that the comparative form involves two persons or things; the superlative involves three or more persons or things. Usually the comparative is formed by using the word *more* and superlative by using the word *most.* There are a few adverbs, however, that form the comparative with *er* and the superlative with *est* (*soon, late, fast, low, far).*

187 Not all adverbs end with *ly;* for example, *close, deep, straight, well, almost, soon, far, late, again, down, near, now, seldom, the, up, ever, never, often, so, there, always, here, not, rather, too.*

Turn **left** onto Reed Lane.
Dan was **often** late for work.

Exercises

A. Form adverbs from the following adjectives.

1. timid
2. positive
3. brief
4. gloomy
5. dull
6. foolish
7. neat
8. false
9. probable
10. poor
11. hard
12. cheap
13. fast
14. warm
15. strange
16. winning
17. solemn
18. favorable
19. innocent
20. smooth
21. pleasurable
22. continuous
23. sleepy
24. mindless
25. greedy

B. Underline all the adverbs in the following passage and indicate whether each modifies a verb, an adjective, or another adverb by writing V, ADJ, or ADV above the word.

> I walked quietly into the house. I was then afraid that Bradley might return soon, so I worked fast. I really feared him. I should have gotten my things sooner, but I was so confused. I still could hardly believe the terrible things that had happened. I was very tired and awfully worried. Suddenly the phone was ringing loudly. I didn't know whether to answer it or not. Only my youngest sister, Claire, knew where I was. Maybe she was calling. I stumbled frantically toward the telephone, but just stood there staring vacantly at the loudly ringing machine. Was it Claire? Maybe it was Bradley. Probably it was neither of them. I was genuinely bewildered. The ringing stopped. I uneasily turned toward the very familiar staircase. I wanted to take my clothes and personal possessions, a moderate request, I think.

C. Select and underline the right word for each sentence.

1. He does (good, well) in school, but he does (poor, poorly) in athletics.
2. I (sure, surely) hope that you know what you are doing.
3. I felt (bad, badly) about embarrassing Melissa in front of Torrence and Elaine.

4. We are (real, really) excited about the upcoming wedding in our family.
5. Mallory is known for her musical ability, but tonight she played (bad, badly).
6. The haircut and new dress give Nan a (complete, completely) new look.
7. Stand (close, closely) to me when he enters the room.
8. We knew that we would have to work (steadier, more steadily) if we hoped to complete it on time.
9. That child's plight is the (more, most) pitiful of all the children we have tried to help here.
10. I think that we can purchase some jewelry (cheap, cheaply) if we buy it from this dealer.
11. I found working with Carmen (pleasanter, more pleasant) than with any of the other assistants I've had.
12. How (quick, quickly) can my car be repaired?
13. Mary was suffering from headaches, and she felt (awful, awfully) that night.
14. You shouldn't feel (bad, badly) about getting the promotion that Debra hoped to have.
15. Little Deanie looked (sweet, sweetly) in her costume.
16. He was dressed (sloppy, sloppily).
17. I was afraid that I had done (bad, badly) on the exam.
18. Nan felt (sick, sickly).
19. The child was sitting there (quiet, quietly).
20. You looked so (guilty, guiltily).
21. We worked (intent, intently) on our projects throughout the night.
22. How (brief, briefly) can you explain it to me?
23. The (poor, poorly) written speech was nonetheless received (well, good) by the audience.
24. Ronald wanted his office to have a (total, totally) different feel.
25. Bryant Gregoire screamed (wild, wildly) at the old man.

D. Decide whether each underlined word is an adverb (ADV) or an adjective (ADJ).

1. Marianne doesn't work well under pressure, but she is a good worker otherwise.
2. He is almost ready for your best ideas to be presented tonight.
3. It seems good that you have come so soon.
4. The tension was unbearably heavy when Kyle entered the room.
5. I felt so good that morning that I could hardly sit still.
6. It was so nice of you to come to my humble home this lovely morning.
7. I understand you perfectly and fully, but you seem odd to my friends.
8. The party was so poorly planned that no one enjoyed it.
9. The music sounded sweet but eerie.
10. He mumbled angrily about Rita's abrupt decision yesterday.
11. I cannot swim well now, but I was formerly a real champion.
12. I was only partially relieved at the news.
13. Most children enjoy playing outdoors, but Karrie almost always preferred to play in her room.
14. The brightest hope in my entire life was that scholarship.
15. We were truly sorry to hear of your recent loss.
16. Jonas was more or less resigned to his fate.
17. She spoke so sincerely that I could hardly turn her down.
18. I would travel anywhere.
19. He lives alone.
20. We were playing a really silly game Tuesday night.
21. Loretta is a stunningly beautiful woman.
22. Life is short.
23. He arrived but was most apologetic.
24. You should be ashamed of yourself.
25. It was an entirely comfortable evening.

Prepositions

188 Prepositions are rather difficult to define. They combine with other words to form prepositional phrases. A preposition shows the relation of a noun or pronoun (the object of the preposition) to another part of the sentence. Prepositional phrases always begin with a preposition and are completed by a noun, pronoun, or noun equivalent—the object of the preposition, which can be either singular or compound. Prepositions can consist of more than one word. Table 2-10 is a list of common one-word prepositions. Table 2-11 lists common prepositions consisting of more than one word.

Her arms were **above** her head.
Among friends there should be no awkwardness.
From now on, there will be no coffee breaks **before** 10:00 **in** the morning.

Prepositional phrases can act as adjective phrases or adverbial phrases. This text will not go into an analysis of those functions because that would be of little valuc to the CR.

Table 2-10
Common One-Word Prepositions

about	by	over
above	concerning	past
across	down	round
after	during	since
against	except	through
along	for	throughout
among	from	till
around	in	to
at	inside	toward
before	into	towards
behind	like	under
below	near	underneath
beneath	of	until
beside	off	up
besides	on	upon
between	out	with
beyond	outside	without
but		

Table 2-11
Multiword Prepositions

along with	but for	in spite of
apart from	by way of	instead of
as for	in place of	on account of
as to	in reference to	to the extent that
as well as	in regard to	with regard to

189 One of the most confusing aspects of prepositions is that the same words that act as prepositions can act as other parts of speech.

> He left his bicycle **outside** the garage. (preposition)
> Leave your bicycle **outside**. (adverb)
> **But** for this five-dollar bill, I am broke. (part of two-word preposition but for)
> I am nearly broke, **but** I do have this five-dollar bill. (conjunction)
> **To** run a five-minute mile was his goal. (part of infinitive)
> He asked me **to** the dance, but I had other plans. (preposition)

190 **Object of a Preposition**

The noun or pronoun that completes the prepositional phrase is the object of the preposition. It is seldom difficult to locate the object of the preposition once the prepositional phrase has been found. If the object of the preposition is a pronoun, it must be in the objective case. (See the section on pronouns in this unit.)

> Under the **circumstances**, I thought it best to remain in the apartment.
> Monique thought his actions beneath **contempt**.

General Rules for Prepositions

191 Some people consider it poor form to end a sentence with a preposition, especially in formal writing. Most modern authorities, however, consider this practice entirely acceptable, pointing out that a sentence with a preposition at the end is often far more effective and less "stilted" than a sentence with a buried preposition. The CR should follow the preference of the speaker.

Formal

To whom did you speak?

Informal

Whom did you speak to?

Formal

For what committee did you work?

Informal

What committee did you work for?

192 *Different from* is correct when comparing, not *different than.*

Correct

Your position is no different from mine.

Wrong

Your position is no different than mine.

193 Avoid using unnecessary prepositions such as *at* and *of.*

Correct

Where is my car parked?

Wrong

Where is my car parked at?

Correct

His name was taken off the list.

Wrong

His name was taken off of the list.

Correct

Where has he gone tonight?

Wrong

Where has he gone to tonight?

194 Do not use *of* in place of *have* after *might, could, should,* or *must.*

Correct

He could have come to the reception for Professor Dodd.

Wrong

He could of come to the reception for Professor Dodd.

Correct

I might have expected something like that to occur.

Wrong

I might of expected something like that to occur.

195 Do not confuse the prepositions *between* and *among.* Use between for situations in which two share, among for those in which three or more share.

The duties were divided **between** Dianne and Doris.
There was no discord **among** the company's dozen or so employees.

196 Do not use *in* and *into* interchangeably. *Into* indicates movement from one location to another; *in* means inside or within.

He moved quietly from the yard **into** the house.
I put it **in** the safe.

197 Use *plan to,* not *plan on.*

Correct

I plan **to** use the money for a new automobile.

Wrong

I plan **on** using the money for a new automobile.

198 Use *independent of,* not *independent from.*

Correct

Our company was independent **of** their control.

Wrong

Our company was independent **from** their control.

199 *Correspond with* means to write letters back and forth; *correspond to* means to match with something.

Clarke's performance did not correspond **to** my needs.
Miss Miller was happy to correspond **with** my cousin; they became long-distance friends.

200 Use *accompanied with* to indicate being with an object; use *accompanied by* to indicate being with a person.

The tiny gun was accompanied **with** a holster.
Stephanie was accompanied **by** her brother and his wife.

201 Write *angry with* a person, *angry at* a situation.

I was angry **with** Robin about the party.
Mother became angry **at** the situation.

Exercises

A. In the following passage, find the prepositional phrases. For each phrase, underline the preposition once and its object twice.

Everything was quiet in the house, or so it seemed. We stood on the porch debating whether we should knock on the door. Dori peered through the window, trying to see if Mel was there, but everything was dark. We walked around the house. If anyone was inside the kitchen, we would probably hear them. We were looking for any indication that someone was there. Near the garage was Mel's bicycle, and beside it was another bike. I wondered who had been with him. I looked at Dori and asked her if she thought we should just knock on the door. She was torn between running and knocking. I wanted to get away from that house. In my opinion, Mel was not someone I wanted to see. I suggested that we walk to the corner and use the pay phone to call Mel. If he was at home, he'd answer. If not, we could go. Suddenly, across the yard we saw a movement. Someone was among the trees at the edge of Mel's yard. I pushed past Dori to run toward the street. Behind me Dori ran, too.

B. Select and underline the proper pronoun to serve as the object of the preposition in each of the following sentences.

1. He refused to go out with Janet and (I, me).
2. Between Allegra and (she, her), they haven't a dollar.
3. He refuses to do any favors for Rick and (I, me).
4. The ball was thrown close to Neil and (she, her).
5. No one except Adam and (I, me) spoke in defense of Miss Quana.
6. Sometimes I believe that the entire department is set against my secretary and (he, him).
7. That report is no doubt a recommendation with regard to Vincent and (we, us).
8. The Hatchers do not want Terry near their house and (they, them).
9. I think that package is for Nina and (I, me).
10. Grandpa gave tracts of land to Janie and (he, him).
11. Other than Cal, Ernie, and (he, him), no one was interested.

12. Will you go with Jim and (I, me)?
13. The gift was from (she, her) and Miss Gurney.
14. Give it to Lennie or (me, I).
15. He threw the ball toward Colleen and (I, me).

C. Which of the two sentence pairs is correct in each of the following?

1. a. Our small grocery was independent from the large chains.
   b. Our small grocery was independent of the large chains.
2. a. Your attitude is quite different from mine.
   b. Your attitude is quite different than mine.
3. a. I was planning on calling you this week.
   b. I was planning to call you this week.
4. a. Reception duties were divided between Diana, Chris, and Lynn.
   b. Reception duties were divided among Diana, Chris, and Lynn.
5. a. I have no idea where he was at that night.
   b. I have no idea where he was that night.
6. a. We might of tried harder to improve things.
   b. We might have tried harder to improve things.
7. a. The book fell off the shelf and startled us.
   b. The book fell off of the shelf and startled us.
8. a. Did your expectations correspond with reality?
   b. Did your expectations correspond to reality?
9. a. I jumped into the swimming pool without thinking.
   b. I jumped in the swimming pool without thinking.
10. a. Why are you angry with Mona?
    b. Why are you angry at Mona?

D. Write sentences using the following phrases or words:

1. correspond to
2. independent of

3. into the hole
4. in the hole
5. plan to
6. might have
7. between
8. among
9. different from
10. in reference to
11. to the extent that
12. but for
13. around the corner
14. in case of
15. instead of

Conjunctions

Conjunctions are connectors; they join together words, phrases, or clauses. There are three categories of conjunctions: coordinating, subordinating, and correlative.

202 **Coordinating conjunctions** join together elements of equal rank: nouns with nouns, phrases with phrases, independent clauses with independent clauses, and so on. They do not join independent clauses to dependent clauses because they are not of equal rank. The most common coordinating conjunctions are *and, or, but, nor,* and *for.*

> On the shelf **and** under a book you'll find the key.
> Bob **or** I will contact you next month about where the dog might be sleeping. (connects a noun and a pronoun)
> He hoped to go, **but** he had no money. (connects clauses)

203 **Correlative conjunctions** also join elements of equal rank, but they differ from coordinating conjunctions in that they are used in pairs. The most common correlatives include the following pairs: *either...or, neither...nor, both... and, not only...but* (or *but also),* and *whether...or.*

> **Either** Mother **or** Father will come.
> **Neither** the dog **nor** the cat was in the house.
> **Not only** were you upset, **but** you were uncontrollable.

204 **Subordinating conjunctions** connect dependent clauses to independent clauses. The verb to *subordinate* means to place in a lower rank or position. Thus, the dependent clause (or subordinate clause) is of a lower rank than the independent clause (main clause). The dependent clause functions as a single part of speech—as an adverb, an adjective, or a noun. Some of the most common subordinating conjunctions are *after, although, as, because, before, for, if, once, since, till, unless, until, when, whenever, where,* and *wherever.*

> **After** we walked along the path for a few minutes, Gil decided to sit and rest.
>
> We had no idea **where** Joann was staying.
>
> **Unless** there is another reason for delay, we should proceed **whenever** Marsha returns.

Relative pronouns behave like subordinating conjunctions in that they make clauses they introduce dependent, or subordinate. These pronouns include *that, which, who, what, whoever, whom, whomever,* and *whose.*

> The proposal **that we accepted** was a victory for Tom Winters.
>
> **Wherever we go**, we cannot forget such acts of kindness.

Some subordinating conjunctions are more than one word: *as if, as though, as soon as, even though, in order that, in order to, in that, no matter how, so that.*

> **No matter how I try**, I cannot understand these instructions.
>
> **Even though I believe it's a mistake**, I will file the motion for you.
>
> **In order to fulfill his financial obligations**, Ralph took on another job.

205

Noun Clauses

Dependent clauses can function as nouns, which means they can act as a subject, an appositive, an object, or a predicate nominative. Dependent clauses are introduced by subordinate conjunctions, interrogatives, or relative pronouns.

> Subject: **When he intended to returned the borrowed equipment** was not clear to anyone.
>
> Appositive: The idea **that Chad could be elected** was greeted with laughter and sneers.
>
> Direct Object: I didn't know **that he was planning to leave.**
>
> Object of the Preposition: I will give the promotion to **whoever does the best job over the next month or two.**

Predicative Nominative: A new house is **what you wanted,** isn't it?

206 Adjective Clauses

Dependent clauses can function as adjectives; that is, they act to modify a noun.

> I wanted to buy a coat **that was warm but fashionable.**
>
> The book **that I read last week** was frightening.

In the first sentence, the clause modifies *coat.* It tells what kind of coat. In the second example, the clause modifies *book.* It describes or limits the book.

207 Adverbial Clauses

This type of dependent clauses functions in the same way that an adverb functions within a sentence; that is, it modifies a verb, an adjective, or another adverb. Adverbial clauses that introduce a sentence are followed by a comma if they are more than about four words long; if the adverbial clause is short, however, and no misreading of the sentence is likely to occur as result of leaving out the comma, then no comma is used.

> **Whenever I saw him in my shop**, I watched him closely.
>
> **If you know the whereabouts of Mrs. Rose Kimball,** you must inform this office immediately.
>
> **When we arrived** Jane Bennett was waiting for us with her lawyer.

In the last sentence, the comma is not necessary because the adverbial phrase is so short; if a comma were placed after arrived, it would not be incorrect, however.

Adverbial clauses that occur at the end of a sentence may or may not be set off by commas, depending on whether they are restrictive in nature. If the clause is restrictive (that is, essential to the meaning of the sentence), it is not preceded by a comma. On the other hand, if it is nonrestrictive (that is, merely provides additional information) it should be preceded by a comma.

> We can make our flight **if we leave right away.** (restrictive clause, essential to the meaning of the sentence, no comma)
>
> I will give you your receipt **when you have make payment in full.** (also restrictive)

The Bricker family is still living in this town, **although I never see them out and about.** (nonrestrictive and so preceded by a comma)

208 **Conjunctive Adverbs**

Another category of words could be included in either this section on conjunctions or the sections on adverbs. These are conjunctive adverbs (single words) and transitional phrases (more than a single word), which act both as adverbs and as conjunctions. See Tables 2-2 and 2-3 for a list of conjunctive adverbs and transitional phrases. They separate independent clauses and are used after a semicolon or a period, not with a comma. To use a comma would create a run-on.

Correct

We expect to receive a report any moment; moreover, we expect it to contain the information you seek.

Wrong

We expect to receive a report any moment, moreover, we expect it to contain the information you seek.

Correct

We couldn't refuse; in other words, we were stuck.

Wrong

We couldn't refuse, in other words, we were stuck.

Exercises

A. Identify all conjunctions in the following passage and classify them as to type of conjunction: coordinating, correlative, subordinating.

When we arrived at the park, the staff picnic was already well in progress. In fact, we were probably the last to arrive, although we had tried to be on time. I would be surprised if we were ever on time for anything, though. Neither Ellen nor Maggie wanted to go with me to the picnic. They said that any event where no one was under the age of 30 just couldn't be much fun. I made them go along, but I lived to regret that. Not only did both girls complain all the way in the car, but they also ended up hurt when the fight broke out. At one point, I didn't even know where they were. Whenever something freaky like that happens, I just turn to whoever is close to me and see if they know what to do. Since that day in the park, I haven't wanted to let my two girls out of my sight. Either Maggie or Ellen will probably disown me soon, or maybe both of them will decide to do it. Anyway, in order to join in on the festivities, we parked the car where everyone else was parked. The parking area where we parked was kind of in a wooded area, but I thought it would be safe. I had parked there before that day, and nothing had ever happened. What caused the fight I really don't know. Who started it I do know. It was Marty Inman who caused the whole mess. Even though he is a friend of mine, I know what his temper can be like when he is mad. The Marty that I know and care about is not the same man you see when he's angry, believe me. I like him and do see Marty socially, although I am careful when I am with him not to anger him. The fight broke out after Marty saw Bill Omsted take something out of Wanda Hillman's purse. Marty knows that there's bad feeling between Bill and Wanda.

B. Now go back to the above passage and find any examples of noun clauses, adjective clauses, and adverbial clauses. If they are noun clauses, tell how they function in the sentence; if adjective, what word they modify; if adverbial, decide if each clause is restrictive or nonrestrictive.

C. Find a magazine article 3-5 pages long and pick out examples of noun, adjective, and adverbial clauses.

Interjections

209 Of the eight parts of speech, the interjection is the one that requires the least discussion. Interjections are identified easily and offer little or no difficulty. Interjections are words that express mild or strong feeling, and they are followed by either a period or an exclamation point.

Oh, I hope you're right.
Damn! I knew it!

The decision whether to use a comma or an exclamation point depends on the emotion conveyed in the speaker's words. The CR should take care not to overuse the exclamation point, but rather reserve it for situations that clearly demand its strength. Many CRs avoid use of the exclamation point entirely because they do not wish to "interpret" in any way. Follow your own firm's preference on this matter. Interjections can occur within a sentence.

> I hoped to see him again, but, **oh**, I just couldn't go through with it.
>
> Sheila tried to get that promotion, but, **alas**, she was passed over for promotion time and again.

Unit Exercise

A. List the part of speech of each underlined word. If the word is a noun or pronoun, indicate its function in the sentence as well.

> There must have been two hundred kids lined up outside the studio; I asked myself why I had bothered to show up—but then I had had occasion to ask myself that question frequently. Oh, I may as well go ahead and stand here endlessly in the burning sun and take my chances like everyone else. So I stood in the line; in fact, I remained while others started leaving. I was exhausted, but I also felt hopeful, especially each time someone left the line. Finally it was my turn to go inside. For me, this was a monumental turning point in my life. I walked boldly into the dark studio. I wished that either Sandra or he could be with me. There were five hopefuls ahead of me. They had the same desperate look on their faces that I knew I was wearing. I felt despondent. The man in charge shot me a disinterested look and then turned his head immediately to speak with someone else. Waiting was killing me. I heard my name, and I began to tremble. I walked to the stage. For me, this was the moment of truth. Either I could give it my best or I could go blank. I didn't know what I would end up doing; moreover, I didn't know how I would manage. Then the oddest thing occurred: I no longer cared what happened in this audition. I didn't care about the part. I forgot my dreams, my ambitions, my career.

B. Clip an article from a magazine or newspaper and find the subject and verb of each of 10 sentences within the article. Then find at least 25 adjectives and five adverbs.

C. For each of the following sentences, determine the part of speech of every word. For example: He showed me the book, but Jane interrupted our intimate moment.

Analysis: He (pronoun acting as subject)
showed (verb)
me (pronoun acting as indirect object)
the (article)
book (noun, acting as direct object)
but (conjunction)
Jane (proper noun acting as subject of clause)
interrupted (verb)
our (possessive pronoun)
intimate (adjective modifying moment)
moment (noun acting as direct object)

1. I was writing a bunch of checks and lost track of whether or not I even had enough money in my checking account to cover them.
2. We searched throughout the room for the letter from Thomas, but we found it in the car.
3. Neither my mother nor my brother welcomed her into our family when she and George were married.
4. I have no recent photographs of Melinda, although I do have a painting that was done five years ago.
5. Whoever called me did not say where they were or what they wanted from us.
6. Did Matthew claim that Elizabeth and he would sign the papers?
7. In order to maintain the status quo, Mr. Williams instituted a new set of rules.
8. Picture this in your mind.
9. The rolling green hills made a nice picture.
10. He read from a large yellow notebook that was tattered and torn.
11. Where do you think he went?
12. Tell me about this accident that occurred in front of your house.
13. When my computer was turned on, it just blinked and spurted.
14. Lucy Davis and Adam Peterson request an audience with you, and they are very anxious.
15. I will tell her if you don't.

16. That child is always hurting himself.
17. The veterinarian is not in his office on Tuesdays.
18. The four-year-old child was given several household duties.
19. The loud, obnoxious, heavy metal music pounded in my poor ears.
20. Where is my car, Jack?

3
PUNCTUATION

Ultimately a CR's competency will be judged by the quality of his or her transcripts. Whereas Units 1 and 2 are "knowledge" sections, Unit 3 is more utilitarian and lends itself more readily to quick reference.

Punctuation can "make or break" a transcript. Too much punctuation can disrupt the smooth flow of words for the reader; insufficient or misplaced punctuation can alter or obscure the meaning of the words that were spoken. Because the CR's goal is to produce a transcript that will convey to the reader what transpired in the proceeding, it is crucial for the CR to insert punctuation rather than leave it up to a typist, because the CR was *there*! Editing can be performed afterward, of course, to improve quality, but the CR's understanding, even interpretation, should be the basis for punctuation.

A sound rule to follow is: "When in doubt, don't." Generally speaking, too little punctuation is better than too much.

The guidelines that follow are grammatically sound, although a few may differ from the rules set forth for other professions, such as newspaper journalism. The CR will of course follow the preferences of his or her employer when such preferences are established.

End Punctuation

End punctuation, for the most part, will present comparatively few problems for the CR. The period, question mark, and exclamation point are the primary end, or terminal, punctuation marks, although the dash is sometimes in that position. It is important to note that the CR will rarely or, more likely, never use the exclamation point because of the mandate to avoid interpretation.

210 The Period

- The period is used after a declarative statement or an indirect question.

The trial is set for next week.
Mrs. Norbert did not come forth voluntarily.

- The period is used after indirect questions.

I asked if you remember the incident.

- The period is used after a request or mild imperative.

Take the stand, sir.

- No period is used when a sentence is interrupted before it can be completed.

A. Mr. Bates said —
B. John Bates or Jacob Bates?

- No period is used after items in an enumeration that are not complete sentences.

We requested that he deliver the following items for the past five years:

1. tax records
2. paid invoices
3. accounts receivable
4. accounts payable

If the enumeration is *within* the sentence, commas or semicolons may be used:

He has, on separate occasions, stated (1) that he does not remember the incident, (2) that he acted in self-defense, and (3) that he was not ever present.

We set forth the following conditions for reinstatement: (1) the missing equipment is to be returned or replaced; (2) damages must be paid; (3) a letter of apology is to be sent to all department heads; and (4) Mr. Jenkins will be on probation for six months.

- No period is used after a sentence that is included within another sentence.

He stared at me—he's often quite rude—without so much as blinking.

Janis turned to me and whispered, "Don't leave yet, please," and that's why I remained.

- The period is placed inside the end quotation marks.

I told him, "Jim, I just don't know you anymore."

I am reading now from a transcript of a deposition taken on June 5th of this year: "I heard Miss James say, 'You're going to be sorry,' and then she walked away."

Damien said, "Dad shouted at me, 'Get out of here.'"

211 The Question Mark

- The most obvious and most frequent use of this mark is, of course, at the end of an interrogative sentence.

  Did you understand the questions, Mrs. Yeager?
  Is that the truth as you know it?

- The question mark is not used with an indirect question.

  I asked if she went with Mr. Long.
  William wondered what was wrong.

- A question mark is used at the end of a declarative sentence if it is obvious, from the speaker's inflection, that the statement is actually meant as a question.

  You were afraid of him?
  Miss Swanson gave you the money?

- Do not use a question mark after a command "disguised" as a question.

  Will you state your name for the record.
  Would you please advise your client to restrain himself.

  Note: Although these requests are stated in question form, the speaker does not really expect a direct answer. It would be absurd, for example, to expect an answer to the following: "Will you please state your name." One would not answer, "Yes, I will tell you my name." The anticipated reply would be simply a name.

- If it is truly a polite request that may or may not be honored, then the question mark can be used.

  Will you let me know when they arrive?
  Would you tell me if he questions you again?

- A question contained within a declarative statement still retains the question mark.

  Was he being honest? was the question she needed answered.
  Did you see it happen? is what he'll ask you.

- A question mark is placed inside or outside the end quotation mark, depending on the context of the sentence. If the entire sentence, including the quoted matter, is a question, then the question mark is placed outside the end quotation mark.

Did he say to you, "I killed my wife"?
Were Julia's exact words, "He's my brother," or did she say "I think he's my brother"?

- If the quoted material and the statement are both questions, the question mark goes inside the quotes:

Who said, "What time is it?"

If only the quoted material is interrogative in nature, the question mark is placed inside the end quotation mark.

Mary asked Jeff, "Where did you leave the car?"
"Who's responsible for this fiasco?" the officer demanded.

- Repeat the question mark in a list or series of questions, even incomplete ones.

Did Ethan join in? Or Mason? Maybe Carlton?
How did he grab you? By the arm? On the shoulder?

- Do not use a question mark with short parenthetical elements that occur midsentence and are set off by commas.

June Marshall and Faith Scanlon are, shall we say, our contacts within the department, and they have been most helpful.
He should have called someone, wouldn't you think, to help in what was clearly an emergency situation, but he did call for help.

- When testimony is quoted during proceedings, it can be handled as follows:

Q. Did you testify as follows: "Question: Where were you living in September of 1985? Answer: In Boston"?

Note: No period is used after "Boston."

- A question inserted in the middle of a sentence and set off by dashes is followed by a question mark.

Frederic's income is—how do I even know this?—about $125,000 annually.
I want to state clearly—can everyone hear me?—that I knew of Harrison Brown's operations in Brazil.

- Questions that follow a colon, if complete sentences, begin with a capital.

The question is this: Is he your husband or your ex-husband?

What I expect to learn is this: Is Claire the rightful heir?

- Some statements that appear at first glance to be questions actually are not. The CR should avoid using question marks with such sentences.

  I worried how was I getting to Seattle.

  The secretary inquired where her supervisor is going.

212 Multiple Punctuation

Except with quotation marks and dashes, two punctuation marks are not used at the same place in a sentence. In situations where it might seem appropriate for two marks to be used, use only the one that is stronger.

Acceptable

Did Bea say to you, "Millicent is dead"?

Wrong

Did Bea say to you, "Millicent is dead."?

Acceptable

Who was screaming, "I think he's dying"?

Wrong

Who was screaming, "I thing he's dying!"?

213 The Dash as Final Punctuation

If a sentence is obviously not completed, the dash is the final mark of punctuation.

Q. Who told you about —

A. Maybe it was —

214 The Ellipsis as Final Punctuation

It would be a rare situation in which a CR would use an ellipsis as final punctuation. Use a dash, not an ellipsis, to indicate that the speaker was interrupted or trailed off. When a passage is being quoted verbatim, and the person quoting says, "Dot dot dot," then an ellipsis would be used in the place where the dots are read. In such a case, the ellipsis does not indicate an interruption or trailing-off speech, but rather indicates that the quote is not being read in its entirety.

I read from Ben Miller's letter to Emma Sloan, dated December 15, 1985: "I think it would be justice for me to have that money...."

Exercises

A. Punctuate the following sentences.

1. He inquired of me Where did you place the records
2. We heard a rumor and I think it was totally unfounded that you were planning to leave
3. What did he tell you is important for me to know
4. Would you please state your name and address
5. I cannot stand this another moment
6. My sister looked at me I could have died and wept
7. I wrote in my letter to her Were you aware of this problem
8. Oh I thought this was Ms. Tibble's office
9. Can you believe that she answered Yes
10. Mother always asked if we're hungry
11. Did you say to him You don't even know the meaning of the word 'disheartened'
12. Can you describe his face his clothes his physical size
13. Father was didn't you know a difficult man to deal with
14. Where did he go that night was my question
15. I wondered where was my sister and why had she gone
16. Would you describe your job for us
17. With whom did you meet that night where what time why
18. If you want to know where's Daniel I do not know
19. Did you yell The house is on fire
20. Did his note to you say Pamela don't try to find me

B. Write three examples of sentences using each of the following:

1. quotation marks
2. An imperative
3. A request
4. Indirect questions

C. Add end punctuation and quotation marks to the Q and A below:

Q. After consultation with the commissioner, were you told by Mr. Dunn to

A. Mr. Dunn didn't tell me anything

Q. Will you please allow me to complete my question Did Mr. Dunn say to you, Come back to my office after you see the commissioner?

A. You mean in those exact words

Q. In those exact words Did he say that to you

A. If you're talking about

Q. Would you just answer yes or no

A. No

Q. You are telling me that Mr. Dunn never said that to you

A. He didn't, at least

Q. Yes or no, Miss Miller

A. No, then

Q. Your office had a formal set of procedures I believe that is true

A. We had procedures

Q. You were familiar with all of those procedures

A. Of course

Q. And you knew that Mr. Dunn expected you to follow those procedures

A. Did he expect me to follow them Sure

Q. The other people in your office—I believe there were five others in your department—they followed the procedures

A. Are you talking about Sam Balwin Melinda Talbert Who

Q. Your co-workers, Miss Miller.

A. People at my level

Q. Those persons who were in your department, at your level or otherwise.

A. I just think that—

Q. Miss Miller, the question is this: Did everyone in your office know and follow a standard set of procedures ?

A. I think that—how do you expect me to know all this—I think everyone did, I can't tell you what everybody else did just what I did .

Q. All right. Let's establish another thing about those procedural guidelines, and that is --

A. Nobody called them guidelines .

Q. Tell me what they were called .

A. Procedures .

Q. Okay, then, tell me, Miss Miller, were those guidelines in print ?

A. You're asking me if they were typeset .

Q. I am merely trying to establish if the guidelines were in written form and distributed to the staff.

A. I had a copy .

Q. And I can presume that the other staff members had copies as well ?

A. I guess so .

Parentheses

CRs do not use parentheses in the traditional manner that is for asides and parenthetical material. Instead, they are used to describe actions that are crucial to an understanding of what transpired in the courtroom; they do not record words actually spoken.

215 Parentheses are used to describe physical actions.

Q. Did you see him before that day?

A. (The witness nodded her head.)

Q. Are you feeling all right, Mr. Carrio?

A. I—yes—no—(The witness slumped over in his chair, unconscious.)

216 Verbal occurrences in the courtroom that are not taken down verbatim by the CR can be noted in parenthesis.

(The reporter read the last question.)

(There was an off-the-record discussion.)

217 Parentheses are used to indicate recesses and adjournments.

(Court was adjourned at 5:15 p.m.)

(A recess was taken at 9:45 p.m.)

218 Within the parentheses, punctuation should be just as it would be if it were written without parentheses. The material within the parentheses should be a complete sentence.

219 **Enumeration**

Parentheses are used to enclose numbers or letters used in lists or enumerations. If the words used by the speaker are "first," "second," etc., the CR may elect to write out the words in the transcript. If the speaker enumerates by saying "one," "two," etc., the CR should use numerals in parentheses. (See the discussion of formatting in Unit 10.)

> You may find the dependent guilty of (1) murder in the first degree, (2) not guilty by reason of insanity, (3) not guilty because he acted in self-defense, (4) or guilty but acting out of passion without forethought.
>
> The following actions were taken: first, the office was searched; second, his house was searched; third, his car was impounded.

Quotation Marks

When and where to use quotation marks can be a tricky issue for the CR. There will be times when the CR will have considerable difficulty discerning the exact point at which a quotation begins and ends, or, indeed, that there is a quotation at all. Of course, if the speaker is reading from a document, it is obvious that the material being presented is also being quoted; however, many situations will not be nearly so obvious.

The following guidelines are intended to assist the CR in handling quotations. Always be conservative and use quotation marks only when reasonably certain the material is being quoted verbatim.

220 A period is placed inside the end quotation mark, whether double or single.

> Vera told Claudette, "You will never be able to pull this off."
>
> Michael told me, "Jeanette, you are and always will be a child."
>
> The transcript reads as follows: "Roger Oulette told us, 'you can have this old thing.'"

Note: Both single and double quotation marks follow the period in this sentence.

221 A comma is also placed inside the end quotation mark.

"Come along with us for a joy ride," Holden urged.

Nanci cried, "Please, Joel, don't leave," but he wouldn't listen to anyone.

222 Always place a semicolon outside the end quotation mark. The CR will have infrequent uses for the semicolon in conjunction with quotation marks, but it is important to know how to handle such situations if they do indeed occur.

Mother said to me, "We have no use for those people"; however, I did not share her view.

Mr. Edmond said to his wife, "Our children are on their own now"; nonetheless, she refused to agree to sell the large family house.

223 A colon also is placed outside the end quotation mark. This too will probably be an infrequent occurrence.

"We shall overcome our productivity losses": this is a typically American viewpoint.

Doris demanded, "Tell me where my daughter is": that is all she said to me.

224 A question mark is placed either inside or outside the end quotation mark, depending on the content of the sentence.

- If the entire sentence, including the quoted material, is a question, the question mark should be placed outside the end quotation mark.

  Did Vernon say to Miss Adams, "I have your keys"?

  Did the memo declare the following holidays: "April 1-11 this office will be closed, and regular hours will resume on April 12"?

- If only the quoted material is a question, the question mark is placed inside the end quotation.

  Ruth turned to Stephanie and asked desperately, "Can you tell me where my son is?"

  We inquired of him politely, "What do you want, Mr. Hopkins?"

- If both the sentence and the quoted material are questions, the question mark goes inside quotes.

  Who asked, "What time is it?"

Stanley said to his father, "I have no intention of paying these bills"!

- If only the quoted material is exclamatory in nature, then the exclamation point is placed inside the end quotation mark.

It is obvious that "Patriotism forever!" doesn't incite the crowds as it once might have.

The child screamed, "Grady's hurting me!" so often that no one paid much attention to her wails.

225 Split quotations are handled by setting off the interrupting words (for example, words like *he said* and *he replied*) with commas. The second part of the split does not begin with a capital letter unless it is a proper noun or adjective or the pronoun *I*.

226 Do not use quotation marks with indirect quotes.

I asked Joe if he had decided to accept the job.

They told me that our house had been robbed!

Note: The above sentences, if direct quotations, would read as follows:

I asked Joe, "Have you decided to accept the job?"

They told me, "Our house has been robbed!"

227 It is frequently impossible to distinguish between a verbatim quote and an indirect quotation.

He said, "Sure."

OR:

He said sure.

I told Emory, "We weren't ready to leave when Gil arrived."

OR:

I told Emory we weren't ready to leave when Gil arrived.

Q. What did you tell your father?

A. I told him everything's just fine.

OR:

A. I told him, "Everything's just fine."

Q. What did you say when he asked you to spy for him?

A. I said, "No."

OR:

A. I said no.

In the above sentence pairs, the inclusion or omission of quotation marks makes no distinguishable difference in meaning. In the sentences that *do* use quotation marks, there is no clear indication that the words are being quoted verbatim. Omitting the quotes would make no difference; however, this often is not the case. The omission or inclusion of quotation marks can indeed affect the meaning conveyed to the reader. Because the CR should have in mind at all times rendering to the reader what really happened and what was actually meant, the CR will have to make some difficult decisions regarding quotations. Some CRs use quotation marks sparingly and only when they cannot avoid doing so; however, quotation marks can be useful in producing an accurate transcript, despite their difficulty and ambiguity at times.

228 The CR often will be able to tell whether a direct quote is present or not by the content of the transcript, that is, by considering what is said before and after the section in question.

Q. What did your brother say about James Fields?
A. He said, "He's behaving very strangely."

In the sentence above, the second *he* obviously refers to James Field; there is no confusion possible. With or without the quotation marks, the meaning is the same. However, consider the following:

Q. What did your brother say about his own physical condition?
A. He said he's been feeling much better recently.

In the sentence above, insertion of quotation marks would change the meaning of the sentence. Notice the change in the sentence below:

A. He said, "He's been feeling much better recently."

The addition of the quotation marks indicates that *he's* refers to someone other than the speaker. Obviously, such an interpretation would be erroneous given the content of the question.

229 Rambling constructions that contain some quoted and some nonquoted statements can be rendered most easily understood by using quotation marks, even when they are not absolutely necessary. Note the difference in readability between the following passage with and without the quotation marks.

I was planning to say to Dave I want a divorce, but then he came home with his brother, so I didn't want to say that to him, not with Ken there. Instead, I said I am going to my sister's for a while, because I thought that way he would agree and it wouldn't be as awkward. Dave said sure, go ahead and go. When are you coming back? I said I didn't know. Then Dave's face turned red, and I knew trouble was coming. Dave started shouting come here, right now, and I started toward the door. Ken said to Dave to let me go, but Dave said no way.

The above passage is understandable as it stands, but reading is made smoother by inserting quotation marks.

> I was planning to say to Dave, "I want a divorce," but then he came home with his brother, so I didn't want to say that to him, not with Ken there. Instead, I said, "I am going to my sister's for a while," because I thought that way he would agree and it wouldn't be as awkward. Dave said, "Sure, go ahead and go. When are you coming back?" I said I didn't know. Then Dave's face turned red, and I knew trouble was coming. Dave started shouting, "Come here, right now!" and I started toward the door. Ken said to Dave to let me go, but Dave said, "No way!"

230 Sentences with personal pronouns can cause tremendous confusion, as the presence or absence of quotation marks can completely change the meaning.

Q. Did you tell Joseph, "You took the money"?

OR:

Q. Did you tell Joseph you took the money?

Obviously, the first version is saying that Joseph took the money, whereas the second version is saying that the speaker took the money. Usually, the content of the transcript will make it obvious to the CR which version is correct. If this is not the case, and the CR cannot decide, the sentence can be written in a third, rather noncommittal manner.

Q. Did you tell Joseph, you took the money?

231 Sometimes doubt is cleared instantly by the speaker's use of the word "quote" and sometimes "end-quote." If this occurs, the CR knows exactly where to insert the quotation marks. Do not, however, actually write in the word "quote" unless it is part of a phrase or clause that precedes that quote, as in the second example below:

Q. What did she say in her letter to you dated January 5, 1984?
A. She said, and I am reading directly from the letter itself, "I intend to leave you everything when I die."

Q. What did Mr. Boswell say to you and Donna Pietra?

A. He said, and I quote, "The two of you will be promoted to floor supervisors."

Q. Those are his exact words, then?

A. Yes, exact words.

Q. And what did you reply?

A. I said I was looking forward to the opportunity.

- Writing the word quote and/or unquote is certainly an option and sometimes the best one.

He was, quote/unquote, nuts.

232 If it is clear where a quotation begins but the CR cannot fathom where the quotation ends, the CR can omit the quotation marks, using a capital letter preceded by a comma to show where the quotation begins and leaving out any indication of where it ends. It is preferable not to have to do this, of course, but it may be the only solution.

Q. What did the man say to you?

A. He said, You had better hand over that wallet, if you can understand what that means.

The question is whether the quote ends after wallet or after means. This is one way to handle this uncomfortable and bewildering situation; however, if your employer prefers another way of handling it, follow your firm's preferred method.

- For long quotations, that is, those that continue for more than a single paragraph, place open quotation marks at the beginning of each new paragraph; however, do not use any end quotation marks until the quoted material is complete. This means that the end quotation mark would be used only once for that quote—as a final quotation mark. This would be applicable when long excerpts are read and when quoting readback testimony.

Q. I read from your earlier testimony, Mrs. Reed. This is what you said yesterday:

Q. Where were you on the night of January 10, 1990?

A. I was with my mother and sister. We were at my sister's house out in Rockville.

Q. How long were you there?

A. About six hours, I think.

Q. Do you remember saying that, Mrs. Reed?

A. Yes, I remember it.

233 Quoted phrases, terms, and fragments of quoted material are set off with quotation marks.

> The columnist refers to this event as "Nightmare on Main Street."

234 Technical terms, that is, terms not widely understood by the general public, can be set off with quotation marks, but this practice should not be overdone. For example, in a maritime case, a multitude of maritime terms will inevitably be used, but these should not all be set off with quotation marks. To do so would "dot" the transcript making it hard to read, and also wear out the CR. Only terms that are odd or unique to the case should be set off.

> The editor was expecting to receive the "blues" that day. (a publishing term)
>
> The pilot contacted the controller, his hands off his "intercom link" to see if TWA 229 could approach the runway.

235 Titles of various works, both short and long, are enclosed in quotation marks. Many, such as book titles, are traditionally underlined to indicate that they are to be italicized in print, but the CR can use quotes in place of underlining. There is only one exception: court cases, which are underlined by most CRs (though not all). Use quotation marks to enclose the titles of the following:

short stories
poems and poetry collections
essays
plays
magazines
pamphlets and periodicals
movies
television programs, both series titles and specific episodes
songs
books
newspapers and tabloids
articles
radio shows
titles of chapters or parts of a book
reports
works of art (statues, paintings, sculptures)
names of trains, planes, ships, boats

Note: Some CRs elect to underline the titles of plays, magazines, movies, TV shows, books and newspapers to be in keeping with their "standard" handling; follow your firm's preference.

236 Foreign terms that are unfamiliar to the general public should be enclosed in quotation marks. Conversely, foreign words or terms that have become commonplace should not be set off. Table 3.1 lists some of the foreign terms that are in common use and do not have to be put in quotation marks.

They had reached an impasse.
My per diem rate was $500.
His "mal la tete" was his common complaint.
He was a practitioner of "feng-shui," which I think is a form of magic.
Some are a judgment call: I wished him "bon appetite" and left.
OR
I wished him bon appetite and left.

Table 3.1

Foreign words or terms that have become in incorporated into use in the English language.

a cappella	cafe au lait	et cetera	papier-mâché
adieu	canape	faux pas	par excellence
ad libitum	cancan	gauche	passé
à la carte	carte blanche	gendarme	passim
à la mode	caveat	gratis	patois
alfresco	chanson	gringo	per annum
alma mater	chapeau	habeas corpus	per capita
alter ego	chaperon	hara-kiri	per diem
amour	château	impasse	per se
ante bellum	consomme	julienne	persona grata
a priori	cordon bleu	lamé	pro rata
apropos	cul-de-sac	maestro	protégé
attaché	debacle	magnum	purée
au gratin	defacto	Mardi Gras	raconteur
au jus	demitasse	ménage	résumé
au naturel	denouement	metier	risqué
bateau	dinero	naive	sahib
bijou	dossier	nee	sauté
bona fide	double entendre	nil	séance
bon mot	eclair	noblesse oblige	soiree
bon voyage	en bloc	nome de plume	versus
briquette	en route	padre	via
cafe	erratum	panache	vice verso

237 If a translation of a term is contained within a sentence, it too should be placed in quotation marks.

> Mrs. Tremblant's "joie de vivre" —or "love of life" was evident to anyone who knew her.

238 Do not use quotation marks with names of diseases or technical words or terms in general use.

> The effects of the hormone somatotropin are varied.
> The landing gear was not operational.

239 When dealing with words in their roles as words, quotation marks are used. These are introduced by expressions such as *the term, the expression, the word(s),* and *known as.* When the expression *so-called* introduces a word or phrase, quotation marks are not necessary, but the CR may choose to use them.

> The term "conclusion" does not have the same literary color as does the word "denouement."
> The expression "serious money" is best used to describe amounts that are larger than that!
> The phrase "driving me to distraction" predates psychological researchers.

The quotation marks are used only for the first occurrence of the term or word, not every occurrence.

> *Note:* Some terms are used repeatedly in courtroom sessions, and the CR would be justified, perhaps advised, not to use quotation marks with such stock phrases.

The terms *preponderance of the evidence* means simply the greater weight of the evidence.
The word *negligence* implies lack of ordinary care and prudence.

240 Slang terms or words used in a special sense may be enclosed in quotation marks. The CR should use quotation marks for such terms carefully and conservatively.

> Barry was just a "home boy" to us.

241 Nicknames are sometimes set off in quotation marks.

> Louis Anton, known as "Fingers" to the neighborhood kids, was less a hero than a joke.
> Vanessa "Legs" Davis is an incredible dancer.

242 Short quotations are introduced by a comma; long quotations are introduced by a colon. Quotations of several lines (usually ten or more) may be single-spaced and indented an additional ten spaces on each side. CRs who prefer to avoid single-spacing may indent long quotations five spaces on both sides and retain double-spacing. A third method is to set the quotation like regular text, starting each paragraph of quoted material with a quotation mark and using the end quotation mark only at the end of the final paragraph of the quotation.

243 Letters and numbers written *as* numbers or letters, and so labeled, are enclosed in quotation marks.

> The letter "a" did not appear on my son's report card.
> The figure "150" was higher than expected.

244 Irony or sarcasm may be denoted with quotation marks, but the CR should use this method quite sparingly, if ever.

> Q. How would you describe his treatment of Carmen?
> A. Oh, he was a real "sweetheart" all right. He beat her up a couple of times a month or more. He couldn't hold a job. Yes, he was a "darling."

245 A CR may, on rare occasions, have to quote poetry. Lines of poetry in a transcript are usually not set line for line but run in, with a slash (virgule) between lines. Like other quoted material, poetry is set off by quotation marks.

> As the poet said, "Love can only flourish in the hearts of the enlightened."
> "Or I shall live your epitaph to make, / Or you survive when I in earth am rotten."

Remember: Excessive use of quotation marks, or use without sound cause, can ruin the physical appearance and smooth reading of a transcript. Such abuse can also, more seriously, change the meaning of what was spoken. Thus, the CR should give special consideration to when and how to use this particular mark of punctuation.

Exercises

A. Insert quotation marks where necessary. Some changes in punctuation and capitalization may also be needed.

Q. What did he say to you?
A. He said I can be influenced.
Q. Was that his exact word—influenced?

A. Yes, that's what he said. Then he winked.

Q. How did you respond?

A. Thanks but no thanks I said.

Q. Didn't you ask him what do you mean by that?

A. No. I said I knew what he meant.

Q. Was that the end of the conversation?

A. That day, yes.

Q. You had a subsequent conversation?

A. The next night I went to see The Shooting Party at the Star Cinema. I was going with my friend Susan Josef, whom I call Winky.

Q. You saw Mr. Alexander there?

A. I saw him afterward. We were at a coffee shop and he walked in. He walked over to my table and said he wanted to speak to me for a minute.

Q. What did you say then?

A. I said okay.

Q. And then what happened?

A. He said he was desperate. He needed my help.

Q. Did he explain?

A. He said I need your help. There's no one else I can turn to now. Then let me think oh, he started crying and saying please, please, don't turn away. He just kept repeating that. I wanted to get away from him. I never liked him or trusted him, but he was out of control by that time. I finally told him to please stop it. He didn't stop, though.

Q. What did you do?

A. I started walking away. I walked toward the bus stop.

Q. So you were outside the coffee shop?

A. Yes. He and I had walked outside to talk.

Q. You left your friend?

A. Yes, I did. I was frightened and just wanted to get away, and I forgot all about her. He ran after me shouting you little tramp, come back here right now!

Q. Did you answer him?

A. No. I ran into an apartment building where I knew there was a pay phone. I called my brother and told him where I was and please come pick me up, Andy, I said.

Q. What did Andy say?

A. He said he was on his way. Stay where you are and scream for help if you need to he told me.

Q. Didn't you have a job for the next day?

A. Yes. I had a small part in a movie, just a few lines, but it was in a movie called Over Yonder From Whence We Came.

Q. Had you appeared in any other movies?

A. Just one—Riverton Smith and Unger Black was the name of it. It wasn't much of a movie. But I've been on a couple of TV shows—The Carol Burns Hour and Try Your Luck.

Q. Back to that night. Did your brother arrive?

A. Not before Alexander found me. He grabbed me by the arm—I thought he'd break it—and pulled me into an alley. He threatened to cut a big X across my face for abandoning him.

B. Correct any improperly used quotation marks and insert any that have been omitted. Punctuation and capitalization may also need to be altered.

Q. Did you say Zachary you didn't do that correctly?

A. No I said I didn't know if I had done it properly or not.

Q. Did you tell him it's your fault?

A. No, I didn't. I said, "The report was his responsibility and he didn't do any supervision at all." I felt that if I hadn't done it properly, it was partly his fault.

Q. Did he agree with your evaluation?

A. He said, "Nothing."

Q. He refused to discuss it; is that what you're saying?

A. Yes.

Q. What report was this?

A. The new personnel manual entitled This Is Your Firm!

Q. Did you write the entire manual?

A. Everything except the section called Medical and Dental.

Q. Who wrote that section?

A. My so-called supervisor.

Q. Did Zachary ever answer any of your questions.

A. He was perpetually, as his secretary always told me, unavailable. He did write me a note, however, which I couldn't even read. I can't distinguish his m from his n or his a from his o. His numbers are worse. A 3 looks like a 5 or an 8 and a 1 looks just like a 7. It was a fiasco. I took it to him and said would you like to interpret this for me.

Q. What did he say to that?

A. He said, "That was my problem, not his."

C. Find 10 examples in newspaper or magazine articles using foreign terms.

D. Find 5 examples of split quotations in published matter.

The Apostrophe

The apostrophe has three primary uses: (1) in contractions, (2) in possessives, and (3) in unusual plurals and verbs. The contraction is one of the less difficult marks of punctuation and should give the CR little trouble.

246 **Contractions**

The apostrophe indicates the omission of letters in words that are written as contractions. Although contractions are frowned on in formal writing, the CR can hardly avoid them in oral testimony.

Q. The hearing is scheduled for two o'clock this afternoon; is that right?
A. There's nothing in the subpoena that would determine that.
Q. I can't believe that you didn't hear anything. Are you quite sure you shouldn't change your testimony?
A. I'll change nothing.

Note: o'clock (of the clock), *there's* (there is), *can't* (cannot), *didn't* (did not), shouldn't (should not), *I'll* (I shall or I will).

247 The apostrophe can indicate the omission of numerals.

Q. Was Jennifer born in '71 or '72?
A. No, she was born in November of '73.

Note: The number 19 has been omitted from the years in the above sentences.

248 **Possessives** (See also Unit 2)

Most singular possessives are formed by adding an apostrophe and an *s.*

The judge's decision was overthrown today.
The clerk's error cost us a day's proceedings.

Note: An alternate form of the possessive uses the word *of* instead of *'s.*

The decision of the judge was overthrown today.
The error of the clerk cost us the proceedings of a day.

249 Singular nouns that end with an *s* can be put in the possessive form by adding an apostrophe only (*James' decision*) or by adding both an

apostrophe and an *s* (*James's decision*). Some strongly prefer just the addition of the apostrophe in such cases; others follow this rule: If there is an extra final *s* sound *spoken* in the possessive form, then the *'s* should be used (pronunciation would be *"Jameses"*).

Ross' sedan was stolen last night and he doesn't expect to recover it.

Tess' hair is the envy of all the girls in her school.

OR:

Ross's sedan was stolen last night and he doesn't expect to recover it.

Tess's hair is the envy of all the girls in her school.

Consistency is important; the CR should establish a preference and follow it throughout a transcript.

250 The apostrophe is never used for possessives of personal pronouns (*my, mine, your, yours, our, ours, its, hers, theirs, their, whose, his*).

Correct

Yours is the better plan.

Wrong

Your's is the better plan.

Correct

Several houses in the neighborhood were robbed, but ours never was.

Wrong

Several houses in the neighborhood were robbed, but our's never was.

251 A frequent source of confusion is the difference between *whose* (possessive form) and *who's* (contraction of who is); between *its* (possessive) and *it's* (contraction of it is); and between *your* (possessive) and *you're* (contraction of you are).

Correct

If the book wasn't Tom's, whose was it?

Wrong

If the book wasn't Tom's, who's was it?

Correct

You say that you're his legal guardian?

Wrong

You say that your his legal guardian?

Correct

My car needed its oil changed.

Wrong

My car needed it's oil changed.

252 **Plural Possessive**

Those that end with *s* are formed by adding an apostrophe.

The five managers' secretaries attended the meeting.

My three daughters' bedrooms were all upstairs.

253 Some plurals do not end with *s*. These are made possessive by adding both an apostrophe and an *s* to the end of the word, just as one would form the possessive of a singular word.

The children's grades were falling.

Many women's health histories were incomplete.

254 The singular and the plural forms of words often sound exactly the same. In practice, the CR must distinguish what form is correct, and this is done by examining the context of the transcript.

255 In forming plural possessives, it is essential that the CR first know how to form plurals! When in doubt, consult your dictionary.

256 To form the singular possessive of a compound word, add an apostrophe and an *s* to the last word in the compound construction.

The commander-in-chief's orders came to us last night.

Stratford-on-Avon's memorial to Shakespeare attracts countless tourists.

My father-in-law's business is thriving.

257 Possessives of word groups are formed by adding the apostrophe and *s* to the last word of that word group.

Three Boys Who Cook's food is better than you'd expect.

Crusaders Club of Smithville's funds were depleted by the gala event.

258 **Joint vs. Individual Ownership**

- Joint ownership is indicated by adding *'s* to the last name of the group.

Phil and Ramon's grocery has never been robbed in its 27 years of operation.

John and Marie's Chrysler uses more gas than does their Toyota.

Note: In both the examples, a single object is owned by two persons.

- Individual ownership is indicated with *'s* added to each name.

  Phil's and Ramon's groceries have never been robbed.

  John's and Marie's Chryslers use more gas than does my car.

  Note: The plurals *groceries* and *Chryslers* indicate that each member of the two parts is an individual owner.

- Sometimes common sense will tell the CR that joint ownership is illogical. It would be unlikely, for example, for two or more people to own, say, a toothbrush or a pair of shoes jointly.

Correct

Joe's and Peter's shoe were found in the wooded area behind the cabin.

Wrong

Joe and Peter's shoe were found in the wooded area behind the cabin.

259 For names of periodicals, organizations, etc., the CR should defer to the organization's actual practice.

Citizens Band
Veterans' Administration
Consumers Union
Johnson's Used Cars

"Reader's Digest" (not "Readers' Digest")
People's Republic of China
National Shorthand Reporters Association

260 **Double Possessives**

The word *of* indicates possession (*the home of Melinda Zerba*) as does the regular possessive form (*Melinda Zerba's home*). A double possessive makes use of both of these forms of possession.

These plans of John's are unworkable.
That car of Peter's is slick.

Note the difference in meaning between the following two sentences:

That photo of Mimi was blurred.
That photo of Mimi's was blurred.

The first example is discussing a photograph of Mimi; the second example discusses a photo that belongs to Mimi, which may or may not be a photograph of Mimi herself. Thus, care must be taken in dealing with double possessives, as meaning conceivably can be altered through misuse.

261 Inanimates can be rendered possessive through the use of an apostrophe and an *s*.

A year's contract was being drawn up.
The train's seats were all filled.

Note: Do not confuse possessives and adjectives.

Correct

Our sales manager resigned.

Wrong

Our sale's manager resigned.
Our sales' manager resigned.

262 **Unusual Plurals** (See Unit 2 on plurals.)

The plurals of letters, abbreviations, symbols, and figures can be formed by using an apostrophe and an *s*.

My *a's* look like my *o's*.

If no confusion results, the apostrophe can be omitted in forming plurals of this type.

During the 1960s campus demonstrations were common.
(preferred to 1960's)
The three-year-old boy recited his ABCs accurately.
His Ps look like Ts to me. (OR P's and T's)

Use an apostrophe if omitting it might confuse the reader.

Your *on's* look like *an's*. (to avoid the odd-looking *ons* and *ans*)
My son made straight A's. (Without the apostrophe, it appears to be the word "As" rather than a plural.

263 Certain verb forms can be created by using an apostrophe and the letter *d* to put a verb in its past tense.

> He X'd out his name from the list.
> My client was not ID'd in the line-up.

Exercises

A. For the following list of words, write first the singular possessive form and then the plural possessive form.

	Singular Possessive	Plural Possessive
child		
week		
lady		
man		
puppy		
mother-in-law		
student		
piano		
turkey		
building		
chief		
window		
scissors		
deer		
tooth		
aunt		
dinner		
movie		
monkey		
moss		
foot		
managing editor		
family		
watchman		
housekeeper		
great-uncle		
taxpayer		
writing		
auxiliary		
witness		

B. Select and underline the correct word for each sentence.

1. I have no idea (whose, who's) going to be elected to office.
2. I don't think (your, you're) grasping the meaning of what I have said.
3. I asked (whose, who's) keys they were, but no one replied.
4. The dog was biting (it's, its) skin relentlessly because of allergies.
5. Do you know (who's, whose) responsible for sending out the invoices at the end of the month?
6. I think (it's, its) going to be a long time before he comes back to this town.
7. (It's, Its) been several years since we were associated with that firm.
8. Have you turned in (your, you're) report to the sales manager?
9. I don't think (it's, its) going to be hard to learn.
10. We couldn't figure out (who's, whose) been tampering with the books.
11. (Who's, Whose) expected to win?
12. The (childrens, children's, childrens') vaccinations were overdue.
13. My car was in better condition than (her's, hers, hers').
14. Our children were well behaved, but (their's, theirs) were positively angelic.
15. Many of the (boys, boy's, boys') uniforms had been stolen.
16. The herd of (deer, deer's, deers, deers') survivability was in question.
17. Did you inquire about (Jame's, James', James's) health?
18. She used five (cupful's, cupfuls) of milk.
19. Douglas suffers from an illness of six (month's, months, months') duration.
20. We visited the (Cox's, Coxes, Coxes') weekend cabin about twice a year.

The Colon

The colon is the punctuation mark of anticipation. It introduces or announces that something is about to follow, something worthy of attention. It marks a break stronger than a comma would indicate, but less strong than the break indicated by a period; and it differs from the semicolon because of its introductory nature.

264 The colon introduces a list that is preceded by words such as *the following* or *as follows.*

> The following paragraphs were rewritten: 10A, 10C, 11A, and 15D.
>
> He wrote in his report as follows: "The company is suffering from a marked decline in sales, especially in the Northeast Sector. The other sectors are doing less business than in previous years, the sole exception being the Gulf Sector."

265 When *the following* is part of a question, use a question mark, not a colon.

> You were asked those questions, and did you answer in the following manner?
>
> You had not seen him in five years, and did you write him as follows?

266 If another sentence (or sentences) falls between the introducing statement and the list, no colon is used.

> At the meeting the items discussed were as follows. The first two items received the most attention.
>
> 1. The annual stockholders' meeting
> 2. Membership drive for next year
> 3. National convention agenda
> 4. Committee on Aging

267 A colon can be used to introduce a short list at the end of a sentence.

> We invited our closest friends: Jay, Tom, Sue, and Sam.
>
> She is taking three courses: English, biology, and French.
>
> Bob purchased two items: a disk drive and a printer.

If the sentence continues after the list, do not use the colon. Use a dash instead on both sides of the list.

> We invited our closest friends—Jay, Tom, Sue, and Sam—to our wedding, but no one else.

She is taking three courses—English, biology, and French—and will take three more courses in the spring.

Bob purchased two items— a disk drive, and a printer— with his new credit line.

If the sentence is inverted, a colon can still be used.

Jay, Tom, Sue, and Sam: they are our best friends whom we invited.

English, biology and French: these are the courses she is taking.

A disk drive and a printer: these are the items Bob bought with his new credit line.

Acceptable

English, biology, and French—these are the courses she is taking.

A disk drive and a printer—Bob bought these with his new credit line.

268 A colon introduces extracts, formal statements, and legal documents.

The applicable law here is Civil Code 13, which reads in part: "Any alteration of the certificate is an act of fiscal piracy."

I read from the record: "I left the airport at 10:30 that night."

269 Use a colon with the speaker's greeting to her or his audience (salutation).

Mr. Speaker:
Sir:
Ladies and Gentlemen of the jury:
Mr. President:
Your Honor:
Friends and Co-Workers:

Note: When using the colon after a salutation, the text that follows should be indented as a new paragraph. If the salutation or greeting is incorporated into the first paragraph, a comma should be used in place of a colon.

270 Use a colon to focus the reader's attention on what follows.

His statement is clear: He is not guilty.

One problem remains: Shall we accompany Mr. Thomas?

With introductory words such as *namely, for instance, for example,* and *that is,* use a comma, not a colon, unless what follows is a complete sentence, in which case a semicolon would be used.

Correct

We ordered five pieces of equipment; specifically, we required two desks, two typewriters, and a file cabinet.

But

We ordered five pieces of equipment, namely, two desks, two typewriters, and a file cabinet.

271 Use a colon to introduce long quotations.

The president of the company addressed his employees by asking: "What are we hoping to achieve? Why are we here? Do we have definite goals outlined? Have you set your priorities for the coming year?"

272 A colon may introduce an appositive in certain constructions.

The family had one major problem: poverty.
The attorney questioned him on two topics: finances and ethics.

Acceptable

The family had one major problem — poverty.
The attorney questioned him on two topics—finances and ethics.

Note: In a different construction, commas would be used.

The two topics under discussion, finances and ethics, were discussed by the attorney and his client.

273 Do not use a colon where it is not necessary. For example, a colon should not be used in a sentence containing a short list introduced by *were* or *are.*

Correct

The persons present were Ms. Jones, Miss Lennox, Mrs. Petersen, and Mr. Baker.

Avoid

The persons present were: Ms. Jones, Miss Lennox, Mrs. Petersen and Mr. Baker.

Correct

You should do your homework, clean your room, and help your mother.

Avoid

You should: do your homework, clean your room, and help your mother.

BUT

You should accomplish the following tasks: do your homework, clean your room, and help your mother.

274 The CR employs the colon to designate speakers in colloquy and for swearing in witnesses.

CROSS EXAMINATION BY MR. HORACE:

By Mr. Horace:

The above-named witness, after having been duly sworn, testified as follows:

Note: Most firms do not use the colon after Q and A, but rather use nothing at all or a period. Use the preference of your firm.

275 With certain introductory phrases and clauses, a colon offers greater clarity than other marks of punctuation.

I should explain the circumstances: We had lost our money, Mort was badly injured, and I was terrified.

Just tell me one more thing, Mr. Jarvis: Were you or were you not aware of their connection to Lang and Company?

276 When a second sentence amplifies, clarifies, or explains the first one, a colon can be used. Note that the first word of the sentence following the colon is uppercased.

I told you several times where I was: I was at the movies.

The officer grimaced when I filed the report: She, too, had been a victim of that crime.

You know you were far closer than mere acquaintances: You were and are intimate friends.

You said that he was rude and arrogant: What did you mean by that?

277 When a question is stated awkwardly, and two questions or statements are related, a colon can clarify what is meant.

Preferred

Perhaps you will remember that her reason is: All through the winter there were problems with the heating system.

Acceptable

Perhaps you will remember that her reason is, all through the winter there were problems with the heating system.

Preferred

The problem we faced was, you may recall: We were not well informed, nor did we know how to get the needed information.

Acceptable

The problem we faced was, you may recall, we were not well informed, nor did we know how to get the needed information.

278 Hours and minutes are set off from each other, by a colon, in written references to time.

We were scheduled to meet at 12:15, but he did not arrive until nearly 1:30.

279 Certain reference materials employ the colon to distinguish between volume and page numbers, chapter, and verse.

He read John 3:16 the first thing each morning.
The article in "American Journal of Neurology" 43:212-225 discusses that condition.

The Semicolon

The semicolon lies approximately midway between the comma and the period in terms of strength. It can act as either a weak period or a strong comma. This chameleon of punctuation can change to meet the requirements of the sentence, but knowing when to use the semicolon instead of the comma or the period can be tricky and must be a learned skill. The CR should make it a rule never to employ this mark without a sound reason. If properly used, the semicolon can clarify meaning and make reading an easier task.

280 A semicolon can replace a period when the following occur:

- Two sentences are closely related in thought.
- They are not connected by a coordinating conjunction.
- They are somewhat brief.

We worried about Amelia; we never worried about Renata.
I thought he was my friend; he was not.

Note: A period could be used instead of the semicolon in the above examples, but it is a somewhat poorer choice because the semicolon indicates the close relationship between the two sentences. On the other hand, a comma would be incorrect; written with a comma the examples would be run-on sentences. (See section in Unit 2 on run-ons and comma splices.)

281 Certain short sentences are heard repeatedly during courtroom testimony (for example: *is that right, isn't that right, is that correct, isn't that true, do you know, do you recall).* These should be preceded by a semicolon.

Correct

You were Mr. Harmon's assistant from 1981 until the end of 1987; is that right?

You knew exactly what Victoria Ellis intended to do with the building she owned; isn't that true?

Wrong

You were Mr. Harmon's assistant from 1981 until the end of 1987, is that right?

You knew exactly what Victoria Ellis intended to do with the building she owned, isn't that true?

282 The CR must distinguish between true compound sentences and those that use "echo questions." An echo question occurs at the end of a sentence and is usually, though not necessarily, negative. Never use a semicolon before an echo question. Echo questions echo the subject and verb of the sentence.

Correct

You were there, weren't you?

You knew that Maurice was in Switzerland, didn't you?

He wasn't able to get the loan, was he?

Wrong

You were there; weren't you?

You knew that Maurice was in Switzerland; didn't you?

He wasn't able to get the loan; was he?

If distinguishing between sentences with echo questions and "regular" compound sentences is confusing, think about the difference between the following:

He was your supervisors; is that correct?

He was your supervisor, wasn't he?

The pause in the first sentence is more defined than the pause at the same point in the second version. The length of a pause is certainly not always a valid test for punctuation, but it may serve well here for identifying echos.

283 The CR must be aware of exactly what a question like "is that correct?" refers to. On occasion, another sentence may be inserted between the two.

Correct

Jonathan's divorce occurred in 1989. You didn't know that he had ever been married. Isn't that the correct date?

Wrong

Jonathan's divorce occurred in 1989. You didn't know that he had ever been married; isn't that the correct date?

284 Traditional grammar would not allow a semicolon after a question. However, this is sometimes acceptable for the CR in certain constructions, complying with the requirement of asking one question at a time.

How did you get to work that day; do you remember?
Can you identify the woman; is that she?

285 When an independent clause appears midsentence, do not use semicolons; instead, treat it as a parenthetical element and set it off with commas or dashes.

Kenneth was Mr. Giroir's only heir, at least that's my understanding, but William intended to dispute the will.

Let me tell you what you should do—my intentions are totally honorable— about Barry's dishonesty.

Also Acceptable

Kenneth was Mr. Giroir's only heir—at least that's my understanding—but William intended to dispute the will.

Let me tell you what you should do, my intentions are totally honorable, about Barry's dishonesty.

286 A semicolon is the preferred punctuation before a conjunctive adverb *(however, indeed, moreover, thus, nonetheless,* etc.) that separates two independent clauses. See Table 2.2.

Correct

He was the master of his home; indeed, he was a tyrant to his wife and three children.

Acceptable

He was the master of his home. Indeed, he was a tyrant to his wife and three children.

Wrong

He was the master of his home, indeed, he was tyrant to his wife and three children.

Correct

Thomas believed in his brother's willingness to help; nonetheless, Thomas maintained control.

Acceptable

Thomas believed in his brother's willingness to help. Nonetheless, Thomas maintained control.

Wrong

Thomas believed in his brother's willingness to help, nonetheless, Thomas maintained control.

287 Use a semicolon before a transitional phrase (*on the other hand, for example, in fact, in other words,* etc) that occurs between two independent clauses. A transitional phrase has exactly the same function as a conjunctive adverb. See Table 2.3.

Correct

George was on one side one day and the other side the next day; in other words, he was terribly confused.

Acceptable

George was on one side one day and the other side the next day. In other words, he was terribly confused.

Wrong

George was on one side one day and the other side the next day, in other words, he was terribly confused.

Note: A period can be used in place of the semicolon before conjunctive adverbs and transitional phrases, but this is considered less desirable than the semicolon unless the sentence is quite long and needs to be broken up.

The task was overwhelming in its complexity, and it will doubtless require endless diligence, effort, research, and literally hundreds of hours of work. On the other hand, nothing worthwhile comes easily, or so it is said.

288 Deciding what punctuation mark to use before an expression like *that is, for example,* or *namely* can be troublesome. The applicable rule is this: If what follows is a complete sentence, use a semicolon; for very long constructions, use a period; if what follows is not a complete sentence, use a comma.

Correct

We were purchasing the shop from Mr. and Mrs. Owens, that is, the stationery shop.

BUT:

We were purchasing the shop from Mr. and Mrs. Owens; that is, we were purchasing the stationery shop.

Correct

I did a lot for my brother and his wife, for example, housecleaning.

BUT:

I did a lot for my brother and his wife; for example, I did their housecleaning.

289 Three or more closely related sentences may be joined by semicolons, although such use should be limited to situations where the sentences are relatively short and closely associated in thought.

We invited Mary; Joe, her brother, came, too; Billy was unavailable.

The water was cold; we were accustomed to moderate temperatures; we swam for less than an hour.

Note: If the clauses are quite short and flow smoothly, commas can be used. Again, the CR should be very careful in using such a construction. It would be a rare occurrence indeed.

Jim came home, he turned on the radio, he lay down on the sofa.

I came, I saw, I conquered.

290 Use a semicolon to separate long subordinate clauses that begin with the word *that.* This is a common occurrence in legal language.

We intend to prove today that the defendant did willfully and intentionally lie under oath; that he did knowingly and maliciously plan and intend to take from the property of Mrs. Williams, his employer, her jewelry and cash; that he, the defendant, did abuse the trust Mrs. Williams had placed in him as a trusted employee; and that the defendant is guilty of all charges listed in the indictment.

291 The semicolon is used to separate two independent clauses that are joined by a coordinating conjunction (that is, in a compound sentence) if one or both of the clauses contain commas. This is a judgment call that is made for the sake of clarity.

> Unless you are convinced that he was telling the truth, you should not sign those papers, Mrs. Rose; and you should wait until further validation can be done.
>
> When we backed the car out of the garage, Lena jumped out of the back door, let out a yell, and ran; but we had no idea what was wrong with her.

292 Use semicolons to separate elements of a series when the elements themselves contain commas.

> The impounded automobiles include a Renault, a French car; two Saabs, Swedish cars; a Jaguar, British; and five Chevrolets.
>
> My former addresses include 23 Yearling Lane, Raleigh, North Carolina; 557-3 Meadow Avenue, Savannah, Georgia; and 1141-4 West End Avenue, New York, New York.
>
> The officers attending the meeting included the president, Tom Mendez; the acting chairman of finance, Carla Parkin; the regional manager, Ellen Immo; and the firm's chief accountant, Jeffrey Unger.

293 Use semicolons to separate references containing commas.

> I will read from Chapter 3, paragraph 7; Chapter 4, paragraph 2; Chapter 6, paragraph 3; and Chapter 9, paragraph 1.

294 Use a semicolon with long enumerations, but not with short lists.

> The plan is to (1) consult with experts in the field who would be able to give us some idea of the market; (2) conduct a formal, wide-range market search; (3) prepare advertisements and solicit new business; (4) go into the project full-force when the market appears ready for us.
>
> BUT:
>
> You may (1) sign the check, (2) return it unsigned, or (3) negotiate further.

Remember that a semicolon is always placed outside quotation marks. When a quotation ends with a semicolon, the semicolon should be omitted entirely.

> He said, “Our victory is inevitable”; however, I do not share his confidence.
>
> She said to him, “You don’t know what’s going on here”; in fact, he hadn’t been home in two years.

Exercises

A. Correct any errors involving colons and semicolons in the following sentences. Some sentences are correct.

1. My son and my two daughters: They are my primary concern.
2. Our marriage was plagued by one problem, money.
3. Mr. Eaton left for France; isn’t that true, but you were unable to go along with him.
4. Carlton Manning: what is your profession and with what firm are you employed?
5. You wouldn’t deceive me; would you?
6. Luci is a clever girl; indeed, she is the most talented student I have ever taught.
7. There is only one issue now, did you steal the money?
8. Maria walked over to Louis, and did she say the following to him:
9. Sheila put three things in her purse: namely, her wallet, a revolver, and a set of keys.
10. We argued often about Freda’s problems: for instance, her tantrums.
11. She instructed her children to stay off the phone, thus, they told their friends to drop by rather than telephone.
12. The following persons are to see me this afternoon: Bring pencil and paper: Jill Conrad, Alicia Grant, Boris Abbott, and David Perrine.
13. He made only this one demand, $15,000 in cash by Friday.
14. Our best secretary was: Miss Twombley.
15. Only two courses were available at that time: sociology and chemistry.

16. How often did he come around, do you remember?
17. He didn't drink before driving that night, did he?
18. Terese purchased four items: paper, pen, dictionary, and a stapler from my shop, and then she went home.
19. We were concerned about Dad's health; in fact, we were frantic.
20. Study the following passages: Section 34, page 185, paragraph 4, Section 71, page 288, paragraph 2, Section 125, page 419, paragraph 6.

B. Write five examples of each of the following:

1. a colon to introduce a short list within a sentence
2. a colon to introduce an appositive
3. a sentence using "for example"
4. a sentence using "is that correct"
5. an echo question
6. a semicolon used before a conjunctive adverb
7. a semicolon used before a transitional phrase
8. semicolons used to separate references containing commas
9. a sentence containing "do you recall?"
10. a colon used to introduce a long quotation

The Dash

The CR's use of the dash should be limited primarily to indicating either a shift in thought or an interruption of some kind. Other uses of the dash acceptable in traditional grammar are considered a poor punctuation choice for the CR or are not permitted at all. Overuse of the dash would indicate, at times inaccurately, hesitancy on the speaker's part. Dashes should not be inserted each time a speaker falters, hesitates, pauses, or slows down. Use the dash discriminately and only when it is the decidedly best choice. The dash should be used with special care when punctuating the words of a judge or attorney.

There are certain situations in which accurate reporting demands use of the dash. It is the CR's task to be alert to these situations and to produce a transcript which, through use of the dash, will more clearly reveal to any reader exactly what transpired during the proceedings.

The dash is a useful tool for preventing misreading in many circumstances.

296 The dash is used to indicate interruption of the speaker by another person. Meanings can be altered by the incorrect use or omission of the dash, and the CR must record interruptions meticulously. Do not use the ellipsis to indicate interruption.

Q. Will you cooperate with this investigation?
A. I will—
Q. Just answer yes or no, Mr. Juarez.
A. I will not be part of this fiasco. No.

Note: If the CR had used a period after *I will*, the transcript would not make any sense. First the witness would be saying that he would cooperate, and then he would be saying he would not. The dash, then, is an essential element in understanding the proceedings.

297 When a speaker is interrupted and then resumes what he or she was saying after the interruption, use a pair of dashes.

Q. Did you discuss this problem with Jim Langley?
A. I discussed only —
Q. Speak up, Miss Adams.
A. —that I had discovered a problem in his bookkeeping.

The resumption does not begin with a capital letter unless it is a proper noun or the pronoun I.

Q. Did you see the—
A. When do you mean?
Q. Right after the fire.
A. Okay.
Q. —the man the police call David M. Smith?
A. Yes, I saw him.
Q. Can you describe the incident—
Mr. Jensen: Your question is entirely too vague.
Ms. Davids: It relied upon the preceding body of questions.
Mr. Jensen: I regard it as vague; why don't you be specific?
Q. (By Ms. Davids): —that occurred on the 15th of last month at approximately 6:30 p.m.?
A. I recall it.

298 When a speaker is interrupted by a person who then continues and completes what the speaker was saying, a pair of dashes is used.

Q. Furthermore, all the accountants in the firm—
A. —had access to the documents? Yes, they all did. But we were all told by our supervisor that we were—
Q. —immune from prosecution?
A. Yes, that's right.

299 Shifts in thought pattern are indicated with dashes.

Q. Where was Sheila at that time?
A. She was —I'm wondering what she has to do with this.

Q. How do you know that?
A. I saw in the files—are you doubting my word?

300 Noticeable hesitancy or doubt is recorded by using a pair of dashes if the hesitancy is bypassed and the sentence resumed, by a single dash if not resumed.

Q. What did the defendant say to you?
A. He said—I think I heard him say— for me to leave.
Q. What was Terrance's relationship to Mr. Barre?
A. He was his—I think, at least, but I'm not sure—his nephew.
The pilot—I'm not sure if it was the pilot or the co-pilot.

301 An abrupt shift is recorded with a dash or a pair of dashes.

Q. Did you hear anything?
A. I was humming—I was happy—humming loudly and couldn't hear a thing other than my own voice.

302 If the speaker suddenly thinks of something else he or she wishes to say, in the middle of a sentence, the dash is used to indicate this phenomenon.

Q. When did you first hear the news?
A. Mrs. Bradley telephoned me at about nine o'clock—she's 85 years old—to tell me about it.
Q. How long did you own the property?
A. I owned it from 1961 until last year—that whole area was virtually unpopulated—when I sold it to Mr. Rocca.

303 If the speaker realizes abruptly that he or she has made an assumption that should not have been made and subsequently expresses that realization, a dash is placed at that point.

Q. When you purchased the equipment from Mr. Yargar—you did purchase the equipment from Mr. Yargar?

A. I did, yes.

Q. Where did you find the diary, Miss Armstrong?

A. I found it in the library—you mean Mary Thornton's diary?

304 Sometimes the speaker will have a sudden recollection; this should be indicated by a dash.

Q. Was he wearing a hat?

A. I don't know if—he did have a hat on.

Q. Why did your mother wish to see Martin?

A. I have no idea why she—oh, it was about her will.

Note: In the first example above, note that the omission of the dash would present the reader with the exact opposite meaning. Look at the difference between the two versions, with and without the dash.

I don't know if—he did have a hat on.

I don't know if he did have a hat on.

The first sentence makes it clear that the speaker has recalled that the man was wearing a hat, but the second version would indicate that the speaker does not know whether he was wearing one.

305 When a parenthetical statement is used, the CR should insert a dash both before and after the parenthetical. The speaker has thought of something in the middle of the sentence, makes the statement, and then resumes with the original statement. Parentheticals may contain *internal* punctuation, which is applied just as it would be if the parenthetical were an independent statement, for example, commas. Parentheticals never contain periods.

I told you—I have several witnesses, you know—that I was at the theatre all night.

Mr. Dunning was president—I worked for him 22 years— and I was his executive assistant for the last 16 years of that time.

For parentheticals that represent a less distinct break, a comma can be used in place of each dash, although a dash is usually acceptable.

He was my friend, and he never doubted my loyalty, for 30 years.

306 Explanatory words that occur in the middle of a sentence can be set off with dashes.

My neighbors—well, actually my former neighbors—borrowed my car on several occasions.

Our summer home—it's more of a small cabin—is located in an area about 125 miles north of this city.

307 Some situations that would seem to call for a colon must use a pair of dashes instead because the sentence continues after the "listing."

The following persons received copies of the report— Alan Zimmerman, Bill Yeats, Rebecca Gold, and Benjamin Thatcher— and all of them will be called to testify in these proceedings.

BUT:

The following persons received copies of the report: Alan Zimmerman, Bill Yeats, Rebecca Gold, and Benjamin Thatcher. All of them will be called to testify in these proceedings.

308 Explanatory words that occur at the end of a sentence may be preceded by a dash, although in most cases a comma would serve equally well.

She was a fragile child—delicate and sickly.

OR:

She was a fragile child, delicate and sickly.

Mr. Pearl is a wonderful teacher, an example to his students, their mentor, their leader.

OR EVEN:

Mr. Pearl is a wonderful teacher: an example to his students, their mentor, their leader.

309 Appositives that contain commas should be set off with dashes.

Sylvia—wife, mother, college professor, and volunteer—has almost no spare time.

Three states—Utah, New Jersey, and Colorado— were not represented at the convention.

310 Serious ambiguity can result unless appositives that occur within a series are correctly punctuated.

Mother, Father, my teacher—Mr. Shaw—Uncle Jim, Sally Li, and Beryl met me that night at Les Fleurs Restaurant.

Note: If *Mr. Shaw* were set off by commas, the sentence would read differently: Mr. Shaw and the teacher would seem to be two individuals rather than the same person. The same principle applies to the following examples.

Maryland, Virginia, North Carolina—her home state—and West Virginia were possible sites for her business.

311 At the beginning of a sentence, an appositive that consists of a series can be followed by a dash. A colon is an alternative punctuation. The same applies to appositives at the end of a sentence.

Her parents, her children, her husband—those individuals' needs were her only real concern in life.

OR

Her parents, her children, her husband: those individuals' needs were her only real concern in life.

Greene Street, Williams Boulevard, Eagle Road, and Simmons Lane—these roadways are under construction.

OR

Greene Street, Williams Boulevard, Eagle Road, and Simmons Lane: these roadways are under construction.

312 Do not use a dash between two closely related sentences. Whereas this practice is sometimes acceptable in other disciplines, it is unacceptable for the CRs purposes.

We were anticipating great success; everything was going along splendidly and smoothly.

Avoid

We were anticipating great success—everything was going along splendidly and smoothly.

313 Do not use dashes to indicate a speaker's slowness, stuttering, or any speech pattern. Dashes would be distracting and unnecessary.

Avoid

I have—not—seen him—in two years.

Correct

I have not seen him in two years.

314 It is not the CR's job to record accents, dialects, and speech impediments. Learn to distinguish between speech patterns and interruptions or shifts that are essential to the meaning of what was spoken.

315 Do not use the dashes for the attorneys' or judge's words unless absolutely necessary, that is, when no other mark can do the job.

316 Be conservative with the use of the dash. A transcript peppered with dashes is visually distracting. Do not use it without a concrete reason and a conviction that it will clarify the transcript's meaning.

The Comma

Proper use of the comma seems to present one of the greater points of confusion. Correct comma use requires a thorough knowledge of grammar, including an ability to recognize the difference between phrases and clauses and the difference between independent and dependent clauses. A misplaced comma can change the meaning of what was said and confuse the reader.

A common misuse of the comma in transcripts is inserting a comma to indicate a speaker's pauses or hesitations. This widespread practice produces a manuscript that is distorted and, ultimately, incorrect in its representation of what occurred and what was said. Whereas many commas do reflect natural pauses, the CR must not attempt to punctuate transcripts on that basis alone.

The three primary uses of the comma (1) to separate, (2) to introduce, and (3) to enclose. The CR should use a comma only when a sound reason for its use can be given; otherwise, omit the comma.

317 A comma is used to separate independent clauses connected by a coordinating conjunction. The comma is placed before, not after, the conjunction. (See Table 2.2.)

Correct

Miss Fields says she was employed by Bates Manufacturing, but they have no record of her working there.

We rode down to Springville, and we spent the day there.

Wrong

Miss Fields says she was employed by Bates Manufacturing but, they have no record of her working there.

We rode down to Springville and, we spent the day there.

We rode down to Springville, and, we spent the day there.

318 If there is no conjunction between two independent clauses, a comma cannot and must not be used to separate the clauses; a period or semicolon should be used.

Correct

The door was unlocked and the key on the floor; I picked up the key and walked right in.

OR:

The door was unlocked and the key on the floor. I picked up the key and walked right in.

Wrong

The door was unlocked and the key on the floor, I picked up the key and walked right in.

Correct

Mr. Blake was not easy to get along with, in my opinion; everyone respected his knowledge and experience, however.

OR:

Mr. Blake was not easy to get along with, in my opinion. Everyone respected his knowledge and experience, however.

Wrong

Mr. Blake was not easy to get along with, in my opinion, everyone respected his knowledge and experience, however.

319 If two independent clauses connected by a coordinating conjunction are very short, or the first one is very short (fewer than five words, for example), the comma is optional. The comma can be omitted when there is no possibility of confusing or misleading the reader.

He walked out and I followed.
We worried but Sonny didn't.

320 Three or more independent clauses can be joined by commas.

Mrs. Yates and her daughter moved to Cleveland in 1986, they purchased a home immediately, and Miss Hunter rented a room from them starting in 1988.

He can resign voluntarily, he can take a leave of absence, or his supervisor may decide to let him go.

321 If two independent clauses are connected by a conjunction and either or both clauses contain commas, a semicolon can replace the comma that separates the clauses. This is a judgment left to the CR and may not be necessary if only one comma is used within either clause. If clarity is enhanced by using the semicolon, by all means use it.

The painting is, in the opinion of Mr. Tremaine, not an original; but he does consider it an excellent copy, one that is worth keeping.

OR:

The painting is, in the opinion of Mr. Tremaine, not an original, but he does consider it an excellent copy, one that is worth keeping.

The second version, although certainly not incorrect, is less effective.

322 At times witnesses or attorneys will engage in what seem to be endless sentences that ramble on forever. It is acceptable for the conscientious CR to separate these long constructions with periods and semicolons. In fact, it is more than acceptable; it is highly desirable, for clarity's sake, to cut up excessively long constructions into shorter ones.

The following is an example of such a rambling passage:

Bring your records of all transactions during the past five years, and be prepared to open these records, but be certain that you have brought everything available and have omitted nothing, but if elements are missing, Mr. Daniels, you must be prepared to explain, if possible, such omissions, and you can be sure that you will be questioned thoroughly.

A CR could punctuate the passage more effectively by replacing some of the commas with semicolons and/or periods.

Bring your records of all transactions during the past five years, and be prepared to open these records; but be certain that you have brought everything available and have omitted nothing. But if elements are missing, Mr. Daniels, you must be prepared to explain, if possible, such omissions; and you can be sure that you will be questioned thoroughly.

The following examples also started as one long sentence containing independent clauses joined by coordinating conjunctions. It has been cut up into smaller sentences by using periods and semicolons rather than commas between some of these clauses.

I thought that he was going to return after a couple of hours; so I told Mr. Ellis to wait for him there, and he told me that he would wait. And then I just let Mr. Ellis sit down in the waiting room, but I didn't watch what he was doing or anything like that, for it hadn't occurred to me that I needed to keep an eye on him, and I knew that Ed Johnson knew him. But I did walk into the waiting room several times to get this or that, and I didn't notice him doing anything except looking through magazines; and once he was looking out the window, sort of staring out as though he was worried. But I didn't want to disturb him, you know.

323 Commas separate items in a series. The items can be words, phrases, or clauses. A series consists of more that two items. The "serial" comma, that is, the final comma before the conjunction, should be used, although some advocate omitting this final comma. For the CR, the only situation in which the serial comma should be omitted is when the two final items are a unit rather than individual items.

Words or terms in a series:

He handed me his application, fees, and identification.
The breakfast specials were blueberry pancakes, oatmeal, and ham and eggs.

Note: There is no comma after *ham* because *ham* and *eggs* is a unit.

Phrases in a series:

The children walk over the bridge, up the hill, down Brewster Lane, and past the IGA.
He hoped to graduate from college, to travel for a full year, to keep a travel journal, and then to return home.

Clauses in a series:

He ate, he slept, he complained, but no one seemed to mind.
We worked all day, we went home at dusk, and we listened to music until time to retire.

324 Omit the comma when the conjunction is repeated in a series.

Either Mamie or Harrison or Nora will get the promotion.

BUT:

Either Mamie, Harrison, or Nora will get the promotion.
She cried and screamed and begged and accused and generally went into a rampage.

BUT:

She cried, screamed, begged, accused, and generally went into a rampage.

325 For clauses in a series, if the conjunction is repeated and the clauses are independent, retain the commas.

We saw him walking toward the pier, but he did not see us, and so we didn't call out to him or try to get his attention.

My sister was planning a visit to Georgia, and she was going to take her son with her, but she just didn't have enough money to take both her son and her daughter.

Note: Semicolons could also have been used in the above sentences after *us* and after *her* because of the internal commas within one or both clauses (see Section 319).

326 Do not use commas if dependent clauses are connected by conjunctions.

When you received the check and when it cleared, did you then spend those funds?

Before he was out of college and before he was working full time, what was his source of income?

Note: There is no reason to put a comma after *check* in the first example or after *college* in the second example.

BUT:

Whatever she does, wherever she goes, she worries about Phillip and Michael.

If there were a conjunction between the two clauses, the comma could have been omitted.

Whatever she does and wherever she goes, she worries about Phillip and Michael.

327 If the elements in a series contain commas within the elements themselves, the commas between the elements should be replaced by semicolons. This is to make the separation between the elements clear.

Correct

We planned to stop in Baltimore, Maryland; Washington, D.C.; New York, New York; Boston, Massachusetts; and Newport, Rhode Island.

Wrong

We planned to stop in Baltimore, Maryland, Washington, D.C., New York, New York, Boston, Massachusetts, and Newport, Rhode Island.

Note: Using a semicolon rather than a comma in such situations is not only desirable but frequently necessary to the meaning of the sentence. In the example that follows, the sentence can be misread to be a list of almost twice as many people as it really includes, a situation clarified by the use of the semicolon.

Members present at the board meeting included Mr. Jaffe, the president of the club, Miss Wallis, the organization's secretary, Tom Carr, the chairman, and Noel Richards.

328 Adjectives in a series that modify the same word or group of words are separated by commas.

> Our pompous, demanding, holier-than-thou supervisor made our work situation intolerable.
>
> The thin, frail, frowning young man is my cousin.
>
> *Note:* No comma is used after the last adjective, that is between the adjectives and the noun that is being modified.
>
> BUT:
>
> The large white house on the corner of Johnson Lane and Bluebell Street is my family's home.

Why is there no comma between large and white in the above sentence? This issue can be difficult to master, as the distinction can seem subtle and not easily discerned. The rule is this: A comma is placed between adjectives that modify the same noun to the same degree. The word "large" modifies white house, not just house; that is why there is no comma between large and white.

There are a couple of "tests" that work well in deciding whether to place commas between adjectives. The CR can use one or the other of these tests—or both—to help in deciding whether or not commas should be used.

Test #1

If the word *and* can be inserted logically between the adjectives, then a comma is used. For example, one would not say the large and white house; thus, no comma is used.

> MORE EXAMPLES:
>
> The angelic little baby was terribly sick. (No comma is needed between angelic and little.)
>
> I thought her a scheming, conniving, disloyal woman. (Commas are used between the adjectives scheming, conniving, and disloyal.)

Test #2

If the order of the adjectives is reversed, is the original meaning retained and does the reversed order sound "right"? If so, use a comma between the adjectives; if not, use no comma.

His big blue eyes grew wide with delight.

To reverse the order of the adjectives would produce the following sentence:

His blue big eyes grew wide with delight.

This does not work well, obviously; therefore no comma is used between big and blue.

The pathetic, drunken vagabond has been homeless for about two years.

Changing the order of the adjectives produces this kind of sentence:

The drunken, pathetic vagabond has been homeless for about two years.

Reversing the order seems to produce a sentence with the same meaning as the original; thus, the commas are correct.

329 Never use a comma before a series begins.

Correct

He implied that we were lonely, neurotic, and depressed.

Wrong

He implied that we were, lonely, neurotic, and depressed.

330 Adjectives that follow the word they modify should be set off by commas.

The woman frightened and cold, seemed disoriented.
The building, stately and grand, would bring a large price.

331 Short introductory phrases (usually four or fewer words) often do not require a comma; phrases of five words or more should be followed by a comma. Even very short phrases must be followed by a comma if confusion could result from omitting the comma.

During 1988 we made only a small profit. (no confusion, no comma)

BUT:

During the summer and fall of 1988, we closed the store. (introductory phrase is long)

For Joseph she was willing to go to jail. (short, no confusion)

BUT:

For Joseph's safety and well being, she was willing to go to jail. (long, comma needed)

Note: if there is a question of clarity, use the comma even with short introductory phrases.

In Springfield, Nevada was considered more like a foreign country than a fellow state. (separates Springfield from Nevada so that the sentence is not read as Springfield, which is in Nevada). This issue is confusing but crucial!

332 Introductory verbal phrases (infinitive or participial) should be followed by a comma.

Working long and hard each day, John had no time for his avocations.

To get along in his company, all you have to do is be absolutely excellent at your job.

Note: Be sure to distinguish between introductory verbal phrases and verbals that serve as the subject of the sentence. There is no comma after verbals that are the subject.

Becoming aware of our shortcomings was not easy. (subject)

BUT:

Becoming aware of our shortcomings, we began to see what we would need to do to improve the situation. (introductory)

To sell the house by the end of summer was our hope. (subject)

BUT:

To sell the house by summer, we would have to do some repairs. (introductory)

333 Direct address at the beginning of a sentence should be followed by a comma. In the middle of a sentence, it should be set off with commas, and at the end of a sentence, it is preceded by a comma.

Mr. Alton, we are prepared to meet with the auditor at his convenience.

I do not recall, Miss Bayer, when he made the formal request; however, I can tell you, maam, that it was before June.

334 Commas are sometimes necessary to avoid possible misreading or slowing down of the reading.

Before, the acquisition would have been impractical.

Note: If the comma is omitted after before the reader might at first see it as the beginning of the prepositional phrase *before the acquisition.* In this case, *before* means *previously.*

Inside, the house was elegant, although the exterior was worn.

Note: Again, the comma prevents misreading *inside the house* as an introductory prepositional phrase.

335 Use a comma after introductory words *(well, yes, no, however, nevertheless, briefly, actually, similarly, unfortunately, nevertheless).*

Actually, she was due to move to New York.
Indeed, we were more than simply displeased.
Yes, it was a risk.

Sometimes careful inspection is necessary. What may appear at first glance to be an introductory word my perform another function in the sentence. Look at the following examples:

Now I understand what you mean.

BUT:

Now, I can see your side of the problem, but it's not my place to sympathize.

In the first sentence, *now* is an adverb (denoting time); in the second, it is an introductory word (used like "well"). Examine the following sentences.

However I try, he will not cooperate with me.
However, he will not cooperate with me.
Well, I like to drink water with my meals.
Well water tastes odd to me.

336 Do not use a comma after a coordinating conjunction that begins a sentence.

Correct

And have you thought about my offer?
But how can you be so happy about this?

Wrong

And, have you thought about my offer?
But, how can you be so happy about this?

337 Sometimes a comma is appropriate after *yes* or *no;* in other situations a period is the appropriate mark. This is determined by the content of the sentence. If yes or no is answering a question but supplying no other information whatsoever, a comma is used. If the answer goes on to supply additional information, use a period.

Q. Is Jason sick?
A. Yes, he is.

BUT:

Q. Is Jason sick?

A. Yes. He has been sick for two weeks, and he has not improved.

Q. Have you lived at that house for more than a year?

A. No, sir, I have not.

BUT:

Q. Have you lived at that house for more than a year?

A. No, sir. I have been living there only two months—since July.

338 Use a comma to separate a statement from an echo question that follows. (See section on semicolons in this unit.)

He is certain of the facts, isn't that correct?

You couldn't identify the man who robbed you, could you?

BUT:

He is certain of the facts; isn't that correct?

You couldn't identify the man who robbed you; isn't that true?

339 Commas set off appositives unless they are restrictive in nature (see exceptions and examples below).

The defendant, Julia Thompson, is too ill to stand trial.

Carl Brown, the principal of the local elementary school, is my brother's closest friend.

- Remember that titles, academic degrees, and abbreviations after a name, such as *Jr., Sr., Esquire, Inc.,* and *Limited,* are appositive in nature and should be set off with commas.

Stanley Bankston, Jr., is our attorney.

Campbell and Sons, Inc., is a local company that's familiar to everyone in our area.

Exception: Roman numerals after a name.

Daniel Bronson Hubbard IV is only a child aged eight or nine years

- Do not set off an appositive that is part of a title, i.e., a historical title.

Alexander the Great is remembered in several plays.

William the Conquerer is the subject of his study.

- Use quotation marks, not commas, to set off a word, phrase, expression, etc., used as an appositive.

The term "indisputable" is not appropriate.

We were told that the phrase "in reply to your letter" is trite and should not be used in company correspondence.

- Set off identifying or explanatory phrases that begin with *of.*

Mr. Henry Zellar, of our Chicago office, is preparing a report.

Miss Jane Dunmore, of British Columbia and London, was visiting her aunt in New York City.

- If an appositive is *restrictive* in nature, it should not be set off by commas. This is an area of confusion for many and often requires extra thought.

Note the differences between the following sentence pairs, the first sentence of the pair contains a restrictive appositive, the second sentence contains a nonrestrictive appositive.

Although I have only a child, my daughter, Theresa Jean, seems a huge parenting responsibility.

Of my five daughters, my daughter Theresa Jean is youngest.

The most exciting year of our lives, 1990, went too fast.

The year 1990 was the most exciting of our lives.

The only song he ever wrote, "The Minute I See Them," was never recorded.

The song "The Minute I See You" was never recorded.

340 If all three elements of a date are used, i.e., month, day, and year, each item should be set off. If only month and year are given, they do not need to be separated by commas. Similarly, no comma is required for inverted dates.

The transaction went through, officially at least, on September 5, 1991.

The transaction was expected to go through in September 1991.

The date on the contract was 6 April 1974.

On May 21st of 1985, my grandfather was married.

On the 21st of May, 1985, my grandfather was married.

341 A comma is used before a short quotation.

Mistress Samuels asked, "Terrence, where have you been for the last week?"

I said to him, "You are not allowed in this laboratory."

342 Set off the word *please* when it occurs at the end of a sentence and sometimes in the middle of a sentence.

Describe the scene for us, please.
Give me that book, please, and then have a seat.

BUT:

Would you please inform me of Jack's whereabouts?

343 Set off *etc.* within a sentence.

His wrote in his journal about his feelings, emotions, activities, hopes, goals, etc., on a daily basis.

344 When city and state are written together, commas are placed after each of them.

We spent our vacation in Miami, Florida, at a luxury hotel.
The conference would be held in Athens, Greece, this year.

345 It is usually preferable not to use a comma in a sentence that has a compound verb but is not a compound sentence.

Fletcher watched as the boys fought but took no action to break up the fight.

BUT:

Fletcher watched as the boy fought, but he took no action to break up the fight. (The addition of a second subject, *he,* makes this a compound sentence.)

346 Parenthetical elements are set off by commas except when dashes seem more appropriate.

He is, I believe, president of the company.
He was, to put it mildly, a poor sport.

347 Company names that employ an ampersand omit the comma before the ampersand.

Hays, Milton & Sach have opened a new office on 25th Street.

348 Introductory dependent clauses are followed by a comma unless they are very short (in which case the comma is optional).

If you can, come to the shop tonight.
Because he failed math, he will attend summer school.
In 1987 we bought a new car. (Optional comma after 1987)

349 Commas follow conjunctive adverbs and transitional phrases.

We felt that the decision was sound; nevertheless, it seemed wise to consult an expert.

Mr. Galvin knew what was going on; in other words, he was fully competent.

350 Elements in an address, except in zip codes, are separated by commas.

The company's headquarters will be located at Suite 502, 112 Main Street, Walker, Arkansas.

My mail should be forwarded to The Yalta Center, 45 South Windward Avenue, Burlington, Vermont 05401.

351 Nonrestrictive elements are set off by commas.

The employee who is honest and works hard will get ahead in this company. (restrictive)

Mr. Warren, who is one of the hardest workers in this company, has just been promoted. (nonrestrictive)

In the first sentence, *who is honest and works hard* is a restrictive clause; that is, it is essential to the meaning of the sentence. Take it out and we have: *The employee will get ahead in this company.* The restrictive clause identifies exactly which employee will get ahead. In the second sentence, Mr. Warren is not identified by the clause. The nonrestrictive clause *who is one of the hardest workers in this company* gives the reader additional information about Mr. Warren, but removing it does not alter the essential meaning of the sentence.

There are two Mr. Carls in my neighborhood, but I am acquainted only with the Mr. Carl who works for Exxon. (restrictive)

Samuel Carl, who is a barber, lives near me. (nonrestrictive)

The plan that you suggest cannot solve our problems. (restrictive)

Plan C, which is the best we have seen, will be adopted. (nonrestrictive)

Children like Amos need special attention. (restrictive)

Our nation' largest cities, like Chicago and New York, will be highlighted in this book. (nonrestrictive)

Note: Clauses that begin with *that* are not set off by commas.

The boy that I saw was tall and thin.

One of the most beautiful places that we visited was Tokyo.

352 Use a comma to indicate contrast.

I wanted to play, not to work.

I expected to receive a little money, but not a fortune.

353 Use a comma to separate identical words when confusion could occur.

I tell you, you are mistaken.
Let Malcom in, in the foyer only.

354 When a numbered list occurs in a sentence, a comma follows the written-out version of the number. If what was said was "one...two...three," etc., numerals in parentheses are used; if what was said was "first...second...third," etc., these ordinals are written as words, not numbers.

I want you to tell us these things: first, when you met Paul Matthieson; second, what he said to you; and, third, why you kept this meeting secret from Silvio.

Do not use commas after the numerals in numbered lists:

The package contained the following items: (1) four pamphlets, (2) three pencils, and (3) an empty envelope.

355 Use commas to set off *for example, for instance, namely,* and *that is* if what follows such a term is not a complete sentence. If what follows is a complete sentence, use a semicolon before the term and a comma after it.

The elements were harsh, for example, the temperature and the wind, in the mountains.

BUT:

The elements were harsh; for example, the temperature was freezing, and the wind gusting.

356 A comma can be used to indicate omitted words that are "understood."

Jan earned $50 doing odd jobs for Mr. Suarez; Zina, $80.
Garreth bought groceries, shoes, and beverages; Tina, cutlery and paper products.

357 Use a comma in numbers over a thousand except in addresses, telephone numbers, document designations, and page numbers.

We sold 3,982 tickets to the concert.
He lives at 11237 Boulder Lane.
Policy no. 58473K-33 has been cancelled.
Dial 425-1160 and ask for Bev.
Turn to page 1156B in Unit 11.

358 Sometimes commas are needed to separate numbers that occur adjacent to one another in a sentence.

> Of 115, 14 were chosen to compete nationally.
> On page 471, 35 persons are listed as missing from that area.

359 Do not use a comma in elements of a single measurement.

> The sacks of grain weighed 40 pounds 10 ounces each.
> My three sons stand 5 feet 11 inches, 6 feet 1 inch, and 6 feet 2 inches.

Unit Exercises

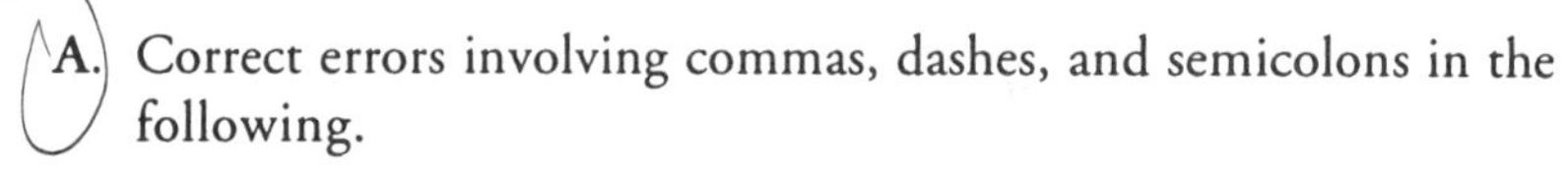

A. Correct errors involving commas, dashes, and semicolons in the following.

Q. State your name please.
A. Eleanor Mary Albert.
Q. In respect to the house at issue here today; you had a purchase agreement with —
A. Nathan Sorrell
Q. And was Mr. Sorrell, the sole owner of the house.
A. I thought he was but, I learned later that his sister, was co-owner.
Q. What is Mr. Sorrell's sister's name Miss Albert?
A. Her name is, Lianne Sorrell Reed.
Q. And, is Reed her married name?
A. Yes, It is.
Q. When did you learn that Mrs. Reed was co-owner of the house, from whom did you learn this?
A. I found out, when Mrs. Reed showed up at my door, she told me herself. Mr. Sorrell never told me, anything about it.
Q. What did she —
A. I was shocked.
Q. say to you that day?
A. She told me that I would have to move out of the house, and that I would have to move out.
Q. Did she tell you why?
A. Well she was talking fast, and acting nervous. She walked, into my house — she didn't even tell me who she was — and just started telling me how I would have to move out of the house, because the sale was not going to take place.

Q. Was this the first time you met Mrs. Reed?
A. Yes. It was actually the first time I even knew that she existed.
Q. What was your response to her, to Mrs. Reed's statements.
A. I asked her, who she was.
Q. What did she say?
A. She said — "I am the owner of this house; and I am not going to sell it to you."
Q. Is that all she said?
A. No, she told me that it had all been a big misunderstanding, but she would give me two weeks, to get out of the house.
Q. And, what was your response?
A. I told her that I had a purchase agreement with her brother Nathan Sorrell, to buy the house.
Q. What was the asking price of the house; do you recall?
A. It was, I think $125,000.
Q. But the offer you made was lower than that; wasn't it?
A. Yes, I made an offer of $107,500.
Q. Did Mr. Sorrell accept —
A. Yes, he accepted my offer.
Q. Was your offer accompanied by any money?
A. Oh yes. I gave him a check for $1000, — a token of good faith.
Q. Did Mr. Sorrell cash the check, or not?
A. He did cash it, yes.
Q. Tell me, Miss Albert was anyone living in the house at the time you made the offer?
A. No. It was vacant at that time and it had been vacant for several months.

B. The following text contains almost no punctuation. Insert commas, colons, periods, question marks, semicolons, or dashes where they would be correct and be the best punctuation choice.

> My wife her sister and her sister's two babies were there when I arrived and they made it clear no more than clear that they did not want me to be there so I just said I'll take my kids and go where are they my wife turned and sneered at me take the little brats Bernard I'm sick to death of having those dirty whining annoying little brats around me anyway and I could use a long peaceful weekend just for myself you've heard of rest haven't you I guess if I strain myself I too can remember how rest feels but right now I don't so take them sir yes please do that the sooner the better What

she said was more or less those words indeed they were probably much stronger, much more vehement than that I was somewhat taken aback although I shouldn't have been because she was never the world's greatest mother at her nastiness so I went from room to room searching. She followed behind me. Let me tell you this: she was not herself, she was wild irrational worse than usual.

4
CAPITALIZATION

Rules for capitalization vary *somewhat* with the occupational setting, and the issue of when to capitalize can be a troublesome one. The following guidelines are tailored to the CR; although a few may not always coincide with those of other professions, most will. The following rules are based on generally accepted rules.

In the CR industry, some sections of depositions are capitalized for reasons of tradition within the industry. In such situations, the CR should follow the preferred format of the firm by which the CR is employed. It is essential, however, that the CR be *consistent* with capitalization within a transcript. It is also important not to allow "tradition" of one's employer or the CR industry as a whole to perpetuate use that is actually incorrect.

The guidelines in this chapter begin with the most general rules and then proceed to more specific, detailed situations. Some of these rules are fundamental to proper English, whereas others are more specific to the CR's needs. Of course, no chapter can cover every possible capitalization issue, and the CR may have to consult the dictionary when in doubt.

360 The first word of each new sentence and the first word of a sentence fragment, when written as though it were a sentence in Q and A, should be capitalized.

Q. Would you describe Bradley Hutchins as a trusted employee?
A. Hardly.
Q. How long had he been with the firm?
A. Too long.
Q. Did Janet Morris telephone you on January 6, 1989?
A. No way.
Q. How can you be so sure?
A. Good memory.

Quotations

361 The first word of a quotation is capitalized even when the quotation begins midsentence.

> The woman begged, "Don't take my son from me!"
> The child told me, "Mommy and Daddy aren't here," and then he said, "You can't come in the house."

362 Do not capitalize the first word of the second part of a split quotation unless it should be capitalized for another reason (because it is a proper noun).

> "We cannot do that, " Mr. Roberts told us, "unless Donna signs those papers."
> "The car was traveling at a speed of about 70," Jacob reported, "despite the stormy weather."
> BUT:
> Mr. Saenger cautioned me, "Unless you and your husband decide soon," and he slammed his fist on the table, "Daniel Rees will make the decision for you."
> "Although I grew up in New York," I said to Nicholas, "California is now my home."

363 In a series of questions in which some are not complete sentences, the items after each question mark are capitalized.

> When did you see Arnold? Where? Was he alone? With someone?
> Did you give him the files? Which ones? How many?

Names

364 Names of persons, including nicknames, are capitalized.

> Janet "Happy Face" Morrison was always the life of the party.
> We referred to Mr. Trask as "Lordship" because he was so demanding and authoritarian.

365 Initials in names are capitalized.

> Kenneth M.J. Peoples has served the H.J. Jones Company for 27 years.
> I called B.J., but there was no answer.

Note: Editorial practice varies with respect to the spacing of personal initials. CRs should close them up as shown above.

366 Designations in names are capitalized; for example, Jr. and Sr.

This automobile is owned by William Grant Towne, **Jr.**, who is my father-in-law.
Is she married to Walt Robertson, **Jr.**, or to Walt Robertson, **Sr.**?

367 Some names contain articles and prepositions, which may or may not be capitalized. There is so much variety in handling these types of names that only a few general rules can be given. In French names that contain le, l', la, and les, these are usually capitalized; de, d', and du are usually not capitalized. There are, however, exceptions, and the best course of action for the CR is to make an attempt to ascertain the accepted capitalization of that name, usually a family preference or tradition.

Jeanne Le Blanc will run for mayor of Lafayette, Louisiana.
Leonardo da Vinci was his hero, the historical figure he most admired.
Alexandra von Halkein is my aunt, but I have never met her.

368 Epithets are capitalized.

The movie was going to relate to the life of Billy the Kid.
I was hoping to see the First Lady when I visited the White House.

369 The names of houses and estates are capitalized.

My family had lived at Five Willows for three centuries.
Grandfather built Billings Manor in 1911.

370 **Titles**

Titles are capitalized when they are accompanied by the name of the person who possesses the title. A title used alone is not capitalized except when it is a part of a formal list or is being used without the name in direct address. Exceptions are the heads of states, U.S. Senators, U.S. Congressmen, and other high government officials. Capitalize President and Vice-President when referring to the U.S. officials or when accompanied by a name. However, adjectives such as presidential are not capped.

Remember: A title is capped when used with the name but, with a few exceptions, is not capitalized when used alone. Other exceptions: Commander in Chief, the Surgeon General, the Postmaster General, Supreme Allied Commander.

I asked the captain for permission to go aboard.
I asked Captain Forrestor for permission to go aboard.
The mayor will attend the celebrations in the park.
Will Mayor Dinkins attend the celebrations in the park?
I will ask the lieutenant when he met with John Stuart.
Tell me, Lieutenant, when did you meet with him?

371 **Academic Degrees**

Academic degrees and their abbreviations are capitalized when written after the name of the person having the degree. They are also capitalized when written out as a complete term. They are not capitalized when they are used in a general sense.

I hope to have my Master's degree by June.
He has been working on his doctorate at Florida State.
Isabel Morales, Doctor of Philosophy, will speak to our group next month.
He'll never get his medical degree, in my opinion.
The job requires a bachelor's in sociology.
Samuel Goldman, D.D.S., is now open for business.

372 **Scientific names**

Capitalize phylum, class, order, family, and genus. Species and subspecies are lowercased.

The scientific name for the rhesus monkey is *Macaca mulatta.*
The subclass Rhizopoda consists of creeping protozoans.

Note: Larger divisions (phylum, class, order, family) are not underlined, but genus, species, and subspecies are underlined in CR transcripts.

373 The common, or nonscientific, names of plants and animals are not capitalized unless a proper noun is part of the name.

The squirrel monkeys are caged in groups of about a dozen.
I bought my son an Irish setter instead of a poodle.

374 Buildings and Institutions

Capitalize the names of specific buildings and institutions including schools; lowercase when using the common nouns alone, even when referring to a specific building or institution. Exceptions would be those with a very special meaning: the House (House of Representatives); the Yard (Scotland Yard), the Garden (Madison Square Garden).

The Chrylser Building is on 42nd Street; is that correct?

The Pitken Society was about 150 years old, and the society was renowned throughout the area.

The Scardsdale Junior High School Parent Association was one of the most active parent-teacher associations in the state.

The Hotel White Horse was a beautiful old building, and it stood next to the only theatre in town, the Paramount Theatre.

We both attended the University of New Hampshire; it was an excellent school.

Note: The word *the* is almost always lowercased, unless it begins the sentence.

375 Organizations

The titles of organizations are capitalized (including clubs, institutions, schools, colleges, commissions, boards, companies, buildings, councils) when referring to a specific one.

The Girl Scouts of America meant a lot to me as a young child.

The Springfield Opera Company needed funding desperately.

BUT:

Has the board of directors met this month?

My club is looking for ideas on how to raise money.

When an organization is named in full in a sentence and subsequently referred to in shortened form either in the same sentence or another, the reference should not be capitalized. Capitalizing the subsequent reference(s) is the practice in some disciplines, but the CR, for the sake of both simplicity and speed, should not make this effort.

The Sharkey Fishery Company closed its doors two years ago, but the company is reorganizing to reopen this year.

Note: The word *company* in its second occurrence does not need to be capitalized.

376 References to the U.S. Government

Words that refer to the U.S. government (e.g., "Government," "Federal") are sometimes capitalized, depending on the preference of the CR's employer or the CR's own preference. The most important consideration is consistency in the use of one or the other style.

The Federal judgeship was a position he had coveted for years.
The Government presented its case well.

Capitalize the names of government agencies, bureaus, offices, and boards.

Civil Service Commission
National Security Administration
Department of Defense
Federal Bureau of Investigation

When subsequently referring to a government agency in a transcript by using a shortened version, capitalize that shorter term.

He was working for the Federal Bureau of Investigation since he graduated from college. When anyone would talk about their work, he would just say that the Bureau discouraged employees from talking about their jobs. He wouldn't tell us what he did in the Bureau, but we knew that he was devoted to the FBI.

Some governmental agencies' names have become so much a part of our society that Webster's says capitalization is optional, for example, social security and medicare. The best rule to follow is this: when referring to a specific government agency as such, capitalize; when referring to a general idea or social program, capitalization is optional. Some find it simpler just to capitalize all the time rather that have to examine each incident individually.

He was hoping to receive some kind of social security income after the accident, but nothing is definite at this time. (capitalization optional)
The Social Security Administration will review your case and inform you of any decisions made pertaining to your situation. (must be capped)
At what age is one eligible for medicare? (optional)
The person in the Medicare office told me this would be covered. (must be capped)

377 **Family Names**

Names designating family relationships are capitalized only when they are used as a substitute for that person's name, when they are used in direct address, or when they are used with the person's name. They are not capitalized when used with a possessive noun.

> Tell Mother that I cannot attend the reunion.
> My mother is away for a few weeks.
> We hadn't seen Uncle Jay or Aunt Millie for months.
> My aunt and uncle had been away for months.
> Describe for us, Grandpa, the house where you grew up.

378 **Product Names**

Trade names are capitalized, but the generic name of the object itself is not.

> His Toyota was about 12 years old, but it was a reliable automobile.
> Herman eats those Nabisco crackers every day at lunch.
> The Xerox photocopier worked better than any other.

Remember: The company name is capitalized, but the name of the object itself is not (e.g., Bayer aspirin, Scotch tape, Cross pen).

379 **Documents**

Titles of books, magazines, movies, pamphlets, television and radio programs, songs, poems, and works of art are capitalized except for articles (*a, an, the*), coordinating conjunctions (*and, or, for, nor*), and prepositions of fewer than four letters, unless one of these words is the first or last work of the title or subtitle. The *to* in an infinitive is not capitalized.

> Reading "The Education of Little Tree" was an emotional experience.
> I grew up on shows like "I Love Lucy" and "Make Room for Daddy."
> Marianne has subscriptions to "Redbook" and "Working Woman," but that's all.

380 Parts of documents are capitalized or lowercased according to their relative size within a document. Major parts (exhibits, volumes, sections, subsections, articles) are capitalized. Minor parts are lowercased (pages, notes, lines, verses). *Paragraph* is lowercased.

Remember: Consistency must be maintained throughout the transcript. If a particular segment title is written without its number, e.g., chapter, section, paragraph, it is lowercased.

I refer to Exhibit 2.

Those words came from Section 21, Subsection 41, paragraph 11.

The first three chapters are well written, but Chapter 4 needs considerable work.

381 Capitalize the name of acts and laws once they have been enacted; however, bills that are yet to become law are lowercased.

Will the education bill pass or not in your opinion?

He based it all on the Civil Rights Act of 1964.

This same rule applies to treaties, resolutions, amendments and other formal agreements.

It was founded on the Tenth Amendment.

The Treaty of Versailles was signed here.

382 Citations of legal cases are capitalized and underlined except for the *v.* or *vs.* (indicating *versus*) and other small words (short prepositions, articles, coordinating conjunctions) that normally would not be capitalized in any title.

We saw, *Rich* v. *Underhill Woods & Forests*, a case similar to the one we are hearing today.

The State of Michigan v. *Todd Garilino* will be heard after *Munson* v. *Department of Public Works.*

383 Capitalize names of specific examinations and court documents.

The jury heard Examination by Attorney Evans on July 18, 1991.

I refer to Plaintiff's Exhibit No. 2.

BUT:

The subpoena was delivered last night.

We have gathered affidavits from several witnesses and plan to subpoena them, if necessary.

Time

384 Capitalize the names of holidays.

We celebrated Easter at Father's country house every year.

Why was the Fourth of July picnic cancelled?

385 Time zones are lowercased except when abbreviated.

Was it five o'clock eastern time or central time?
I think daylight savings time begins in April.

386 Do not capitalize the names of the seasons.

We moved to Bloomfield in autumn of 1977.
The plan was to remain there until summer and then leave.

387 Months of the year and days of the week are capitalized.

The group met every Wednesday night except in December.
The store closed at noon on Saturdays and Sundays.

388 Do not capitalize a.m. or p.m., even when written out.

I asked if he meant 2:00 a.m. or 2:00 p.m., but he didn't answer me.
The note said that the event would take place at six o'clock ante meridiem, but I didn't know what that meant.

Geographic Terms

389 Capitalize divisions of the world and of its surface.

He intends to explore the North Pole over the next 18 months.
We knew there would be trouble in the Mideast, but we couldn't turn down the money.
It was the best we could find in the Western Hemisphere.

390 Names of cities, counties, states, countries, continents, and governing bodies are capitalized when reference is made to a specific one.

In Louisiana counties are called "parishes," the only state that does so.
New York City is the largest city in America, even larger that Chicago or Los Angeles.
I always forget that Australia is considered a continent as well as a country.

391 Names of bodies of water —lakes, rivers, ponds, seas, oceans, etc.—are capitalized when reference is made to a specific body.

The Mississippi River, fed by various other rivers and streams, partially fills Lake Pontchartrain before emptying into the Gulf of Mexico.

The Sea of Denmark's ownership is hotly contested.

BUT:

We loved going down to the river to fish on summer afternoons.

She was afraid of the sea, but we bought a seaside cottage that year.

392 Capitalize the name of specific streets, avenues, boulevards, roads, and highways.

They now live on Hudson Boulevard, which is right off Rome Avenue; it is one of the nicest streets in this city.

Drive down Sellers Lane until you get to Highway 49 and then stay on that road for three miles.

393 Names of specific bridges are capitalized.

The Golden Gate Bridge is part of an impressive landscape.

To get to Manhattan, I cross the Brooklyn Bridge or the Manhattan Bridge; I prefer either of these bridges to the tunnel.

394 The words *room, apartment,* and *floor* are capitalized when used with a number.

The package was delivered to Floor 33, Room 22.

I was in office no. 6 but I moved to no. 9.

Note: The abbreviation for number (no.) is usually not capitalized.

395 *North, south, east, west,* and their various forms and derivatives *(northwest, northern,* etc.) are not capitalized except when they refer to a recognized geographic area or section.

Just drive south for about six miles to find the school.

The western edge of the stadium is reserved for handicapped persons.

We were planning to move out West, perhaps to California.

We couldn't persuade Marlena to leave the Northeast.

They spent most of their time at a villa in the south of France.

396 The terms *state* and *city* are capitalized when referred to in an institutional or corporate sense, but not when referred to simply as a place.

The State of Wyoming will press for extradition.

I will be living in the state of Wyoming for the summer.

She lives in the city of Urbana, Illinois.
The City of Urbana is seeking government funds for the restructuring.

397 Sections of cities or "nicknames" for areas are capitalized.

The Big Apple offers an endless variety of activities.
The South Side of Chicago is his home.
The Crescent City hosts the Mardi Gras every year.

Note: Do not use capitals except for specific nicknames or specific geographic areas.

The south side of my street has several brownstones.
The western corner of the country is the most populated.
I was looking for an apartment in the southeast section of town.
I found an apartment on the Upper West Side.

A geographical dictionary can be useful in determining specific geographic areas and nicknames for cities.

Religious and Philosophical Terms

398 **Personifications**

There will be probably few occasions for the CR to deal with personifications, but if such instances do occur, the personification should be capitalized. Personifications occur when human characteristics are given to abstract nouns.

When Nature grows angry, our electricity goes out!
We were waiting for Spring to paint the countryside in fresh, bright colors.

399 When referring to a supreme being, *God* is capitalized; when referring to the deities of a polytheistic religion, do not capitalize. When pronouns refer to God, they should be capitalized also.

The Greek gods were actively involved in humans' lives.
His godlike rule over his family was intolerable.
He believed that God would be his guidepost in times of decision.
I prayed to Him each night for guidance, but I was confused by His silence.

400 The names of specific religions, churches, denominations, religious movements, orders, and creeds are capitalized.

He was devoted to the Mother Church.

My mother was a practicing Southern Baptist, but my father belonged to the Protestant Episcopal Church.

His conception of the Last Supper was the subject of his most recent painting.

Note: Do not capitalize such terms as heaven, hell, communion, mass, brother, sister, father, friar (unless they are used with a specific name, e.g. Father John).

401 The names of religious books and holidays and of some religious ceremonies are capitalized.

The King James Version of the Bible is our choice for study.

His life is based on the teachings of the Koran.

She takes Holy Communion every week.

Note: The names of most religious ceremonies are not capitalized.

The boy's bar mitzvah could not be postponed.

Her baptism was a special event in her religious life.

402 The books and divisions of the Bible are capitalized as are well-known scriptures.

We always said the Lord's Prayer before we went to bed.

The New Testament was easier to read than the Old Testament, except for the Book of Revelations.

403 Proper nouns are capitalized, but some of their derivatives—those that have become commonly used in everyday language—are not capitalized. Refer to your dictionary when in doubt.

china (referring to dishes)	oriental rug
plaster of paris	roman numerals
scotch (the alcoholic drink)	biblical

404 **Diseases and Physical Conditions**

Diseases are not capitalized unless named for a person, generally the one who isolated the disease. When in doubt, consult a medical dictionary.

The diagnosis was Parkinson's disease.

My grandmother, unfortunately, seems to be developing osteoporosis, and she also complains of slight angina and migraines.

Except for being a bit arthritic, Mother was as healthy as ever.
I'm a bit hard of hearing, but I am not deaf.

A medical eponym is a disease, condition, test, or drug that is named for a person, usually its discoverer. There is a trend currently not to use the apostrophe and "s"; however, it is not incorrect to retain them.

Patients of the disease leprosy prefer the term Hansen's disease to describe the condition. (or Hansen disease)
We had never heard of Legionnaire's disease until about 1976 or 1977.

405 **Capitalize the pronoun *I*.**

He said I couldn't have my inheritance yet.
Do you think I am unaware of what was going on?

Historical Terms

406 Capitalize the names of historic events, including wars and battles.

The Louisiana Purchase bought much more than just the state of Louisiana.
The Vietnam War is the subject of his more recent research.
Was the Battle of the Bulge fought during World War II?
His son was in Saudi Arabia during Desert Storm.

407 Capitalize the names of historic eras, periods, and movements.

The French Renaissance produced many such artists.
She accused Mr. Ross of being from the Stone Age when it came to sexual stereotyping.

Note: Do not capitalize the word century when listing centuries numerically, e.g., 20th century, fifth century.

408 **Nationalities and Ethnic Groups**

Names of ethnic groups, nationalities, languages, and other formal groups of people are capitalized. Slang terms based on "color" are not capitalized.

The black Democratic representative said that his questions had been addressed satisfactorily.

The Greek language was more difficult for me to learn than was French.

His Nordic heritage was evident in his home furnishings.

I saw a Caucasian man and an Oriental woman enter the building after midnight.

409 Heavenly Bodies

Capitalize names of planets, stars, and constellations except for *sun*, *moon*, and *earth*. When *earth* is used as a planet title, it is capitalized. Do not capitalize generic words.

The Milky Way galaxy is our own, isn't it?

We have been watching for Halley's comet every night this month.

Which planet is closer to Earth—Mars or Mercury?

BUT:

I've searched the four corners of the earth to find them, but I have failed miserably.

410 Signs

Capitalize the exact wording of signs. Putting quotes around the words used in a sign clarifies the sentence for the reader.

The sign said "Keep Off the Grass," but we paid no mind and kept going.

We couldn't find the Exit, and panic set in because the place was on fire.

There was a "No Parking" sign where once no sign was posted.

411 Fragments

Quoted fragments, words, or terms may or may not be capitalized, depending on their nature, but usually are not.

Refer to the quoted matter or use best judgement on an individual case basis.

The newspaper article referred to the murder as "the Highland Park Massacre."

What she said exactly was that she was "under the gun" at work.

412 Vocative O

Capitalize the vocative *O* but not the exclamation *oh.*

The 16th-century poem read, "O Lord, have mercy on me."

BUT:

I was oh so worried about my youngest child.

413 **Named Items**

Names of ships, boats, aircraft, and automobiles are capitalized.

We like to take the "Miss Suzy Q" out in the lake any chance we have, as sailing is our favorite pastime.
The "Spirit of St. Louis" can be viewed at the Smithsonian.

414 **Hyphenated Terms**

Hyphenated words are capitalized or lowercased as they would be if no hyphens were used.

I was not aware of any anti-American sentiment when I traveled there.
The pro-Russian policy was surprisingly popular.

The Courtroom

415 Lowercase the words *jury, plaintiff, defendant, courtroom, jury room* and the term *members of the jury* or similar terms within the transcript. When they are used as a salutation, for example, at the beginning of a jury charge (and set apart from the body of the jury charge), capitalize the first word only (Ladies and gentlemen of the jury...).

The jury will keep in mind what the witnesses have said here today.
You should not address your answers to the members of the jury.
The members of the jury will disregard that last comment.

BUT:

I think, Juror Williams, that you should ask to be relieved of your duties as juror

416 When referring to the judge, capitalize the word *Court.*

The Court will now instruct the jury on the law applicable to this case.
If it please the Court, we would like to call a new witness.

417 When referring to a specific court, capitalize; when referring to a type of court, lowercase.

I am going to take you to court to settle this dispute.
The U.S. Customs Court will have jurisdiction in this matter.
The only time I was in court was when I went to traffic court to fight a speeding ticket.
He was taken to the Fourth Circuit U.S. Court of Appeals to wait for his father, who was a judge there.

418 Capitalize the titles of officers of the court.

The District Attorney should have made that document available to the Defense.
Please, your Honor, may I make a request?

Note: In the above example, some prefer to capitalize *your* as well as *honor.*

We will hear the verdict now, Mr. Foreman.

419 Games

The names of games are capitalized if they are trademarked but lowercased if used in a general way.

We played tennis twice a week together at the country club.
He was a master a Scrabble, but I could beat him at Monopoly.

420 Political Parties and Affiliations

Capitalize the names of political parties and groups when referring specifically to an organized body but not when referring to a general philosophy.

The Democratic candidate was a sure winner.
This country was based on democratic principles.
The Independent Party had a strong backing from the labor unions.
Was Carl Adams an independent candidate, or was he affiliated with one of the parties?

421 Awards

Honors, awards, and other forms of recognition are capitalized.

He gave his Purple Heart to his son.

I thought he had a good chance of winning the National Book Award.

BUT:

I won first place in the road race.

422 Tests

The titles of specific tests are capitalized.

The Wechlsler Adult Intelligence Scale is administered to all prospective students.

Results given are from the Fisher's Exact Test.

BUT:

My biology examination was given on a day when I was too ill to attend.

The child was given several motor and developmental tests.

423 Designators

Capitalize *table, figure, chart, graph* when used with a numeral or letter designator; do not capitalize these words when they are used without a numeral or letter. Even when they include a number or letter, do not capitalize the following: column, case, factor, grade, grant, group, phase, patient, type.

Refer to Table 5 for the results of the study.

The age ranges are listed in column 2 of the table.

The figures are good illustrations of the findings.

Cases 2 and 3 showed similar findings using computed tomography.

424 Enumerations or Lists

It is not necessary to capitalize the first word in an item in a list.

Correct

Were you interested in (a) his money, (b) his position in society, or (c) his companionship?

Wrong

Were you interested in (a) His money, (b) His position in society, or (c) His companionship?

If the items are listed on separate lines, it is optional to cap or not.

I asked John Thomas to explain, in writing and in detail, the following:

1. Where he found the envelope
2. What he did with it immediately thereafter
3. Who opened the envelope

OR

I asked John Thomas to explain, in writing and in detail, the following: (1) where he found the envelope; (2) what he did with it immediately thereafter; (3) who opened the envelope.

425 **Resolved**

After the word *Resolved*, or *Resolved* plus other introductory words accompanying it, the first word thereafter should be capitalized.

Resolved, That the Center for Unity has been of benefit and service to this community.

Resolved by this body, That the laws of this land must be our guide.

Exercises

A. Capitalize as necessary in the following passage.

Q. When did you last see your brother?

A. Last wednesday night, at peterson's cafe. We were going to go out and buy that boat from Joseph's supervisor.

Q. What boat?

A. A little sailboat called "cat's paw."

Q. Did he say anything to you about mayor smith's daughter?

A. He said that she had flipped out.

Q. Are those his exact words?

A. His exact words? I can give you that. He said, "Ruth Smith has totally and completely flipped out."

Q. Did you know that she suffers from epilepsy?

A. I think I remember father telling him something about that—or was it grandpa? Somebody told him that the mayor's wife had it and so did Ruth.

Q. Was Ruth acquainted with Harley Bloud, jr.?

A. I think Harley worked at telley refinery, inc., while Ruth worked there. Harley was a supervisor there, and Ruth was a chemist. They were both in the greenwich building.

Q. What did you know about Harley?

A. Just that he had a master's in chemistry. I think he got his master of science degree the same year as Ruth did and at the same university.

Q. And what college was that?

A. The university of utah. Harley had a scholarship from the state of utah. Ruth used to work for the city of denver, but she left there to go to the refinery.

B. Correct any capitalization errors

1. Melvin ("Mr. brain") Ramsey will receive his juris doctorate next month, but he does not want to go into Law. He wants to go into Politics. He is a democrat, and his Father is big man in the Political Party. He will work as a Professor at the local university for the next couple of years. Although Melvin is White, upper-class, and affluent, he has Liberal ideas and is interested in civil rights.

2. Quincy believed that nature was her counselor, her friend. She refused to take even Aspirin or Tylenol. Her only medicine consisted of herbal remedies and vigorous exercise. She won the Herbert Idelmeyer garden award and was even a rhodes scholar. Quincy placed number 2 in an Orchid-growing contest set up by the New York Botanical Society. The Society presented her with a Certificate. The only other information I have about Quincy is that she is writing a book entitled "Ichabod and Minnie Of the Vale," but I have no idea what this Book discusses. She has written for "The Way Of Nature" as a free-lancer and will arrive here in this Courtroom at 8:00 P.M. today. Oh, yes, she is a member of St. Luke's episcopal church located on highway 22.

3. The trial will take place this Autumn. It is based on Marcantel v. Department of Justice. Have you been subpoenaed? Will you tell the court what you know? Has the Government subpoenaed any of your family? It will begin at 9:00 a.m. Eastern Standard Time.

4. I heard that justice Paul W. Jenkins of Ohio voted along with justice William V. Antony, who wrote, "Reason must prevail in this Case if the scales of justice are to be balanced." There was a report in the "Houston herald" that said otherwise. How did this come to be written in that Newspaper? why? by whom?

5. The Downtown Area is about 15 miles down highway two if you head Northeasterly on the Road. You can find several restaurants, a Convenience store, several Mobil Stations, and a Diner. There is an exit ramp about a Half Mile from Russellville. Turn Right and then look for the first paved Street.

C. Find five examples in written materials (newspapers, magazines, books) of each of the following:

1. laws or bills
2. organizations
3. titles of persons
4. divided quotations
5. Document parts

5
NUMBERS

The choice between using figures or writing out a number in words can be a confusing one, perhaps even more so for the CR because of the requirement to record exactly what was said in the courtroom. The following is a practical guide for determining when to use a figure and when written expression is preferable. We begin with the most basic rule and then proceed to specific exceptions and more detailed examples.

426 Write out numbers one through ten; use figures for 11 and higher. Although there are many exceptions to this rule, this is the "basic rule" upon which other rules lie.

She and her four children left this morning.

She and her 11 children left this morning.

427 Numbers that begin a sentence should be written out unless to do so would be cumbersome, i.e., would require three or more words.

Twenty-three persons were injured in the train derailment.

BUT:

There were 23 persons injured in the train derailment.

Q. How many people attended the rally?

A. Two hundred.

Q. What is the exact population of the city?

A. 26,124 at last count.

428 If an answer in testimony consists of a number alone, the reporter has a choice of words or figures unless, as in the rule above, it would be too long in written-out form.

Q. How many employees were laid off?

A. Thirty-five. (or 35, but the written expression is preferable)

Q. What is your area code?
A. 203.

429 **Decimals**

Use figures for all decimals. For example, if the words actually spoken were "seven point ninety-four," the reporter should write 7.94.

The value of the building was set at $16.9 million.
The animal weighs only 111.34 grams.

Note: If the decimal occurs at the beginning of a sentence, it is still written as a figure. To write it in words interferes with the smooth reading of the transcript.

79.118 was the average score on that examination.
22,335.52 persons will visit the memorial each year.

430 Use figures to express measurements of length, volume, weight, temperature, etc.

45 miles
110 volts
5 feet 10 inches
45 pounds
60 degrees Fahrenheit (or 60°F)

Note: It is sometimes acceptable to write out measurements when employing numbers under ten.

Meggan is about five feet tall.
He grew four inches in one year.

431 Round numbers can be written in either figures or words, preferably words.

We decided to display two hundred paintings for the show.
The country's population is about nine million.

432 Write percentages in figures (except at the beginning of a sentence as prescribed by the previous rule).

The company grew by 45 percent last year.
Only 18 percent of the registered voters went out and voted in last month's election.

433 Years are always written as a figure, even at the beginning of a sentence. Centuries and decades follow the basic rule.

He is an expert on 16th century art.

1953 was the year he came to the United States.

434 Parts of a document are always identified by figures. This rule applies to pages, sections, chapters, lines, paragraphs, etc.

The class will cover Chapters 2 through 4 in its next discussion.

Will the House vote on HR 4522 next month?

435 Numbers in the millions or greater are written as mixed figures and words or, ten and under, as words only.

Correct

The population of the area was 22 million.

He inherited three million dollars from his grandfather.

OPTION:

He inherited $3 million from his grandfather.

He inherited $3,000,000 from his grandfather. (acceptable although not preferable)

Wrong

The population of the area was twenty-two million.

436 **Fractions and Mixed Numbers**

Write out fractions; use figures for mixed numbers. Some CRs prefer to write out mixed numbers as they are spoken, but this seems unnecessarily cumbersome and does not really add to the clarity of the text.

I put in 4 3/4 cups of milk.

I put in four and three-fourths cups of milk.

The latter sentence is acceptable and preferred by many, but it is cumbersome.

I ran 10 1/2 miles yesterday.

Note: It is not up to the CR to "translate" fractions into decimals; for example, to say in the above sentence, "I ran 10.5 miles yesterday.

Money

437 Amounts less than a dollar are written according to the basic rule with the word *cents,* not with the symbol for cents (¢).

Correct

I found 45 cents on the sidewalk.
The cost of the candy has risen by eight cents.

Wrong

I found 45¢ on the sidewalk.
I found $0.45 on the sidewalk.

438 Write in figures money amounts that are mixed dollars and cents.

I had exactly $33.55 in my wallet when I lost it.
The bill was for $274.88, but I had already sent them $115.50.

439 Dollar amounts that are even are written without decimals.

Correct

I had borrowed $225 from my brother.

Acceptable (although not preferable)

I had borrowed $225.00 from my brother.

440 When several dollar amounts are listed, and at least one requires the use of decimals, the decimal is retained for the sake of consistency.

I have deposited the checks in the amounts of $59.10, $74.00, $21.44, $39.71, and $25.00.

441 It is acceptable to use a mixture of words and figures for amounts in the millions and billions.

The shopping center investment is $126 million.
He is worth about $14 million.

442 If the word *a* is used with money expressions, it can be employed in the transcript.

I found a hundred dollars in my purse that I didn't know I had!
Can you lend me a 20-dollar bill? (Option: $20 bill)

443 For foreign money, consult the U.S. Government Printing Office Style Manual, foreign money table.

I found 52 pounds in his hotel room that he'd forgotten he had.
I didn't know if 150 lire was a good price or not.

Dates and Time

444 Dates are written in accordance with what was actually said. The CR must be exact. If numbers are employed, use the slash to separate the numbers that stand for the month, day, and year.

> We moved into the house on 6/15/79.
> We moved into the house on the 15th of May, 1979.
> We moved into the house on 15 May 1979.
> We moved into the house on May 15, 1979.

It is not necessary to use the ordinal when the date is expressed in its "normal" sequence.

> We moved into the house on May 15th, 1979 (use of 15th is not necessary; use simply May 15, 1979).

445 If *a.m.* or *p.m.* is used with time, always employ figures.

Correct

We met at church at 6:35 p.m.

Wrong

We met at church at six thirty-five p.m.

446 Use figures when time is expressed as hours and minutes together.

> The appointment was not until 11:45, but I arrived at 11:15.

447 When the word *o'clock* is used, apply the basic rule.

> The accident occurred at six o'clock in the evening.
> I saw him arrive at 11 o'clock on the dot.

Note: Some prefer to use the numerical here. However, writing "6:00 o'clock" would be like saying "six o'clock o'clock."

448 If the minutes are given before or after the hour, follow the basic rule.

> The time was precisely 25 till four. (OR: 25 till 4:00)
> He always picked me up at a quarter after seven. (OR: quarter after 7:00)

Note: Some prefer the numerical in the above examples, that is, 4:00 and 7:00; if your employer has a preference, follow it. If not, follow your own preference, but be consistent.

449 Military time, or 24-hour time, is written in figures without the use of a colon and is often followed by the word *hours*.

> We were to assemble at 0600 hours.

Addresses

450 Components of addresses are written in figures. Numbered streets under *10th* may be written out or expressed in figures.

One exception is a street address that begins with the word *one.*

The party was held at One Drake Avenue, Mr. Wilke's home.
I passed the truck somewhere on Highway 21.
It's located on Seventh Avenue, but I don't know exactly where.

451 A hyphen is used to avoid confusion between the building number and the street number when both are written as numerals.

Our new address was 224-23rd Street.

452 "Smaller" components of addresses are also written as figures.

Apartment 5B is being painted right now.
You can find his office on Floor 7.

Never use commas in house or building numbers, even if they comprise more than three numbers.

I was looking for 33091 Little Beaver Lane.

453 Zip codes are always written as figures, and there is no punctuation between the state and the zip code.

My mailing address is currently 45 Vera Beach Road, San Luna, Texas 78044.

Note: When using the postal abbreviation for states, do not use a period after the two-letter abbreviation. For example:

TX (postal code for Texas) compare with Tex. (standard abbreviation).
CA (postal code for California) which does not employ the period.

454 Telephone numbers, including area codes, are written as figures. The area code should be separated from the rest of the telephone number by a virgule (or slash).

My phone bill had charges to 416/661-5521, but I didn't know whose number that was.
Our telephone number was area code 212/440-1123.

455 **Roman Numerals** (See Table 5.1.)

- Because citations often use Roman numerals, the CR should learn to use them with both speed and accuracy.

This was done in accordance with Title VI regulations.
Edition VII is the only one that was acceptable.

- Roman numerals with names are not separated from the name they follow by a comma or by any other form of punctuation.

  Napoleon II attempted to invade Mexico; is that correct?
  Richard Alan Ballingham IV will inherit a vast fortune.

Table 5.1
Roman Numerals

Arabic	Roman	Arabic	Roman
1	I	23	XXIII
2	II	24	XXIV
3	III	30	XXX
4	IV	40	XL
5	V	50	L
6	VI	60	LX
7	VII	70	LXX
8	VIII	80	LXXX
9	IX	90	XC
10	X	100	C
11	XI	200	CC
12	XII	300	CCC
13	XIII	400	CD
14	XIV	500	D
15	XV	600	DC
16	XVI	700	DCC
17	XVII	800	DCCC
18	XVIII	900	CM
19	XIX	1,000	M
20	XX	2,000	MM
21	XXI	3,000	MMM
22	XXII	4,000	MV
		5,000	V (or [illegible])

456 Adjectives

Numbers as adjectives should be hyphenated, still adhering to the basic rule for numbers.

My 80-year-old father lives with me and my husband.
The five-time winner was not nominated this year.

457 When expressing measured units puts two numbers adjacent to one another, write out one and use figures for the other. Choose the less cumbersome arrangement.

We ordered sixteen 24-ounce cans to be delivered Tuesday.

Note: 16 twenty-four-ounce cans is more cumbersome and thus, not the version of choice.

James found five 18-pound sacks rather than the standard order.

458 **Numbers in a Series**

When a series of closely related numbers includes some that should be written out and others that should be expressed in figures according to the basic rule, disregard the rule and be consistent.

Their scores were 5, 12, 31, and 47 of a possible 50.
We met on the 5th, the 12th, and the 30th of the month.
He was paid three, then four, then six, and finally twenty times.

459 **Addresses**

- Components of addresses are written as figures. Numbered streets under 11th may be written out or expressed in figures.

We were supposed to meet in Room 203, but Reva did not show.
Apartment 3D is now vacant.
We drove along Highway 41 for about two hours before getting on Interstate 67.
She lived at 154-17th Street for five years before moving to Ninth Avenue (OR: 9th Avenue)

Note: A hyphen is used in the last example above to prevent confusion between the building and street numbers.

One exception is a street address that begins with the word *one.*

That sounds like a posh address—One Park Avenue!
Drive the car around to One Divens Lane.

- Do not use commas in house or building numbers.

Correct

Meet me at 10275 Bluegrass Road.

Wrong

Meet me at 10,275 Bluegrass Road.

Organization numbers follow the basic rule unless accompanied by No. or Number.

Q. Were you a member of the Seventh Division in the Pacific?

A. No. I served in the 23rd Artillery.

The First Methodist Church of Denver will be the scene of the wedding.

Mrs. Simms, did your husband belong to Teamsters No. 6?

Note the difference in meaning of the two sentences below:

We ordered 25 hundred-gram bags from Smith Brothers.
We ordered 2,500 gram bags from Smith Brothers.

These two sentences mean entirely different things, which illustrates the importance of the CR taking extreme care in number use.

460 Plurals

Although plurals of figures can correctly be written either with or without an apostrophe, it is preferable not to use the apostrophe unless confusion would result from omitting it. As always, it is crucial that the CR be as consistent as possible within a transcript.

I could not distinguish between his a's and his o's.

Note: To leave out the apostrophe in the above sentence would certainly cause confusion.

The 1970s were the best time in my marriage, but the 1980s saw the end of it all.

Note: It would be very awkward to use the apostrophe to form plurals in the following construction ('70's and '80's).

The '70s were the best time in my marriage, but the '80s saw the end of it all.

461 Ranges

Write ranges in figures if one of the numbers is greater than nine.

We will travel in Europe for 8 to 12 months.

462 Subject-Verb Agreement

Measurements are written as a singular unit, and the verb is singular.

Five milligrams were administered every morning.
A hundred feet is a long drop.

463 **Commas Within Numbers**

The comma should be inserted in figures of a thousand or greater. Some CRs omit the comma in four-figure numbers, but this practice should be confined to numbered documents and addresses.

The House will vote on HR 3411 this afternoon.
They found 1,287 persons in an auditorium that holds only 950 persons.

Note: Some CRs distinguish between *twelve hundred* and *one thousand two hundred*, which is actually the same number. This distinction would appear to be unnecessary hairsplitting, and to feel obliged to write *12 hundred* rather than *1,200* is unnecessary and does not read well at all. This *(12 hundred)* construction should be avoided.

Governments and Organizations

464 Organization numbers follow the basic rule.

Exception: Those preceded by Number or No.

He attended the First Baptist Church regularly.
Local no. 2 had a strike vote last night, but I don't know the results of the vote.
Troop 14 has the best attendance record.

465 Sessions of Congress also follow the basic rule.

This same issue was debated by the Third Congress.
At the opening of the 97th Congress, we heard from the distinguished Senator.

466 Successive governments also follow the basic rule.

The historian was consumed with interest in the Third Reich.
The 19th Chang Dynasty was renowned for its promotion of the arts.

467 Television channel numbers are written as figures.

Channel 2 has the best news, I think.
The broadcast will be carried by Channel 14, WLIC radio.

468 Exhibits in court are numbered with figures.

Please attach the map as Exhibit 2 to this deposition.
Exhibits 200 through 210 are available for your examination.

Miscellaneous

469 To avoid confusion: It is important to remember that the CR avoid constructions that could result in confusion or mistaken interpretation.

POOR:
I think four or five hundred people were present.

The above sentence can be interpreted as either four people or five hundred people.

BETTER:
I think 400 or 500 people were present.

470 Social Security Numbers are always written as numbers.

Q. Do you know your social security number, Miss Grant?
A. Yes. It is 211-47-3339.

Exercises

A. Correct any errors in the use of numbers in the following:

Q. Where were you going when the accident occurred?
A. I was going to my office. It's Room Five, Twenty-Five Mill Street.
Q. Were you alone?
A. No. My daughters were with me.
Q. What are their ages?
A. Melissa is five, and Alicia is eleven. I also had my neighbor's daughter in the car with me.
Q. How old is she?
A. She is fourteen, I think. She might be fifteen by now.
Q. And were those girls going with you to their office?
A. No, I was dropping them off at summer camp.
Q. Where was this camp?
A. On Highway Fifty-Five, just off Interstate Ninety-Three.
Q. What is your age, Mrs. Wilke?
A. Thirty-one.

Q. How long have you lived at your present address?
A. I've been there only 4 or 5 months.
Q. Where did you live prior to that?
A. I have only a two-year lease on my apartment now.
Q. I asked you where you lived previously.
A. 1011 Timberlane Drive, Memphis, Tennessee, 28934.
Q. How long did you live there?
A. 5 years.
Q. What were you carrying in your trunk?
A. I had 10 25-pound sacks of potatoes.
Q. Why were you carrying them?
A. I got them from the farmer who lives out by my parents' house.
Q. Were they all for you?
A. No. I was going to divide them with my 4 sisters and 2 brothers. I got them cheap. The whole bunch only cost me eleven dollars and 50¢.
Q. Were you paying attention to your driving that morning?
A. Sure.
Q. No distractions.
A. Just the radio. I always listen to Channel one twelve on the radio to hear the weather.
Q. Were you carrying a lot of money with you?
A. I had about fifteen hundred dollars with me.
Q. Why were you carrying that kind of cash with you?
A. Two hundred belonged to my office—petty cash. The rest was mine. I planned to deposit 7 hundred and fifty of it in my bank. I had to be at work by eight 30 a.m. I intended to go to my bank on my lunch period.
Q. Where does your husband work?
A. He is deceased.
Q. Where did he work?
A. Construction work out of Local Number twenty-two.
Q. When did he die?
A. April first, 1984.
Q. What is your present annual income?
A. My salary is fifteen thousand five hundred dollars per year at present, but I am due a raise in about 4 months.
Q. Did you receive any insurance benefits as a result of your husband's death?
A. Yes, I did. A hundred thousand dollars.

Q. What bank did you use?

A. The 1st National Bank.

Q. Where is it located?

A. One Grange Street.

B. Correct any errors in the use of numbers in the following:

The 1st patient, a forty nine year old woman, was first seen at the clinic on the seventh of July. The clinic is located at 10542 West Forty Third Street, Apartment twenty-two. She weighed two hundred twelve pounds, and her height was five feet six inches. She came in at ten thirty in the morning. We found her cholesterol to be dangerously high at 266. Triglycerides were 477 and inorganic phosphorus at five point 22. Glucose measurement was a hundred and twenty-seven. The patient's file is no. four-seven-zero-zero-eight AG. We asked her to return in three weeks for a follow-up examination because she was put on an exercise program and diet of twelve hundred fifty calories a day. The examination took about two and half hours, and the patient was unusually nervous and uncooperative. When she returned for a follow-up visit a month or 2 later, she had actually gained fourteen pounds. The patient had edema and ascites; her white cell count was elevated.

6
ABBREVIATIONS

As with most punctuation decisions, the CR must rely to a large degree on what is spoken for decisions regarding abbreviations. Actually, abbreviations are used rather infrequently in transcripts with only a few exceptions. When the CR is in doubt, it is generally better not to abbreviate.

471 Do not use an abbreviation to begin a sentence.

Number 52 is ambiguous. (not No. 52)

EXCEPTIONS:

See next section for words that are always abbreviated.

Titles

472 The following titles are always abbreviated when followed by a name or names:

Mr. Mrs. Messrs,. Jr., Sr., Esq. a.m., p.m. B.C., A.D., Ms. Dr. *Doctors* can be used, although *Drs.* is preferable.

Note: Miss and its plural (Misses) are not abbreviated.

Messrs. Jones and Smith were responsible for the donation of a large amount of money for the hospital fund.

Misses Johnson and Taylor had already arrived when I got there.

Drs. Cooper and Drake concur with my diagnosis.

473 Titles that occur in a sentence without a name are written out rather than abbreviated.

I saw my doctor this morning, but he wasn't here for very long.

Tell me, Mister, do you know who I am?

474 Titles other than those listed above (#472) are not abbreviated.

Captain Tilton will be promoted soon.
I had taken several courses from Professor Chang.
Taylor wrote a letter to the superintendent, but he has received no response other than a call from the office manager.

475 Abbreviations written after names are written with periods.

Martha Cole, D.D.S., is my older sister; didn't you know?
Joseph L. Soames, Ph.D., will conduct the seminar.

476 When part of a name, abbreviate *Jr.*, *Sr.*, and designations such as *III.*

Mr. Carl J. Davis, Sr., has been appointed to the board.
Bennett Rawlings III has written about a dozen books.

Note: Do not use *Jr.* or *Sr.* in abbreviated form unless the complete name is used.

George Junior does not wish to follow in the footsteps of George Senior by working in the lumber industry.

477 **Proper Names**

Write out parts of proper names as they are spoken. Do not abbreviate.

We turned north on Rodgers Road. (not Rodgers Rd.)
Morrison Building is the town's tallest. (not Bldg.)

478 **Abbreviated Organizations**

When government agencies or other organizations are called by abbreviations rather than their full names, they are written without periods.

The AMA guidelines are clear on this subject.
We applied for a HUD loan to purchase our new house.
The UN will vote this afternoon on the issue of sanctions.

OTHER EXAMPLES:

GMAC (General Motors Acceptance Corporation)
NEA (National Education Association)
FBI (Federal Bureau of Investigation)
CBS (Columbia Broadcasting System)
WBRZ, WWFL, WXAB, WWL (television and radio stations)

479 **Acronyms**

Acronyms are written without periods.

Is it true that he attended NATO meetings in 1985 and 1986?
She joined WAVES because she didn't have a career or any other means of support.

480 **Clipped Forms**

No periods are used with clipped forms.

My math exam was a breeze!
The prep school was exclusive in reputation only.
My phone was working just fine last night.
Chemistry lab met once a week at 5:00 p.m.

Time and Dates

481 *A.D.* and *B.C.* are written with caps and periods. *a.m.* and *p.m.* are written with periods and lowercased.

482 Do not abbreviate days of the week or months.

We met every Tuesday night.
I received dividend checks in February, June, and October every year for 15 years.

483 Do not abbreviate units of time, regardless of whether they are used in singular or plural form: weeks, years, seconds, minutes, days, hours.

Company Names

484 The ampersand can be used in company names only if the company or organization itself uses the ampersand in its official title. If uncertain, write out the word *and.*

Mother refused to shop for groceries anywhere except at A & P.
We used AT&T for our long distance service even though my brother worked for Sprint.
Morrison and Sons is where I always had my car repaired.

Note: Never use the ampersand as an abbreviation for the word *and* in any other usage.

Wrong

Carl Reed, Joseph Parker, & Marcus Klein began their company in 1980.

485 *Company* and *Incorporated* can be abbreviated or not, depending on what was said or on the preference of the firm for which the CR works. Listen to what is said. If *Inc.* ("ink") is what you hear, then write *Inc.*; but if the word is spoken in full, write it out. The same rule applies for *Corporation* vs. *Corp.* If what was spoken is the full word, write it out; if *Corp* was said, use the abbreviated form. As always, be consistent.

General City Gravel Co., Inc., closed its doors after 50 years of prosperity.

The Charles Company employs more women than men.

Measurements

486 It is preferred that units of measurement not be abbreviated.

We traveled more than 1,500 kilometers across Canada.

My study measured only 11 feet 6 inches by 14 feet.

487 Although it is tempting to use certain symbols and abbreviations, the CR should write out the following:

percent	not %
Fahrenheit	not F
centigrade	not C
degree(s)	not °
at	not @
plus	not +
equal to	not =
minus	not -

Note: Fahrenheit is capitalized, but centigrade is not.

488 Names

Do not abbreviate personal names.

George (not Geo.)

William (not Wm.)

Note: if the official name of a company customarily uses an abbreviated name in its title, use of the abbreviation is acceptable.

Geo. Trant & Sons

Wm. Black, Inc.

Geographic Names and Terms

489 The abbreviation for *United States* is written with periods and closed up, that is, with no space between the *U* and the *S.*

The U.S. delegation will send a representative to the funeral.

490 The abbreviation *D.C.* is written with periods and closed up.

We had to attend a conference in Washington, D.C.

Note: The U.S. Postal Service specifies a two-letter form without periods (DC, NY, etc.) for use with zip-code addresses, but this form should not be used in transcripts.

491 In geographic names, do not abbreviate *Fort, Port, Point* or *Pointe, Mount, New* (as in New York, New Orleans, New Jersey), *North, South, East,* or *West.* Many agree it is acceptable to abbreviate *Saint* to *St.*

He moved to St. Louis to get away from his father.
We lived in Fort Meyers, not Fort Payne.

Note: Saint is not abbreviated when used in the name of a saint (Saint Thomas Aquinas).

492 Common Latin Abbreviations

The abbreviation *e.g.* (meaning "for example"), *i.e.* ("that is"), and *etc.* ("and so forth") are written with periods. The abbreviation *et al.* ("and others") has a period after *al.* but no period after *et,* which is not an abbreviation but the Latin word for *and.* Some CRs prefer not to use *etc.* but to write it out in full: *et cetera.*

The typical New England state, e.g., Massachusetts, is steeped in American history.
The informal admonition, i.e., the chancellor's speech, had the desired effects on the student body.
The suit was filed by James Reel and the Anderswitt Motor Company, et al.

493 Chemical Symbols

Chemical symbols are written out without periods. The subscript numbers must be written properly, that is, lower than letter symbols.

H_2O and CO_2 are the two most prominent products of mammalian respiration.

494 **Laws, Articles, Sections**

Do not abbreviate laws, sections, bylaws, articles, and other such document titles.

> The basis for this judgment can be found in Section 34.
> Article 523 clearly regulates such activities.

495 **Medical Terms**

The CR is limited by what is actually said. It is not the CR's duty to expand medical abbreviations but rather to "get it right" as used.

> His EKG was within normal range.
> We did tests for BUN, CBC, GFT, and ACTH.
> CT showed no abnormalities.

496 **Plurals of Abbreviations**

Most plurals are formed simply by adding an *s*, although an apostrophe and an *s* are used (1) to avoid confusion or (2) with abbreviations that employ periods.

> Their IQs are as high as ours, I think.
> IUDs were commonly prescribed by Dr. Collins.
> BUT:
> There are only three Ph.D.'s on staff.

497 **Number**

The word *Number* can be abbreviated when used with a numeral.

> She lives in Apartment no. 7B
> The winners were nos. 312 and 411.

Note: If the CR prefers to write out *Number*, this is acceptable.

498 **Versus**

When used to refer to court cases, *versus* can be abbreviated as *v.* or *vs.*

> Do you think this case resembles that of Jones *v.* Battery?

499 **Academic Degrees and Designations**

Such designations are written with periods (no space between the letters).

> Dr. Davidson, D.D.S., is opening his office on June 1st.

He will have his B.S. by June.
She has given up on her M.A. for now.

500 **Letters**

No period is used when letters are written as letters.

Exhibit A was admitted into evidence.
His o's looked like a's.

Exercises

A. Correct any errors in abbreviations. If a sentence is correct as is, leave it intact.

1. Samuel Balin, PhD, will address the student body of St. John High School next week.
2. We were in the gym playing basketball, but Paul and Marijo were in the lab working on an assignment.
3. It felt like 100° in the kitchen, but it was only about 85° F.
4. The US flag is flying at half-mast this entire week in recognition of our national tragedy.
5. We lived in Apt. 7, 14 N. Willow St., but our bldg. was sold, so we moved to Giles Boulevard.
6. I met with Mrs. James Jackson and John Rowell on Nov. 9th.
7. The consultation lasted from 10:30 AM until 4:45 PM.
8. I'm being audited by the IRS!
9. We toured the Smithsonian in Washington, DC, but we saw only a small part of the huge place.
10. Do you work for Dr. Morales or for Prof. Hadelmann?
11. Did you report to Lt. Cole, as you were instructed?
12. List your name, address, & telephone number at the top of the page.
13. He is rather tall—about 6 ft. 3 inches, I'd guess.
14. I made an appointment to see my dr. this Fri. afternoon.
15. Hey, Mr., move your car out of my way!
16. Akemi Fujio, MD, was injured this morning in an auto accident out on West Mountain Hwy.

17. He refused to name his son Rutherford J. Adamson, Junior, because he hates the name himself.
18. My favorite radio station is W.U.L.V.
19. He joined the co. in Jan. or Feb. of 1967.
20. Isn't Ft. Walton Beach on Santa Rosa Island?

7
WORD DIVISION

The following are a few basic rules about word division. No attempt has been made to present a comprehensive treatment of the subject, as the dictionary is always available. Remember: Word division should be kept to a minimum!

501 Divide a word at the end of a line only when it is absolutely necessary. A page dotted with end-of-the-line hyphens is visually distracting and does nothing to facilitate reading.

502 Never divide words at the ends of more than three consecutive lines.

4 consecutive hyphens:

> We left Jacksonville very early in the morn-
> ing that day. I think it was before sun-
> rise. The sky was blue and we were extraor-
> dinarily excited about making the trip to Mary-
> land.

503 Words are divided according to pronunciation, that is, between syllables. One-syllable words cannot be divided (force, self, poach, hope, sense, chaste, straight). Watch out for words that appear, at first glance, to have more than one syllable *(jogged, gasped, punched),* but do not and therefore should not be divided.

504 Do not divide a word if a one-letter syllable would result (*enough, around, elapse).*

505 A two-letter syllable is acceptable at the end of a line but not at the beginning of the next line. Thus, it would be acceptable to break *en/dure, de/duce,* or *re/view,* but the following breaks are not acceptable: *want/ed, church/es, comput/er.*

506 Hyphenated compound words are divided only at the hyphen *(self-/sufficient, cross-/country, well-/being, brass-/collar, braille-/writer, long-/term, full-/time).*

507 Words containing prefixes or suffixes should be divided between the root word and the prefix or suffix *(joy/fully, un/happy, dis/jointed, anti/war, mid/point, other/ness, pseudo/classic, non/linear, semi/quantitative, pre/moisten, super/achiever).*

508 When adding a suffix results in a double consonant, the word can be divided between those two consonants (*run/ning, occur/ring, beg/ging, trap/ped, hit/ting, grab/bing, let/ting, strap/ping, transfer/ring, forget/ting*).

509 Do not divide words of fewer than six letters *(eject, water, money, enact, input, undo, midst, smelt, perky, petty, pshaw, punks, quack, okay, bumpy, proxy, area, open, chaos)* regardless of whether the words contain more than one syllable.

510 Proper names should not be divided unless there is no way to avoid doing it. In names that use initials, divide after the initials (*W.F./Gillis, William F./Gillis*). Divide other names between the given name and the surname (*William/Gillis*). Word processing systems often automatically split proper names, but this problem can be remedied by putting in a "hard break" to avoid improper splits. The same is true of dividing dates, addresses, and proper names. (See Sections 511-513.)

511 Never divide contractions, abbreviations, figures, or abbreviations used with figures.

Wrong

I wanted to attend the seminar, but I could-
n't find a babysitter.
The file said that the animal weighed only 515
g last Tuesday.
She expected to have earned her Ph.
D. by the end of the year.

512 Avoid dividing dates and street addresses.

Avoid

If I remember correctly, it was January
17, 1991.

Acceptable

If I remember correctly, it was January 17,
1991.

Preferable

If I remember correctly, it was
January 17, 1991.

Avoid

We were residing in a tiny apartment at 75 West
Boyd Street.

Preferable

We were residing in a tiny apartment at
75 West Boyd Street.

513 Divide place names between the city and the state (New Orleans/Louisiana). Do not divide between *New* and Orleans.

514 Never divide the last word of a paragraph or the last word on a page.

Exercise

Assume that the following words occur at the end of a line of type. Decide in what way(s) each should be divided or if it cannot be divided at all. Use slashes to indicate the permissible breaks.

alas	touchy	department
self-induced	flanked	clothing
enjoyment	elect	saltwater
emission	can't	breakfast
should	misused	potential
firsthand	clapping	elusive
Quebec City, Quebec, Canada	George F.Billings-Tate	San Francisco, California
St. Louis, Missouri	January 1990	creepy
unwilling	distillery	director
Madrid, Spain,	cannot	peaked
memorial	editor-in-chief	November 21, 1956
didn't	vested	joined
miracles	22 pounds	cease
reenactment	shouldn't	criminal
announce	assistance	erupt
hazard	221 Fifth Street	counterfeit
slammed	indisputable	
New York City, New York	Sharon W.B. Markham	

8
COMPOUNDS

What would seem to be a fairly simple issue is one that causes many CRs to spend an inordinate amount of time in debate. Should a compound word be written open (as two words), hyphenated, or written solid (as one word)? In recent years there has been a tendency away from hyphenation, but there are many situations in which the hyphen is still correct. The dictionary can be useful in many cases, but certainly not in all. For one thing, dictionaries sometimes disagree among themselves; for another, many terms are not listed because they are "temporary" compounds created for the specific occasion, e.g., Maria-like gestures; and, finally, many terms sometimes are hyphenated and sometimes not, depending on how the compound functions within a given sentence.

The following are some basic rules about compound words:

515 Hyphenate compound adjectives, including those that are "created for the occasion."

> The long-term relationship between Earl and Edna has been very special.
>
> Their friendship has been a here-today-gone-tomorrow affair.
>
> Tom is a first-time owner of a Ford vehicle.
>
> The ten-year-old feud between the Browns and the Greens has finally ceased.
>
> She had that I-know-something-you-don't-know look on her face.
>
> I know Bill received under-the-table money for doing that job.

516 Use a "suspension" hyphen for two or more adjectives that have the same base, and that base is used only once. The suspension cannot be used in compounds that do not contain a hyphen.

> The new company is looking for part- and full-time employees.
>
> The realtor will be showing three-, four-, and five-bedroom homes.

Unacceptable

She was working to improve the school's inter- and intracollegiate sports programs.

Correct

She was working to improve the school's intercollegiate and intracollegiate sports programs.

517 Hyphenate written-out numbers from 21 through 99. Do not hyphenate larger numbers.

Twenty-one students will receive scholarships.
One hundred ten dollars is a good price for that jacket.
Eighty-eight members attended the meeting.

518 Hyphenate fractions in their written-out form when they are used as adjectives. If a fraction functions as a noun, hyphenation is optional.

A two-thirds majority is required for passage of the law.
One half of the strawberry pie was eaten by Tim. (or one-half)

519 Do not hyphenate an adverb that ends with *ly* and the adjective or participle it modifies.

She seemed to be a highly motivated worker.
The poorly constructed house is for sale.

520 Do not hyphenate a compound adjective whose first element is the comparative (with er) or superlative (with est) form of an adjective.

He was a clean-shaven, courteous young man.
I cannot imagine a cleaner shaven young man than Bradley. (comparative)
Bradley is the cleanest shaven young man I have ever met. (superlative)

521 A compound adjective that is hyphenated when it precedes the noun it modifies often is not hyphenated when it functions as a predicate adjective.

Mr. Dawes is a well-known author of regional history books.
Mr. Dawes, an author of regional history books, is well known.
My deep-rooted fear was hard to overcome.
My fear was deep rooted.
The Advertising Department needs an up-to-date calendar.
The calendar is not up to date for the Advertising Department.

522 Sometimes a word is hyphenated to indicate a different meaning from the meaning of the word as written without the hyphen. Such situations involve the prefix *re.*

We went down to the Caribbean to recreate and relax.
He will have to re-create the broken sculpture.

I could not hear your last remark.
I will re-mark the test papers in consideration of the new information.

The patient will recover from major surgery.
The teacher will re-cover all arbitraries and derivatives.

523 When a prefix is attached to a proper noun or proper adjective (i.e., one that is capitalized), hyphenate the word.

The anti-American sentiment has grown in the past few months.
In your pre-Timothy days, you dated a lot of different young men.

524 Do not hyphenate verbs to join them to prepositions, although the same terms, when functioning as nouns or adjectives, are hyphenated.

Can you follow up on this report?

BUT:

Allen did a follow-up report for me.

525 Most prefixed words are written solid, even those that create double vowels.

preempt
reeducate
preemployment
preexisting

BUT:

Some double vowels are hyphenated:

anti-immunoglobulin
pre-engineered

526 Use a hyphen with the prefix ex when it means former

ex-convict ex-husband
ex-girlfriend ex-President Nixon

527 Use a hyphen between a prefix and a number.

pre-1980's post-1985 mid-'90s

528 Hyphenate terms that are formed by using letters as prefixes.

A-bomb T-shirt T-bill T-bone steak U-valve

Note: X ray (Noun) X-ray (Verb & Adjective)

529 Exhibit labels employing letters and figures are hyphenated.

Exhibit No. F-1 Plaintiff's B-3 Exhibit C-3

530 A hyphen can sometimes prevent confusion.

He was driving a fast-moving van.

BUT:

He was driving a fast moving-van.

Terry Wilson was a mean woman-beater.

BUT:

Terry Wilson was a mean-woman beater. (Meaning that he only beat *mean* women?)

In her hand she held a strange looking glass.

BUT:

In her hand she held a strange-looking glass.

531 Hyphenate to avoid tripling a letter.

Correct

We heard a bell-like sound in the distance.

Wrong

We heard a belllike sound in the distance.

Open, Hyphenated, and Solid Compounds

The following examples show the same terms written differently, depending on the term's function in the sentence. Take careful notice of the difference.

532 **ad-lib • ad lib**

My ad-lib performance was well received.
I couldn't ad-lib, so I just walked away.
Janie's speech was ad lib.

533 **air conditioning • air-condition**

My air conditioning in my car works.
I am planning to air-condition my apartment.

534 **all get out • all get-out**

The residents of Lilly Lane wish those dogs would all get out of here.

They ran like all get-out when they saw Mickey coming.

535 **all-or-nothing • all or nothing**

Jon's all-or-nothing philosophy created problems in the organization.

I didn't care if I received all or nothing for my work; I did it for fun.

536 **All right • alright**

Phil did all right on his History 204 final exam.

Note: Alright is generally considered incorrect. Use all right.

537 **all-time • all time**

The all-time high for rain was last year.

I will remember that day for all time.

538 **all together • altogether**

The seniors are all together for a picture to be put in the "Hornet."

There were altogether too many people in the room.

539 **already • all ready**

The proposal has already been discussed with the board members.

The students were all ready for the exam except for Patricia.

540 **anyone • any one**

Mr. Talley would talk to anyone who would listen to him.

Any one of the three applicants is well qualified for the position.

541 **anyplace • any place**

You may sit anyplace in the auditorium.

I will meet you at any place or at any time you choose.

542 **anytime • any time**

"You can do that anytime," he told me.

Rodney may call at any time on Sunday.

543 **anyway • any way**

I didn't want to go anyway.
I will help in any way on the project.

544 **around-the-clock • around the clock**

An around-the-clock vigil was held to honor our Persian Gulf veterans.
We studied around the clock for two days.

545 **away • a way**

I will be away from the office for a week.
It is my goal to find a way to pacify him.

546 **awhile • a while**

Stay awhile, and enjoy the air-conditioning.
A while ago he said it was 99 degrees.

Note: If the term is preceded by a preposition, use the two-word version.

547 **back out • backout**

There was a motorbike right behind my car, and I was not able to back out of my parking space.
His backout was a surprise to no one.

548 **back room • backroom**

The back room is where I store my transcripts.
Backroom activity stopped when Mr. Garcia returned.

549 **backup • back up**

My backup Stenograph machine goes everywhere with me.
My backup was Marta, but she was unreliable.
I want you to back up the recorder; push this button.

550 **bailout • bail out**

The fiscal bailout caused jubilation in the company.
His bailout scheme frightened me.
The community people will bail out Mr. Gray, a longtime resident of Maryville.

551 **bareback • bare back**

His sunburn came as a result of skiing bareback over the weekend.

He sat out in the sun until his bare back was sunburned.

552 **blackout • black out**

Mrs. Barnes experienced a blackout in church.

We would always black out the names on the document.

553 **blastoff • blast off**

The blastoff was set for Friday, but the weather forced it to be cancelled.

I saw Darryl blast off in his new car.

554 **blowup • blow up**

A witness had a blowup in court last week.

I couldn't even blow up a balloon because I was so weak.

555 **breakdown • break down**

Her breakdown was anticipated by her colleagues.

I will break down the sentence and identify the parts of speech.

556 **break-in • break in**

A break-in was reported a 2:22 a.m. on Thursday, June 12.

I lost my key, so I had to break in.

557 **breakout • break out**

The prison breakout sent a wave of fear through the area.

Everybody will break out in a sweat when the temperature is 110 degrees.

558 **breakthrough • break through**

There has been a major breakthrough in medical research for AIDS.

I tried to break through his barrier of silence.

559 **breakup • break up**

The breakup between Bernie and Alicia was difficult for Ruth to accept.

Mayor Browne did not want to break up the Council meeting, but a tornado was reported in the area.

560 **broken-down • broken down**

His horse was a broken-down nag.
The car had broken down on Western Acres Road.

561 **buildup • build up**

The buildup of arms is of concern to all of us.
She is trying to build up her muscles through proper exercising and proper dieting.

562 **burnout • burn out**

Student burnout can happen in the first year of college
I thought his enthusiasm would burn out eventually, but I was mistaken.

563 **buyout • buy out**

The corporate buyout was done secretly and suddenly.
Mr. Jennings will try to buy out the remaining inventory.

564 **catch-up • catch up**

Mona's catch-up efforts had her working 18 hours a day.
Jamie will catch up with the class through the assistance of her teacher.

565 **cave-in • cave in**

The cave-in resulted in the loss of 14 lives.
The hole will cave in without some support.

566 **changeover • change over**

The changeover went smoothly, but we disliked Mr. McLaughlin.
Tennille will change over to the Court Reporting Course next term. (Court Reporting Course is a particular course of study.)

567 **checkout • check out**

Checkout time at the motel is 11:30 a.m.
Dakota will check out the china at the Cross Country Mall.

568 **checkup • check up**

Last October I had a checkup at a well-known clinic.
I didn't appreciate having him check up on me.

569 **cleanup • clean up**

The Cleanup Committee does a superb job!
I told Brandon to clean up his room before our guests arrived.

570 **comedown • come down**

The job was a big comedown from owning his own business.
Jim's mother asked him to come down from the attic.

571 **coming-out • coming out**

Her coming-out party was a dismal affair.
We were coming out of the restaurant when a child was hit by a pickup truck.

572 **cover-up • cover up**

The financial cover-up was found by the CPA.
He couldn't cover up his lack of skills.

573 **crackdown • crack down**

The crackdown affected everyone in the plant.
The new teacher tried to crack down on absenteeism.

574 **crackup • crack up**

Route 6 was the site of a crackup between a Buick car and a GMC truck.
We told him he would crack up if he didn't slow down.

575 **cutback • cut back**

My cutback on luxuries became effective immediately.
I tried to cut back on my expenditures.

576 **downright • down right**

His nephew is downright mean when he plays with other children.
I studied for six hours, but I just couldn't get my math down right.

577 **drawback • draw back**

My only drawback is that the apartment is on the other side of campus.

One drawback to his idea was our lack of expertise.

We decided to draw back to our starting point and make new plans.

578 **drive-in • drive in**

There is no drive-in theatre in my hometown.

I couldn't drive in because the snow was too deep.

579 **dropout • drop out**

The dropout rate falls by about a half of a percent each year.

The college dropouts in Miss Lilly's class were very low in number.

Miss Lindsay will not drop out of the gymnastic competition.

580 **dry-rot • dry rot**

If we don't take care, the cloth will dry-rot.

The dry rot has ruined my Senior Prom dress.

581 **easygoing • easy going**

She was an easygoing, likeable, friendly instructor.

Six years of college were not easy going for me.

582 **ego-trip • ego trip**

It looked as though Helene would ego-trip over the constant compliments from Mr. Hernandez.

The pageant was a much-needed ego trip for Brittany.

583 **everyday • every day**

In the everyday working world, commuting is common.

Elizabeth was self-disciplined and attended class every day when she went to college.

584 **everyone • every one**

I requested that everyone R.S.V.P. in two weeks.

Every one of my pencils needed to be sharpened.

585 **fallout • fall out**

The political fallout that followed the investigation had profound effects.
A neighbor saw the little girl fall out of her bedroom window.

586 **far-off • far off**

The far-off hunting area is frequented a lot.
We knew that a layoff was not far off.

587 **first-class • first class**

First-class accommodations were provided for the dignitaries.
He will fly first class when he goes to Hawaii.
My first class on Mondays is English.

588 **first-degree • first degree**

The grease caused first-degree burns on Ms. Redd.
He was found guilty of murder in the first degree.

589 **flare-up • flare up**

The Bronzz Chemical Company allows one flare-up before an employee is terminated.
I knew that the announcement would flare up discontent.

590 **follow-up • follow up**

His follow-up was incomplete.
My follow-up method will guarantee accuracy.
If I follow up with an offer, I may be the new owner.

591 **forasmuch as • for as much as**

Forasmuch as I paid for those shoes, I plan to wear them a lot.
We expected the painting to sell for as much as $2,500.

592 **foul-up • foul up**

The computer's foul-up caused major problems.
An inexperienced employee could foul up the computer.

593 **freshwater • fresh water**

The freshwater harbor is threatened by runoff.
When we arrived at the cabin, there was no fresh water.

594 **getaway • get away**

When Officer Bowwen caught the getaway unit, it was a dark blue truck.

I told him he wouldn't get away with such fraudulent practices.

595 **giveaway • give away**

Mrs. Thornton's giveaway scheme proved to be very expensive.

The grocery giveaway was a box of T-bone steaks.

Mrs. Yoos will give away many handouts at the seminar.

596 **go-ahead • go ahead**

The pilot was given the go-ahead signal for takeoff.

I told Pearl to go ahead with the twenty-fifth anniversary plans.

597 **handout • hand out**

We weren't asking for a handout, just for a fair chance.

Julia was planning to hand out pamphlets to anyone who would take one.

598 **hit-or-miss • hit or miss**

Arturo's hit-or-miss approach got him fairly good results.

My plan was at best done hit or miss.

599 **holdup • hold up**

The holdup was at Green and 14th Streets.

She could not hold up under such pressure.

600 **inside-out • inside out**

Phil's inside-out clothes didn't bother him.

Jimmy's T-shirt was inside out.

601 **knockout • knock out**

Lester gave his opponent a knockout punch that really did knock him out.

Lightning can knock out the entire electrical system.

602 **know-how • know how**

His know-how and my money combined to make us successful.

Cornelia did not know how to use the portable telephone.

603 **layover • lay over**

Ingrid will have a six-hour layover in Evansville.
We will lay over in London for three days.

604 **long-term • long term**

The long-term benefits at the company are excellent.
Our president was concerned about profits over the long term.

605 **lookout • look out**

The lookout fell asleep and didn't see anything at all.
Amy will ask Jennifer to look out for the vacation offers.

606 **makeover • make over**

The makeover process required three full hours.
It is important that we make over the system for calling members in ABWA.

607 **makeup • make up**

The makeup test was far more difficult.
Jennie will be allowed to make up her punctuation quiz.

608 **markup • mark up**

The owner put a markup of 25 percent on the clock.
We were planning to mark up the prices after the first of the year.

609 **middle-class • middle class**

Our middle-class neighborhood was alarmed by their presence.
We are members of the middle class.

610 **mixup • mix up**

The mix-up came about because of a communication error.
I will mix up the vegetables for a vegetable pizza.

611 **off-the-record • off the record**

Counsel for the plaintiff made off-the-record comments.
The judge said his comments would be off the record.

612 **payoff • pay off**

The payoff was not the end of the extortion.
Josephine will pay off the balance of her car loan in December.

613 **pickup • pick up**

The pickup was made on time, but not by me.
Mr. Ruttledge will pick up my car and wash it for me today.

614 **playback • play back**

The playback proved my contention that he was out of bounds.
I wanted to play back those five minutes in slow motion.

615 **printout • print out**

A salary printout for School Unit 236A is available at the unit office.
The printer will print out one page of the transcript in 15 seconds.

616 **recollect • re-collect**

I recollect seeing Teddy on the Fourth of July.
Because the check was no good, we had to re-collect payment.

617 **recover • re-cover**

We hoped he would recover from his surgery by September.
Emily will re-cover her dining room chairs with needle point.

618 **release • re-lease**

Roger will release the nightclub schedule the first of September.
Ann will re-lease the apartment for another.

619 **roundup • round up**

The roundup was incomplete but was counted a success.
Liz will round up as many references as she can in the next fortnight.

620 **run-on • run on**

When you proofread the material, check for run-on sentences.
The speech didn't run on as long as we had feared.

621 **setup • set up**

I realized that the entire situation was a setup to deceive me.

The Charleston Room is all set up for the conference.

622 **shutdown • shut down**

The plant's shutdown caused significant unemployment in the town.

The entire plant will shut down for two weeks in November.

623 **shut-in • shut in**

All of the shut-in residents of Mayville received a Valentine's Day card from the Mayor.

We knew it was hopeless to try to shut in every teenager in the town after dark.

624 **sign-off • sign off**

Sign-off was at midnight.

Albert will sign off Channel 10 at noon.

625 **snapback • snapback**

The snapback came sooner than anticipated.

Beth will snap back after she has physical therapy.

626 **sometime • some time • sometimes**

Jeff will call me sometime next month.

I needed some time to think about the situation.

Sometimes we go to the Christian church for Sunday services.

627 **standby • stand by**

He was always on standby on Saturdays.

We tried to stand by and watch, but we gave up and went home.

628 **standoff • stand off**

There was a standoff between students and campus police.

The children should stand off from the fireworks on the ground display.

629 **takeover • take over**

The corporate takeover was unexpected.

Miss Gray will take over Mrs. Haack's classes during her leave of absence.

630 **turndown • turn down**

Her turndown altered my plans for the future.
No one would turn down that attractive offer.

631 **upper-class • upper class**

Her upper-class attitude made her unpopular with the staff.
The upper class at Bingg High School has excellent ACT scores.

632 **walkout • walk out**

A walkout is planned unless our terms are met by midnight.
The bookkeeper will walk out unless he receives a raise.

633 **workout • work out**

I do a 60-minute workout each morning and each evening.
Judy said the plan will work out for all her colleagues.

634 **zip-code • zip code**

Before I took the letters to the post office, I had to zip-code them.
More than one zip code is used for the New York areas.

Exercises

A. In the sentences below, no hyphens have been used. Insert hyphens where they are needed.

There were two hundred persons present, although we were expecting a much smaller number. Seventy five invitations had been mailed to full time staff members. No family members were supposed to attend the formal attire only dinner, but Mr. Evenna brought along his father in law and his nine year old son. A full figured woman went up to the podium, accompanied by a darkly handsome young man and a strikingly gorgeous, fair haired young woman. The woman was well known, but not through my current employment. I knew her through my ex husband. Back in the mid 60's, she used to speak at the university. Her name then was Ora Nielsen. She had a troll like face and a pumpkin shaped body, bright orange colored hair, and lips painted purple. She was an impossible to forget presence wherever she went.

Although Ms. Nielsen now had white hair, I was able to recognize her immediately nonetheless.

B. Select and underline the correct version in each sentence: open, hyphenated, or solid.

1. The (breakup, break-up, break up) of the company brought a lot of changes.
2. (Forasmuch, For as much) as he already confessed to the crime, my work is simplified but not finished.
3. I liked to (work out, workout, work-out) at the local gym at least three times a week.
4. Jason was (altogether, all together) baffled by his father's odd behavior.
5. Oscar needed (sometime, some time) to contemplate the proposal before offering his support.
6. We were (already, all ready) to depart when the telephone rang.
7. A few moments passed before Darren was able to (recover, re-cover) from the blow.
8. My criticisms were strictly (off-the-record, off the record).
9. I didn't expect Mr. Arla to (turndown, turn down, turn-down) the proposal, but he did.
10. No (make-up, make up, makeup) exams are given without a valid excuse.
11. His mechanical (knowhow, know-how, know how) made Marco popular around the neighborhood.
12. I told Ivan that there wasn't (anyplace, any place) for him in our organization, not now or ever.
13. An (around the clock, around-the-clock) vigil, though not necessary, seemed wise at the time.
14. I couldn't afford to (air condition, air-condition) my car that summer, so I suffered.
15. The (cleanup, clean-up, clean up) was accomplished by a group of students from junior high schools in the area.
16. His (long-term, long term) goals weren't known to me, but my supervisor knew what was going on.
17. We were afraid that Joni would (mix up, mix-up) the exam scores.

18. The (printout, print-out, print out) didn't supply the information we needed.
19. After Rolph's illness, Gil had to (takeover, take-over) as chairman for the rest of the term.
20. I told Berta that I'd return after (awhile, a while), but she insisted that I remain.
21. Verna thought it would be (alright, all right) if we borrowed the book, but she was mistaken.
22. I didn't expect (anyone, any one) of those gadgets to work.
23. Coco and Willis met (everyday, every day) at noon for three years.
24. The plan was never given an official (go-ahead, go ahead).
25. The (walkout, walk-out, walk out) was unsuccessful because so many refused to (cooperate, co-operate).

C. In this exercise, the underlined part is either correct or incorrect. If it is correct, write down "correct." If it is incorrect, write down the correct form.

1. Can Johnna re-sort the mail?
2. The wedding party will be coming out of the church soon.
3. Which checkout lane will you go through, Arthur?
4. Mr. Alwardt is such a nice, easygoing man.
5. Does your neighbor have a new pickup truck?
6. Evelyn, will you buy Harlene a new T-shirt when you go to the fair?
7. Did you think the speaker was anti-Jewish.
8. Since Bill has a preexisting medical condition, do you think the company will hire him?
9. John, do you think we should cut back on credit card charges?
10. Is the drop-out rate at Mary's school 10 percent?
11. Did he intend to wear that jacket inside out?
12. Eileen does first-class work on all her projects.
13. Everyone should sign up for the quilt giveaway.
14. There is a fallout shelter under Jim Jay's house.
15. Everyone of my new tires was slashed last night.

16. Tim will go ahead with his house plans.
17. Arlene's ex-husband lives in San Francisco.
18. Do you think this decade will bring about a breakthrough in genetic engineering?
19. I think Larry will backout of the deal at the last minute.
20. My husband said there will be a shutdown at his plant in August.
21. I have the setup for the carnival ready.
22. Lizzie went to the top of the look-out tower.
23. Dad will recover the tomato plants tonight.
24. Edna asked if she could payoff her bill early.
25. Please come down to Florida this winter to visit.

9
HOMONYMS AND OTHER CONFUSIONS

Naturally, because a CR depends on what he or she hears, homonyms and near-homonyms can be a particularly troublesome area. Many English words that sound exactly alike or somewhat alike have totally different meanings and different spellings as well. It is only through understanding the possibility of such confusions that the CR can avoid making some embarrassing errors. The following are some word groups that can be troublemakers. This list by no means covers all troublesome word pairs—there are many more. However, the following presents a fairly simplified definition of each that, although not attempting to be comprehensive, gives a basic idea of proper usages.

635 **accede • exceed**

accede *(v):* to agree, acquiesce, consent
exceed *(v):* to go beyond a limit or boundary

Mary will accede to the purchase price if she can move on Labor Day.

If Sue can exceed the $1 million real estate sales this year, she will win a trip to the Bahamas.

636 **accent • ascent • assent**

accent *(n):* distinct pronunciation; emphasis; a printing mark to indicate stress of a syllable or pronunciation; *(v):* to emphasize
ascent *(n):* advancement; an upward slope
assent *(v):* to concur or agree; *(n):* agreement

His heavy accent made it nearly impossible for the CR to feel confident about the accuracy of his notes.

After 30 years at YZX, Edward has ascended to the title of vice president.

Her ascent to high office was accomplished with integrity.
The board members assent to an 8 percent raise for all certified employees of Unit 631A.

637 **accept • except**

accept *(v):* to believe; to take willingly; to receive as one's own
except *(v):* to exclude or exempt; *(prep):* other than

Professor Johnson will accept a position in the English Department at UCLA.
Everyone was at the party except the Garrett family.

638 **access • excess**

access *(n):* entrance or approachability; *(v):* to gain entrance
excess *(adj):* more than needed or specified; too much; *(n):* superfluity; overindulgence

Ryan has access to Wally Stadium on campus.
Polly has an excess of reporter paper at home.

639 **adapt • adept • adopt**

adapt *(v):* to adjust to
adept *(adj):* skilled; *(n):* an expert
adopt *(v):* to accept as one's own

It is difficult for Melissa to adapt to the farm community.
That attorney is adept at getting low bail for his clients.
The Willsons would like to adopt a baby boy and name him Matthew.

640 **adherence • adherents**

adherence *(n):* ability or willingness to cling to or support
adherents *(n):* advocates or supporters

The adherence of the Booster Club is fantastic!
Verna's political adherents number in the thousands.

641 **adverse • averse**

adverse *(adj):* unfavorable; in opposition (to)
averse *(adj):* reluctant; having a feeling of dislike or dread

The adverse publicity did not keep him from running for office again.
Jane's husband's mother was averse to the referendum.

642 **affect • effect**

affect *(v):* to influence; *(n):* emotional response (psychology)
effect *(n):* result; *(v):* to cause to happen

The hot weather will really affect the growth of the corn in the Midwest.

The effect of the thunderstorm was damaged crops and light flooding.

The new chairman will effect a dramatic policy change.

643 **aid • aide**

aid *(v):* to assist or help; *(n):* assistance
aide *(n):* a person who assists or helps

Boy Scout Troop 999 will aid with "Operation Cleanup."

We Care Nursing Home will hire 12 new aides during August.

644 **aisle • isle**

aisle *(n):* lane
isle *(n):* small island

Neither the electric scooter nor the electric wheelchair could go down a couple of the aisles because of some circular displays.

The issue is whether the isle falls within U.S. jurisdiction.

645 **allude • elude**

allude *(v):* to make reference to
elude *(v):* to avoid

I would prefer that you not allude to my former wife.

Ronald will elude the constable as often as possible.

646 **allusion • elusion • illusion**

allusion *(n):* reference
elusion *(n):* escape; avoidance
illusion *(n):* an erroneous belief; something unreal

My speech included many allusions to our past difficulties.

His elusion of creditors kept him moving from place to place.

I realized their appearance of affluence was a careful illusion.

647 **altar • alter**

altar *(n):* an elevated structure used in religious ceremonies
alter *(v):* to change or modify

There is an altar in the small chapel and the large chapel of the Community Central Church.
The lady at the bridal shop told me that there would be no charge for altering my dress.

648 **aver • avert**

aver *(v):* to affirm
avert *(v):* to turn away from; prevent; turn aside

Can he aver to the truthfulness of his statement?
We can avert a strike if both parties will compromise.

649 **bail • bale**

bail *(n):* security for release of an arrested person; *(v):* to secure a person's release from jail; to extricate; to remove water by scooping or dipping.
bale *(n):* a bundle of goods; evil influence; suffering; *(v):* to package in bales

The bail for Rodd Jones was $100,000.
John, Nick, and Otis will bale hay in a 40-acre field this afternoon.

650 **bare • bear**

bare *(adj):* uncovered, empty; *(v):* to reveal
bear *(n):* a large mammal; *(v):* to carry; to withstand

I wanted to bare my soul to Laura, but she was preoccupied.
My bare feet got so hot walking across that concrete patio when it was 110 degrees outside.
Josie will bear the huge burden of raising three children as a widow.

651 **bazaar • bizarre**

bazaar *(n):* carnival or marketplace
bizarre *(adj):* weird, strange

A Presbyterian church in Springfield always plans a bazaar and a soup supper on Veterans Day, November 11.

The woman's bizarre behavior alarmed her neighbors.

652 **beside • besides**

beside *(prep):* near or next to
besides *(prep):* in addition; *(prep):* other than

Beside the house is a three-car garage.
Besides the large urban centers, will other areas be represented at the event?

653 **biannual • biennial**

biannual *(adj):* occurring twice a year
biennial *(adj):* occurring once every two years

A local financial institution will schedule biannual meetings for May and November.
The association's biennial conventions will be in Denver in 1986; in San Francisco in 1988; in Boston in 1990.

654 **bloc • block**

bloc *(n):* a group united by some common belief or cause
block *(n):* a city square; a piece of wood; a hindrance; *(v):* to prevent from passing

The Soviet bloc alleged that a violation of the Geneva Convention had been committed.
I need one more block of wood that is 3 inches in width for my bookshelf.
I have some friends in Denver, Colorado, that live 15 blocks from one another.

655 **blond • blonde**

blond *(adj):* of a fair or pale color; *(n):* a person with fair hair
blonde *(adj):* of a fair or pale color; *(n):* a girl or woman with fair hair

Blond furniture was really a fad many years ago.
The blonde lady, Susie Row, is 22 years old.

656 **boar • boor • bore**

boar *(n):* a wild hog; a male swine
boor *(n):* a crude and distasteful person
bore *(v):* to make a hole or passage; to make weary by being uninteresting; *(n):* a dull or tiresome person or thing

The Wingate boy showed a boar at the local country fair.
Although handsome, Cal is a boor.
I can't bore a hole here because the wood is too hard.
Ronnie became very bored listening to genealogy.

657 **breach • breech**

breach *(v):* to violate or break; *(n):* a break or interruption; a violation
breech *(n):* the lower or back part of a thing; the part of a gun behind the barrel

The XYZ Company will breach the contract if the first order is not filled by midnight.
He hit me with the breech of his rifle.

658 **breadth • breath • breathe**

breadth *(n):* width; scope
breath *(n):* air inhaled and exhaled
breathe *(v):* to inhale and exhale; to pause or rest

Ken's breadth of knowledge in accounting was very impressive.
As soon as I catch my breath, I will call 911!
My therapist told me to breathe at all times while I exercise; it is not, according to him, healthy to hold your breath when you exercise.

659 **brunet • brunette**

brunet *(adj):* of a dark-brown or black color; *(n):* a person with dark hair
brunette *(adj):* of a dark-brown or black color; *(n):* a girl or woman with dark hair

The brunet contestant won the title of "All American Male."
The brunette woman is a waitress at a local nightclub.

660 **business • busyness**

business *(n):* industry, function, field of endeavor
busyness *(n):* the state of being busy or active

His computer business had thrived for five years.
Janice's busyness kept her from worrying.

661 **cannon • canon**

cannon *(n):* a big gun; *(v):* to fire a cannon
canon *(n):* a religious regulation

They will fire a cannon at the Frontier Days festival.
The canon of meatless Fridays was observed by my family.

662 **canvas • canvass**

canvas *(n):* a rugged cloth
canvass *(v):* to examine or to solicit; *(n):* the act of canvassing

The tarpaulin for the limestone spreader was made of canvas.
Volunteers will canvass Myville for donations for the Labor Day telethon.

663 **capital • capitol**

capital *(adj):* very serious, excellent; relating to one's assets; *(n):* net worth; uppercased letter of the alphabet; a city serving as the seat of government
capitol *(n):* a building in which state or federal legislative bodies meet

His ideas sound good, but he has no capital to carry out his schemes.
Does he understand that he has been accused of a capital offense?
My apartment, which is at 1417 State Street, is only 13 blocks from the capitol.

664 **carat • caret • karat**

carat *(n):* a unit of weight for precious stones (variant of karat)
caret *(n):* a proofreading symbol used to show where something is to be added or changed
karat *(n):* a means for measuring the fineness of gold

The carat weight of the stone was unusually small.
Please insert a caret with another zero to state the exact amount of the loan, which is $100,000.
Until the karat purity of the gold can be measured, I cannot offer a price on the jewelry.

665 **causal • casual**

causal *(adj):* relating to cause and effect
casual *(adj):* informal

The size of inventory has a causal effect on price.
Their relationship appeared to be a casual friendship.

666 **cellar • seller**

cellar *(n):* a basement
seller *(n):* one who sells

The cellar is where the canned fruits and vegetables are stored.
The seller of the ranch-style house has lowered the price to $78,000.

667 **censer • censor • censure**

censer *(n):* a container for burning incense, usually in a religious setting
censor *(v):* to examine, looking for something objectionable; *(n):* a person who examines materials for something objectionable
censure *(n):* a reprimand or condemnation; *(v):* to criticize

The censer fell over, but David ran to pick it up.
She worked as a film censor for the government before she came to this country.
My opinion is they will censure her for immoral conduct.

668 **cession • session**

cession *(n):* a concession or yielding
session *(n):* a meeting or meetings

Thanks to her impressive income, we made an unusual cession-unlimited credit.
The ladies at the Business and Professional Women's state convention will be in session from 9 a.m. to 5 p.m. on Saturday.

669 **Chile • chili • chilly**

Chile *(n):* a South American nation
chili *(n):* a sweet or hot pepper; a sauce of chilies and meat (also spelled chile or chilli)
chilly *(adj):* cool

Do you have any desire to take a trip to Chile?
Most cooks in the American Southwest know how to make chili.
If it is going to be chilly tomorrow, I will wear a long-sleeve dress.

670 **chord • cord**

chord *(n):* several tones sounded together
cord *(n):* several strands of material twisted together; electrical cable; ribbed fabric; an anatomical part resembling a cord; a unit of wood cut for fuel; *(v):* to pile up wood in cords; to bind with a cord

She always messed up the G chord in that musical piece.
My neighbor sold me a cord of wood for $30.

671 **cite • sight • site**

cite *(v):* to refer to or quote from; to call upon officially to appear
sight *(n):* a spectacle; a panoramic or unusual view; vision; judgment; *(v):* to look at; to take aim
site *(n):* a place or location

I will cite a case from the "Northeastern Reporter."
The doctor told me that my sight has not deteriorated.
The site I have purchased to build a new house is along Highway 30.

672 **coarse • course**

coarse *(adj):* rough, crude, of inferior quality
course *(n):* route; planned program of instruction; *(v):* to traverse; to pursue

The fabric he used was too coarse.
The course for the road rally was set up by Ernie.

673 **complement • compliment**

complement *(n):* something that makes whole or satisfies; *(v):* to be complimentary to
compliment *(n):* an expression of praise or admiration; *(v):* to offer approval or praise

The red-and-green scarf will complement the red suit that I plan to wear to the Christmas party.
Miss Wirth, assistant director, complimented the faculty on how professional they looked yesterday.

674 **comprehensive • comprehensible**

comprehensive *(adj):* of large scope
comprehensible *(adj):* understandable

Henry asked the auditor to do a comprehensive audit of the records.
Henry made a long speech, but his meaning was incomprehensible to me.

675 **comprise • compose • constitute**

comprise *(v):* to contain
compose *(v):* to form or produce
constitute *(v):* to set up or compose

The graph comprised dollar figures for 1980-1990.
The graph was composed of dollar figures and percentages.
The graph constituted an evaluation of the company's health.

676 **confidant • confident**

confidant(e) *(n):* a person to whom one talks intimately
confident *(adj):* sure

I am confident that Jane can be trusted as a confidante.

677 **conscience • conscious**

conscience *(n):* an awareness of morality
conscious *(adj):* aware

It seemed to me, from our long discussions, that he had never developed a conscience.
The new students are so conscious of my principles; I commend them!

678 **continual • continuous**

continual *(adj):* occurring over and over again
continuous *(adj):* without interruption

His continual interruptions annoyed the speaker.
The continuous humming sound came from the apartment above us.

679 **consul • council • counsel**

consul *(n):* a government official appointed to live in a foreign country and to represent the appointing country
council *(n):* an assembly; governing body
counsel *(n):* advice; an attorney; deliberation; *(v):* to advise

The State Department will appoint a new consul immediately after his resignation.
Do you think there will be a council meeting tonight?
The counsel for the plaintiff comes from a town 50 miles from here.

680 **core • corps • corpse**

core *(n):* central part of something
corps *(n):* a group of persons having the same occupation, activity, or direction; military subgroup
corpse *(n):* a dead body

The university's core courses include several of the social sciences.
The Army Corps of Engineers monitor the level of water released through the gates every 12 hours.
The corpse was taken to Niles Funeral Home.

681 **corespondent • correspondent**

corespondent *(n):* an individual charged as being a paramour in a divorce suit
correspondent *(n):* an individual who is involved in writing letters or one who is a news reporter

Mr. Davis hesitated to question the person named corespondent in the Buckley divorce.
Harry Walker served as Rome correspondent for two years.

682 **descent • dissent**

descent *(n):* lineage or ancestry; a downward slope; attack; derivation
dissent *(v):* to have a different opinion; *(n):* a difference of opinion; ideological nonconformity

Aunt Tipple is taking my descent back to the 1800s.
Two of the members felt they should dissent on the matter.

683 **die • dye**

die *(v):* to end biologically; to expire; *(n):* singular of dice
dye *(v):* to color; *(n):* coloring matter

He threw the die and got a snake-eye, the winning roll.
When I die, I would like to be laid to rest in a mausoleum.
Do you think Nancy will dye her hair blonde?

684 **discreet • discrete**

discreet *(adj):* exercising careful judgment
discrete *(adj):* made up of distinct or unconnected elements

I will be discreet when I talk to Janice about personal hygiene.

The problem will be easier to solve if it is broken into discrete parts.

685 **discus • discuss**

discus *(n):* a heavy disk thrown as a test of strength and skill
discuss *(v):* to explore a topic in conversation or writing

The state discus competition is slated for 10:15 a.m. at an Indiana university.
I discuss grammar and punctuation with my students every day.

686 **dual • duel**

dual *(adj):* two
duel *(n):* contest; *(v):* to fight a duel

The driver education car had dual controls.
The duel traditionally took place under the old oak trees.
The contestants will duel with rapiers.

687 **elicit • illicit**

elicit *(v):* to bring out; to derive
illicit *(adj):* forbidden or disapproved

I will elicit help from the upperclassmen for the school play.
He swore that there was nothing illicit about his behavior with her.

688 **emerge • immerge**

emerge *(v):* to rise; to become clear
immerge *(v):* to plunge into; to become intensely involved

The truth will emerge when Jason goes to the office with the principal and one of his parents.
Ms. Gorbea immerged herself in the project to the extent that we seldom saw her.

689 **emigrate • immigrate**

emigrate *(v):* to leave one's native country to live elsewhere
immigrate *(v):* to move to a country that is not one's native country

He made the decision to emigrate rather than live under the new government.

Cheami's immigration to the United States came immediately after high school graduation.

690 **eminent • imminent**

eminent *(adj):* outstanding; famous
imminent *(adj):* about to occur

The speaker, Dr. Lowell Colemann, is an eminent physicist.
His election was considered imminent.

691 **envelop • envelope**

envelop *(v):* to enclose or surround
envelope *(n):* a wrapper or covering

When we have fog, it usually envelops the whole town.
Be sure to use the two-letter state abbreviation on the envelope when you type the address.

692 **exercise • exorcise**

exercise *(v):* to use; to exert; to use regularly to strengthen or develop; *(n):* the act of bringing into play; carrying out as per an agreement; bodily exertion for physical fitness
exorcise *(v):* to expel; to free oneself of

Every United States citizen should exercise his or her right to vote in the November election.
Exercise should be a part of daily routine in everyone's life.
He hoped his new life would exorcise his memories of the past.

693 **faint • feint**

faint *(v):* to lose consciousness; *(n):* sensation of dizziness and weakness; *(adj):* weak; cowardly; dim
feint *(n):* something feigned; *(v):* to make a pretense of

After having severe pain, Mr. Wright fainted in a gym.
His feint didn't work on this particular opponent.

694 **farther • further**

farther *(prep):* at a greater distance
further *(adj):* additional; *(v):* to advance or promote

It is farther for me to meet you in Chicago than it would be to meet you in St. Louis.

I had to have further information before I could make a decision.

695 **faze • phase**

faze *(v):* to upset or disturb
phase *(n):* period, stage, or cycle; *(v):* to introduce or carry out in stages

His ranting didn't faze Martha, but it drove Jude mad.
What phase of the project are you working on right now, Barbara?

696 **flair • flare**

flair *(n):* an ability or talent; style
flare *(n):* a glaring light or fire; a sudden outburst; *(v):* to shine; to become angry or excited

Mona just didn't have a flair for fashion.
The WBT truck driver put a flare along Interstate 1 to show that his unit was disabled.

697 **flaunt • flout**

flaunt *(v):* to display
flout *(v):* to scorn; to treat contemptuously; *(n):* an insult

The math teacher liked to flaunt his publications.
Edward flouted the association's rules and principles with an embarrassing regularity.

698 **foregone • forgone**

foregone *(adj):* past
forgone *(v):* to abstain from

Her release was a foregone conclusion.
Carl had forgone making any profit from the sale.

699 **foreword • forward**

foreword *(n):* a preface or introduction
forward *(adj):* bold; advanced; in front; *(v):* to send; to promote; *(prep):* in the direction of the front; *(n):* in sports, a player who is at the front of the formation

The foreword of Hogan's book was to be written by his associate, Warren Bourgeois.

The postmaster will forward my mail to my new address, 123 Hill Boulevard.

700 **formally • formerly**

formally *(prep):* done in traditional style
formerly *(prep):* previously

He formally withdrew from the campaign after the diagnosis.
Did you know that Jeremy Johnson was formerly known as John Jeremiah?

701 **foul • fowl**

foul *(n):* a breaking of a rule; *(adj):* distasteful, offensive; obscene; dirty; *(v):* to rot; to obstruct; to make dirty
fowl *(n):* any variety of bird

The referee called an exceptional amount of fouls at the basketball game last night.
Oscar hunted fowl, but he refused to hunt deer or moose.

702 **gilt • guilt**

gilt *(adj):* covered with gold; *(n):* gold or something that seems to be gold
guilt *(n):* a consciousness of having done wrong; culpability

The only items in the estate that interested me were the gilt-edged picture frames.
Mother's guilt became overwhelming.

703 **gorge • gouge**

gorge *(v):* to fill to capacity; *(n):* a narrow canyon
gouge *(v):* to shamefully overcharge; to poke; to scoop out a groove or channel; *(n):* a groove; a chisel

All of the family will gorge on Aunt Rita's cooking; she is superb!
We could see something bright red down in the gorge, but we couldn't be sure what it was.
I told her she had gouged my eye, but she turned away.

704 **grate • great**

grate *(n):* a framework of parallel or crisscrossed bars used for various purposes; *(v):* to annoy; to rub noisily; to rub into small pieces

great *(adj):* something significant or large; distinguished; grand

He dropped his keys down into the grate.
The infant's crying clearly grated on Aunt Patrice's nerves.
It is great to hear that Virginia will resume her college studies at Eureeka College.

705 **grisly • grizzly**

grisly *(adj):* causing horror or distaste
grizzly *(n):* species of bear; *(adj):* somewhat gray

The grisly scene caused Jenny to run out of the theatre.
How much do you think the grizzly in Yellowstone Park weighed?

706 **hangar • hanger**

hangar *(n):* a structure designed for storage, usually of aircraft
hanger *(n):* a device from which something is suspended

The hangar was damaged when a four-passenger plane ran into it, but the plane inside was undamaged.
I use durable plastic hangers for my heavy winter garments.

707 **heal • heel**

heal *(v):* to mend; to bring back to health
heel *(n):* the back of the foot; the bottom part of something; a contemptible person

The cut on Linda's arm just wouldn't heal.
Miss Gale's heel was injured in the auto accident.

708 **hew • hue**

hew *(v):* to shape or cut with blows
hue *(n):* color; aspect

He used a small hatchet to hew the wood.
The hues in the hot-air balloon are all bright and cheerful.

709 **hoard • horde**

hoard *(v):* to store up; to keep to oneself; *(n):* that which is hoarded
horde *(n):* a large crowd; a swarm

My friend will hoard her tomatoes.
There was a horde of people at the semiannual sale.

710 **incite • insight**

incite *(v):* to move to action; to stir up
insight *(n):* discernment; ability to see clearly

Mr. Miller will incite his employee to strike.
Tien's grandmother often offered insight and advice to us when we had problems.

711 **incredible • incredulous**

incredible *(adj):* unbelievable
incredulous *(adj):* unbelieving

The stuntman's incredible feats pleased the crowd.
The incredulous crowd stared silently at the stuntman's feats.

712 **ingenious • ingenuous**

ingenious *(adj):* unusually clever
ingenuous *(adj):* natural; without guile

Beth is ingenious when it comes to surprising people on their birthdays.
Although Edith seemed ingenuous, she could be manipulative and deceitful.

713 **insipient • incipient**

insipient *(adj):* stupid
incipient *(adj):* just starting to exist

The insipient woman insisted on a refund despite her obvious abuse of the appliance.
Her incipient disease showed only a few effects.

714 **lead • led**

lead *(v):* to guide or direct; to be first; to open or begin; *(n):* the one in front position; a clue; a metal
led *(v):* past tense and past participle of the verb lead

Ann will lead the church choir at the Easter service.
Following his lead, we got through those difficult passages.
I needed a No. 2 lead pencil to take the examination, but all I had was a pen.
Gracie led the search party to the site of the plane crash.

715 **lesser • lessor**

lesser *(adj):* smaller, less, or less important
lessor *(adj):* someone from whom one leases something

I chose the dessert with the lesser amount of calories.
The lessor, Mr. Johnson, is my uncle.

716 **liable • libel**

liable *(adj):* responsible
libel *(n):* unflattering, malicious, or damaging portrayal (written or printed)

Zetta was liable for the destruction of the vase.
I didn't think the comments in my letter could be considered libel!

717 **lightening • lightning**

lightening *(n):* relieving; lessening
lightning *(n):* atmospheric electricity

My paperwork has lightened since my aide was employed.
The thunder and lightning interrupted the football game.

718 **loath • loathe**

loath *(adj):* reluctant
loathe *(v):* to detest

Principal Mason will be loath to fire Mr. Timmons, but it will be in the best interest of the students and the school to take this action.
I didn't loathe Mr. Wollin, but I couldn't respect him or really like him.

719 **loose • lose**

loose *(adj):* not firmly attached
lose *(v):* to suffer the loss of; to fail to win; to get rid of

Joann's dress is loose because she has lost 25 pounds.
He knew he would lose his role if he missed rehearsal.

720 **mantel • mantle**

mantel *(n):* top of a fireplace
mantle *(n):* cape or cloak

The crystal vase fell from the mantel when the wind blew in.
The mantle of leadership was passed to James Rutherford.

721 **medal • meddle • metal**

medal *(n):* a piece of metal given for commemorative or religious purposes or as an award
meddle *(v):* to interfere in matters not one's concern
metal *(n):* any of various opaque, durable, ductile substances that are good conductors of heat and electricity

He treasured his athletic medals and would never have thrown them out.
Uncle Pat like to meddle in Tim's business.
My brother Jay deals in precious metals— gold, silver, and nickel.

722 **monetary • monitory**

monetary *(adj):* having to do with money
monitory *(adj):* serving to warn

The monetary units for all nations may be found in an up-to-date dictionary.
The monitory tone of his letters concerned me.

723 **nauseous • nauseated**

nauseous *(adj):* causing nausea
nauseated *(adj):* experiencing nausea

Sheila flinched at the nauseous spectacle.
Sheila was nauseated by what she witnessed.

724 **naval • navel**

naval *(adj):* pertaining to a navy or ships
navel *(n):* a depression in the middle of the abdomen; a central point

A naval commander will speak to a group of seniors in April.
My aunt told us to use mineral oil to clean the baby's navel.

725 **palate • palette • pallet**

palate *(n):* the roof of the mouth; sense of taste
palette *(n):* a board on which an artist mixes colors
pallet *(n):* a mattress or temporary bed; a portable platform; a wooden instrument with a flat blade

I burned my palate when I was eating French fries.
The artist's palette held only various shades of the same color.
There are Hotpoint dishwashers sitting on pallets in the warehouse.

726 **passed • past**

passed *(v):* past tense of pass
past *(adj):* bygone; *(n):* a time that has gone by; *(prep):* beyond; *(prep):* at an end

Every student passed the math exam.
Jolene is a past president of Zonta.

727 **peak • peek • pique**

peak *(n):* the high point or top; *(v):* to bring to a conclusion or reach the maximum; *(adj):* at or near the maximum
peek *(v):* to glance; to look furtively; *(n):* a brief look
pique *(v):* to cause resentment or anger; to arouse; *(n):* resentment; wounded pride

The peak of Edwin's running career could be his senior year in college.
The feud peaked with Nell's decision to leave.
Will you take a peek at my new Cutlass.
Dawn was piqued when Jim never came to take her to the show.

728 **peal • peel**

peal *(n):* a loud sound; *(v):* to give out peals; to resound or ring
peel *(n):* the rind or skin of a fruit; *(v):* to remove the outer layer

The peal of the church bells occurred at noon on Sundays.
The orange peel lying on the floor caused Gretchen to slip.
Aunt Helen peeled 20 pounds of potatoes for potato salad.

729 **pedal • peddle • petal**

pedal *(n):* a foot lever; *(v):* to use pedals; *(adj):* pertaining to the foot
peddle *(v):* to offer for sale
petal *(n):* the part of a flower that is usually the colorful part

Joshua, a first grader, can pedal his bike for 1 mile nonstop.
Greg was anxious to peddle his goods, and his enthusiasm was catching.
The flower girl dropped petals of roses along the runner.

730 **peer • pier**

peer *(v):* to look closely and searchingly; *(n):* someone of equal status
pier *(n):* a supporting structure; a structure on or in the water

I peered at the address on the envelope but couldn't make it out.
Mrs. King's peers gave her an excellent evaluation.
Pier 19 is frequented by John, Jeff, Jason on weekends.

731 **personal • personnel**

personal *(adj):* having to do with a person; private
personnel *(n):* employees, staff

Tara takes care of Mrs. Light's personal business.
The personnel stay at school until 4:05 p.m.

732 **plaintiff • plaintive**

plaintiff *(n):* the complaining party or parties in a litigation
plaintive *(adj):* expressive of sadness or suffering

Mr. Ryann represented the plaintiff, Joe Gray.
The plaintive wails seemed to come from the wooded area.

733 **precedence • precedents**

precedence *(n):* something given higher importance; preference
precedents *(n):* actions of the past that may serve as an example or rule to justify similar actions in the future

Precedence will be given to all seniors who plan to attend college in the fall.
Precedents do not suggest a large settlement in this case.

734 **principal • principle**

principal *(adj):* most important; *(n):* a person of leading authority; a capital sum; the person primarily responsible
principle *(n):* a law; a doctrine; a code of conduct

Todd's high school principal resigned.
The principal plus interest will be $81,610.29.
My principles wouldn't allow me to go along with that scheme.

735 **rational • rationale**

rational *(adj):* able to think logically
rationale *(n):* an explanation or reason

Our decision to move seemed like a rational one at the time.
Amy's rationale for buying a Toyota was the excellent gas mileage.

736 **reign • rein**

reign *(n):* the time during which one has power; sovereignty; *(v):* to rule.
rein *(n):* a strip of leather used to guide a horse; something that controls or guides; *(v):* to stop or slow down

Father reigned over the entire family like an emperor.
I pulled at the reins, but the horse continued to gallop wildly through the field.
Ellen's parents tried to keep a tight rein on her social activities.

737 **respectfully • respectively**

respectfully *(prep):* in a manner showing respect or deference
respectively *(prep):* in the order named

Uncle John spoke to all our relatives respectfully at the Waddington Reunion.
The interviews will be conducted with Miss Hardwood, Mr. Benton, and Mr. Cooper, respectively

738 **right • rite • wright • write**

right *(adj):* correct; *(n):* privilege; *(v):* to make amends for; to restore; *(prep):* correctly; immediately
rite *(n):* ceremony
wright *(n):* a suffix meaning worker
write *(v):* to compose

We were trying to right all the wrongs we'd done.
Masonic rites are scheduled for 7:30 p.m. tonight.
The playwright filed suit alleging copyright violations.
I will write a letter to Cecelia and mail it Saturday.

739 **role • roll**

role *(n):* capacity; function

roll *(n):* a rotating movement; a list of names; *(v):* to rotate on an axis; to turn over and over

The role of assistant superintendent was very clear to Mr. Martin.
At the end of the school day, Kathy will take her roll sheet to the office.

740 **rote • wrote**

rote *(n):* a routine, mechanical way of doing something; *(adj):* mechanical
wrote *(v):* past tense of write

His rote recitation held no emotion or understanding and moved no one.
Malea wrote her essay on physical therapy.

741 **shear • sheer**

shear *(n):* one blade of a pair of shears; *(v):* to cut or trim
sheer *(adj):* thin or transparent; steep; pure; *(v):* to deviate or turn aside

A new pair of shears will trim the hedge quite nicely.
I had to shear off about a quarter of the excess.
My sheer nylons look very nice with my business suit.

742 **sleight • slight**

sleight *(n):* skill, deceitful craftiness; trick or stratagem
slight *(adj):* slim; frail; insignificant; *(n):* an act of discourtesy; *(v):* to neglect

She interpreted his early departure as a sleight to avoid further questioning.
There will be a slight delay in our departure.

743 **stationary • stationery**

stationary *(adj):* unmoving or unchanging
stationery *(n):* writing paper and envelopes

Riding a stationary bike is a daily exercise for Paul.
The letters CEW were on Connie's new stationery products.

744 **taught • taut**

taught *(v):* past tense of teach
taut *(adj):* tight

I have taught legal terminology for many years.
The rope was too taut during our move, and it marred my piano.

745 **throe • throw**

throe *(n):* violent spasm
throw *(v):* to toss; *(n):* the act of tossing

The child appeared to be in the throes of agony.
I can throw a softball from first to second base.

746 **timber • timbre**

timber *(n):* lumber
timbre *(n):* a distinctive quality of sound

Arlene owns 15 acres of timber north of town.
Her timbre in the Schubert songs was rich and lovely.

747 **treaties • treatise**

treaties *(n):* formal agreements
treatise *(n):* a written discussion

Treaties on environmental issues have been signed with a dozen countries.
Professor Sanda's treatise on the ethics of capitalism will be published.

748 **troop • troupe**

troop *(n):* a group of soldiers; a collection of people or things; *(v):* to walk, especially in a group
troupe *(n):* a company, especially theatrical; *(v):* to travel in a troupe

The Girl Scout troop will go on an overnight outing to Spittler Woods.
He was working on a history of the German theatre troupe.

749 **trustee • trusty**

trustee *(n):* someone to whom something is entrusted; one who legally administers on behalf of another person
trusty *(adj):* dependable; *(n):* a trusted person who is granted special privileges, especially a convict

Alexandria has been appointed a trustee for the estate of Walter Wellington.

Ben always called Peter his trusty sidekick.

750 **waive • wave**

waive *(v):* to surrender voluntarily
wave *(n):* a swell of water; a curve; a surge of emotion; a hand gesture; *(v):* to flutter; to gesture in greeting or farewell

He waived his right to an attorney.
He waved farewell to us as he drove away.
Class, please wave as the plane with our servicemen and servicewomen approaches the runway!

Exercise

A. Select and underline the correct word or words in each of the following sentences.

1. Hayley, an (ingenious, ingenuous) young woman, trusted Lenny and told him her personal business, which he later used against her.
2. The proposed (cite, sight, site) for the municipal auditorium has stirred up a controversy.
3. Try as I might, I could find no (insight, incite) into the problem, not even from talking with my best friend, C.J.
4. This arsonist has (alluded, eluded) the law until now.
5. My (conscience, conscious) demanded that I come forward with everything I knew about the crime.
6. He (cited, sighted) numerous (precedence, precedents) for the action.
7. What a (capital, capitol) idea!
8. Thomas made no secret of the fact that he was (adverse, averse) to your plan.
9. Morris has had (monetary, monitory) problems ever since he lost his job last year.
10. The (ascent, assent) to the waterfalls is steep and rocky.
11. We tried to (boar, boor, bore) holes in the brick wall to mount the painting.
12. (Censer, Censor, Censure) meant the end of the Senator's career.

13. This applicant's salary demands (accede, exceed) the company's financial ability.

14. Was such disclosure considered a (breach, breech) of confidence?

15. Manfred's (boarish, boorish, borish) manners caused his wife great embarrassment.

16. The patient's (breath, breathe) was irregular and faint.

17. We walked over to the (capital, capitol) building together at 3:15 p.m.

18. Did Mr. Gray give his (ascent, assent) to these changes?

19. I just couldn't (bare, bear) to see his humiliation; I left the room.

20. Jamie offered to (canvas, canvass) the eastern part of town so that the quota might be met.

21. The attorney frequently (alluded, eluded) to Jim Mason's past record.

22. The (cannon, canons) of the church have been challenged before.

23. Jacob's idea, hailed as an (ingenious, ingenuous) achievement, saved the company a bundle of money.

24. The orchestra was (lead, led) by a last-minute substitute that evening, causing an uneven performance.

25. My in-laws never tried to (meddle, medal, metal) in our marital problems.

26. Lee's cousin was (loath, loathe) to testify against a member of his family.

27. Willie and I (pealed, peeled) potatoes until our hands were sore.

28. The (plaintiff, plaintive) sounds may have been from someone who was injured or sick.

29. My grandmother (hoarded, horded) family photographs and memorabilia, allowing no one to see her treasures.

30. The kids slept on (palates, palettes, pallets) in the basement.

31. I couldn't resist taking a (peak, peek) into the newly decorated room.

32. Betsy's constant complaining (incited, insighted) discontent in the entire office staff.

33. Harold's interest in astronomy (peaked, peeked, piqued) and then declined.

34. Calling Ned all those awful names could be considered (liable, libel).

35. The interest payable on the loan was twice the amount of the (principal, principle).

36. The sun shone on the (medal, meddle, metal), blinding me for a moment.

37. Barlow couldn't (pedal, peddle, petal) up the hill to our house.

38. The room was done in various (hews, hues) of pink and green.

39. A (hoard, horde) of people gathered at the hall of justice to see the infamous criminal.

40. Kane (flaunted, flouted) his wealth rarely, but he was outrageous when he did.

41. My problems seemed to (envelop, envelope) me in a cloud of gloom and depression.

42. Although I knew of his resignation weeks before it occurred, Franklin's announcement was not made (formally, formerly) until June.

43. I (gorged, gouged) myself on pizza until I felt sick.

44. Maria's (flair, flare) for floral design was useful to us.

45. I had intended to (cite, sight, site) several authorities in my argument.

46. We were never (conscience, conscious) of any subversive activities.

47. Jeanne (fainted, feinted) an attack on her brother and then slugged Carmine.

48. I had to get permission from Jane Dunham to give Mr. Clary (access, excess) to the files in my office.

49. Although he is a popular young man, Mack's suspension is considered to be (eminent, imminent).

50. We watched a (grisly, grizzly) horror movie on cable television.

51. The headmaster demanded strict (adherence, adherents) to the established code of conduct.

52. The student (council, counsel, consul) will meet every Tuesday afternoon; class representatives were elected last month.

53. Maynard (gorged, gouged) a hole into the wood with a screwdriver.
54. Ben felt like a (heal, heel) when he told Jennifer the bad news.
55. Cory was finally (emerging, immerging) from his depression, but then a disaster occurred that put him back down again.
56. The chairman certainly pulled the (reigns, reins) on his ambitions.
57. The (shear, sheer) fabric of the curtains enabled us to see what was going on in the dining room.
58. Charita's personal (stationary, stationery) was an elegant ivory parchment trimmed with gold.
59. Professor Behrmann seldom called (role, roll) in his morning classes.
60. Tony never (flaunted, flouted) his bankroll at work, but it was a different story when he went out in the evening.
61. The (elicit, illicit) photographs were published years after they were taken.
62. Because there was an (access, excess) of office supplies, no orders were made for a couple of months.
63. Although no insult was intended, Miss Emmanuel felt we had (sleighted, slighted) her and her family.
64. We tried to secure the trunk with a piece of (chord, cord), but it was hopeless.
65. His (eminence, imminence) in his field is evidenced by the number of awards he has won.
66. All of my (allusions, elusions, illusions) about Josh's character were shattered abruptly that night.
67. When my brother was tense or angry, he'd go out to the field and (bail, bale) hay or do something else physically rigorous.
68. Green (die, dye) dripped all over the carpet and left ugly stains.
69. No one expected Robert to (accede, exceed) to his former wife's enormous financial demands.
70. (Adverse, Averse) publicity disturbed the candidate for mayor.
71. Lunch consisted of (chili, chilly), crackers, and soda.
72. Hal had (emerged, immerged) himself in his work.

73. Jena felt that her intellectual development had been (stationary, stationery).

74. The film was rated as obscene by the (censers, censors, censures).

75. Dr. Mimi's (consul, council, counsel) to Jan was that she should go ahead.

76. The book's (foreward, forward) helped me understand what the author was attempting to say.

10
THE FINAL PRODUCT

751 Paragraphing

The purpose of paragraphing is basically the same as that of punctuation: to make reading easier, clearer, and smoother. A new paragraph signals a shift or change of some kind. Often a speaker will go on at considerable length—in jury charges, opening and closing remarks of the attorneys, etc. The CR should break up such long passages into smaller units, or paragraphs, for the reader's sake. A page of unbroken lines appears forbidding.

Although there is no ironclad number of lines or sentences that comprise the ideal paragraph, some general guidelines can be set forth. A single paragraph should run no longer than eight to ten lines and no shorter than four to five lines. One-sentence paragraphs are considered undesirable. There are, of course, situations in which they cannot be avoided.

Often a speaker seems to ramble on and on about a single subject. Even in long recitations of this kind, there are natural breaks—shifts in topic, tone, and approach. The CR should be alert to these logical points for paragraphing.

Some situations demand paragraphing regardless of the length of the resulting paragraphs. For example, during Q and A, it is common for another speaker to enter: the Court may ask a question or make a comment, or another attorney may raise an objection. This is called colloquy. The CR should start a new paragraph for each new speaker and for each new person addressed.

752 Enumerations

Enumerations can be handled in one of two ways. A short enumeration is incorporated into the body of the sentence that introduces it; a lengthy enumeration is set off from straight text, with each item in a separate paragraph.

The second format is commonly used for courtroom material like the following:

1. Components of the jury's decision
2. Terms of stipulation
3. Grounds for making a motion
4. The judge's opinion
5. The judge's charge

Note that the items in a lengthy enumeration are not followed by periods unless they are complete sentences.

Enumerations may occur numbered or unnumbered. For those that are numbered, if the speaker used ordinals (first, second, third, etc.), write out the words rather than using numerals. If the speaker used one, two, three, etc., use figures.

> First, you do not have the facts straight; second, you are misinterpreting the applicable law; third, you are jeopardizing your own reputation and career.
>
> BUT:
>
> I have to say to you that (1) you do not have your facts straight; (2) you are misinterpreting the applicable law; and (3) you are jeopardizing your own reputation and career.

Remember to use semicolons to separate items in an enumeration when the enumeration is incorporated within the sentence.

753 Spacing

The following are a few rules for spacing correctly within your document:

1. Space twice after each sentence, whether the sentence ends with a period, a question mark, an exclamation point, or a quotation mark.
2. Space twice after a colon, except in expressions of time (e.g., 4:35 p.m.) and in citations (e.g., Genesis 5:12).
3. A dash is written by typing two unspaced hyphens. There is no space before the hyphens and none after—unless the dash occurs at the end of a sentence.
4. Do not space before or after a virgule, except when it is used to separate lines of poetry.
5. Space once after a semicolon and once after a comma.
6. Do not space before a comma, semicolon, colon, closing quotation mark, closing parenthesis, or period.

7. Do not space after an opening quotation mark or after an opening parenthesis.
8. For long quotations, indent an additional five to ten spaces from the left margin. Some use an indentation of five to ten spaces on the right side as well. Use an opening quotation mark at the beginning of each new paragraph, but use a closing quotation mark only at the end of the final paragraph of the quotation, not at the end of each paragraph.

754 Proofreading

Proofreading your work is one of the most important steps in producing a first-class document. Although it is sometimes difficult to put forth the effort, this step deserves full attention and extreme care.

There are basically two types of errors: content errors and mechanical errors. Content errors are problems with logic—when the words are technically correct but do not make sense. Lack of consistency is another kind of content error. Mechanical errors include typos, punctuation problems, capitalization errors, and mistakes in formatting.

Because the two types of errors are so fundamentally different, it is highly advisable that the work be read at least twice—once for content and once for mechanical errors. Reading for content means making sure the words make sense. This process is completely different from searching for mechanical errors. The following are a few suggestions for effective proofreading:

1. Proofreading demands concentration and thus should be done at a slower speed than one's normal reading speed.
2. Some CRs find it helpful to use a ruler under the line being proofread to increase concentration.
3. When pondering over punctuation, remember that less is usually, though certainly not always, preferable to more.
4. Do not hesitate to use reference materials to the degree necessary (see Unit 12). A good dictionary is an indispensable tool for the CR.
5. Use the American rather than the British spelling, for example, civilization, not civilisation.
6. Always use the preferred spelling of a word. This is the form given first in the dictionary entry.

7. Check numbers with extra care.
8. Watch for homonyms or easily confused words (for example, their, there, and they're; to, too, and two; your and you're; its and it's), as misuse can result in embarrassing errors.
9. Do not spend an inordinate amount of time debating whether compounds should be written open, hyphenated, or solid. Use your dictionary, and if the term in question is not in the dictionary, assume it is written as an open compound (i.e., separate words).
10. Remember to paragraph for the sake of your reader. Make an effort to find suitable points at which to break up long passages.
11. Use standard proofreading symbols and use them correctly (see Illus. 10-1 and 10-2).
12. After corrections have been made, proofread to ensure that the corrections have been made properly without introducing new errors.

Miscellaneous

There are many things a CR must know and do other than those presented in this text. For example, a sound understanding of legal terminology is essential, but this is gained through courses and experience. Nonetheless, a few last-minute notes of a miscellaneous nature will be made here—in no particular order—to tie things up that may have been omitted earlier.

755 **The CR's Worksheet**

The CR should provide his/her scopist or transcriptionist with information peculiar to the transcript being prepared. This worksheet can be arranged either in alphabetical order or in order of occurrence, although many scopists and transcriptionists find an alphabetical list easier to work with. Correct spellings of persons' names are essential to the worksheet, as are other proper names, such as names of towns, companies, etc. Technical and/or medical terminology that is not general knowledge should also be included. Of course, the worksheet should state clearly the title-page information, i.e., the court and case number, etc.

756 **Nonwords**

Witnesses often mumble something that the CR should include in the transcript. Of course, the CR should not attempt to record every sound made by every witness, but certain utterances can be indicated. For example,

uh-huh (yes)
huh? (what?)
unh-unh or uh-uh (no)

Illustration 10.1

The following are proofreading symbols standard to every profession. Those that seem to have no application to the CR industry are not included here.

¶	New paragraph
no ¶	No new paragraph
	Delete
	Close up
	Delete and close up
#	Insert space
	Transpose
][	Center horizontally
	Center vertically
=	Align horizontally
||	Align vertically
[	Move to the left
]	Move to the right
	Move up
	Move down
	Move as shown
	Connect copy
(stet)	Let it stand (used in margin)
......	Let it stand (used within text)
(sp)	Spell out the numeral or abbreviation
^	Caret—used to indicate where material is to be inserted or to mark the position of an error
lc	Lowercase (used in margin)
/	Lowercase (used within text)
	Make all lowercase letters
cap	Caps (used in margin)
≡	Caps (used within text)
	Insert comma
⊙	Insert period
	Insert apostrophe (or single quotation mark)
	Insert quotation marks
?	Insert question mark
!	Insert exclamation point
(:)	Insert colon
;	Insert semicolon
=/	Insert hyphen
1/M	Insert dash
{ }	Insert parentheses
[/]	Insert brackets

Illustration 10.2

The following passage shows how proofreading symbols can be used to make corrections in your work.

When I got home, my Husband and my Son were scramming and shoutting, fighting over something but I didnt know what. I heard their voices even before I got in the house.

I called out, Sam, Sam, What's going on in there? but noone answered me. so I went into the house through the back and realized that they were in the living room. I saw Sam backed up agianst the wall with my husband striking at him. Sam had his hands up over his face He was trying toprotect himself from my husband's blows.

The Court: Mrs. Freemont, could you please speak a little louder.

WITNESS: Yes, Your Honor. Sorry

THE COURT: Continue with your account, then.

Q. Your husband--is he Sam's father?

A. No. am's father died when Sam was just a BABY. I married Sheperd when Sam was 12 yrs old.

Q. All right, Mrs. Freemont. What happened when you entered the living room?

A. I started yelling at Sheperd to stop. Just kept on striking out at Sam, sometimes hitting and sometimes not. I began to pull on Shep myself to try to get him away from Sam, and at first he paid no attention to me; but then he turned around and slapped me hard across my face. I could seethat Sam was going to jump on Shep, and I was afriad that Shep would kill my son. I was right. Sam jumped on Shep's back, but Shep easily threw him off. Sam was lying on the floor whn Shep put his boot on Sam's chest and pushed down. Sam was screaming in pain. That's when I picked up the vase and hit Shep on the head. It didn't know him out, though, and he turned on me. He hit me repeatedly until I could hardly see straight. In the mean time, Sam had run out of the room and had gotten Shep's rifle. He pointed it right at Shep and said to him-and these are his exact words-he said, "Stop hitting ma or I'll shoot! Shep laughted and lunged at Sam. Then I heard the gun go of. It was horrilbe. Sam was crying, and Shep was just lajying there on the carpet. I thought he was dead, but when I leaned over him, he grabbed my ankel.

757 Format of a Deposition

CRs can find themselves in a variety of settings other than the courtroom; whatever the circumstances, the final product must accomplish its goal of reproducing, in written form, what was said and what transpired. There is an elastic format, seen in several variant styles from state to state, that accommodates most hearings, depositions, and other situations. The CR's employer will specify the details.

The first page of the format usually includes the name of the court, the case or docket number, the names of plaintiffs and defendants, the name of the deponent included in that particular volume, and finally the name of the CR who did the recording. Following the title sheet is usually the appearance page, on which are listed the names and addresses of all attorneys involved in the deposition. Also included are the names of people who were present waiting to be deposed in subsequent hearings, paralegals, or perhaps third party attorneys who play no role in that particular deposition. The next page consists of legal explanation(s) for what transpired during the deposition. Finally, the deponent is identified, and it is stated that this individual has been sworn. The questioning attorney is identified and the Q and A begins.

This is a general, loose idea of format; but it must be stressed that the CR will follow the format of his/her employer and state. There is generally a final sheet asserting the CR's impartial status.

758 Examinations

The CR should identify carefully each type of examination being conducted, e.g., Direct Examination, Cross Examination, Redirect Examination, Recross Examination, Voir Dire Examination, Rebuttal, Surrebuttal, Examination.

759 Computer-Aided Transcription

Because the computer has in its memory steno brief forms and their English equivalents, the CR can have a rough-copy transcript on which adjustments and corrections can be made before the machine prints the final copy or copies, However, the computer cannot replace the CR's need for sound grammar and punctuation skills. The CR must construct a good, accurate personal dictionary so that misspellings will not be perpetuated.

Most computer-aided transcription systems, although fast, will be faster still in the future and will demand even more sophisticated English skills from their users.

Exercise

The following exercise is part of a deposition. As stated in section 757, the format will vary from firm to firm and from state to state. As you type the question-and-answer material, use the correct spelling, capitalization, commas, periods, semicolons, and hyphens. Apply all rules that you have learned up to this point.

Follow these guidelines:

1. A deposition will normally be bound at the left side.
2. Only 25 lines of typing on an 8 1/2 by 11 inch sheet of paper.
3. Double space the Q and A.
4. Each Q and A starts on a separate line.
5. Start the Q and A at the left margin with 5 spaces from the Q and A to begin the text. If there is any carryover of the Q and A, go back to the left margin.
6. If you use paper that is not ruled bond paper, the left margin should be 1 3/4 inches; and the right margin should be 3/8 inches. DO NOT GO OUTSIDE THE MARGINS!
7. If you use a piece of typing paper that is not numbered at the left-hand side, start typing on line 8.

A. QUESTIONING BY MR. BROWN

Q. Will you state your name, please sir.
A. Yes, sir, My name is William Robert Taft.
Q. Will you spell your name, please letter by letter Mr. taft.
A. William, W-i-l-l-i-a-m; Robert, R-o-b-e-t, Taft, T-A-F-T.
Q. You are a resident of Chicago, Illinois; is that right?
A. Yes, sir. My street address is 1296 Irving Park road.
Q. Mr. Taft you were born in the mid-30s?
A. Yes sir. I was born in 1935.
Q. If in any way I state any facts that are not up-to-date, will you correct me, please sir?
A. Yes, Mr. Browne.
Q. You entered medical school out east about 1955 and re-entered school in 1960 after a three-year stinte with the United States army?
A. That is correct, sir.
Q. You are a doctor of—
A. Radeology.

Q. —radiology. OK, sir. That means you are an expert in radiology, or you are an X-ray specialist?

A. Yes, sir.

Q. Do you no a Mr. James.

A. Mr. Ashton James from Rockford?

Q Yes sir.

A. Yes sir, I do.

Q. How is it you know Mr. James; or how did you become acquainted with Mr. Ashton James?

A. I first met Ashton about—

11
CUMULATIVE EXERCISES

A. Correct all errors in the following:

Q. Would you state your full name for the record please?
A. Benjamin Michael O'Keefe
Q. What is your home address Sir?
A. I live at 52 Bailey Dr., Millerville Tennessee.
Q. And your age Mr. O'Keefe.
A. I'll be 80 in July, which means I'm--
Q. What is your present age?
A. 79 now.
Q. Where were you born at?
A. Brooklyn New York.
Q. Are you married?
A. I was married for thirty-nine years, but my wife her name was Sarah, died 5 yrs. ago.
Q. You are a widower then, is that correct?
A. Oh no, I'm married again; just last year, To this pretty young woman whose my wife now.
Q. What is your wifes name?
A. Sarah Baker O'Keefe.
Q. Your current wife's name is Sarah?
A. I'm sorry, her name is Theresa Sampson O'Keefe.
Q. Is she here? In this room today?
A. Yes, She is.
Q. Did you make a trip over seas last September?
A. Yes, I went to Ireland and Scotland.
Q. How did you travel?
A. I went with the Gate's, my friend's and neighbor's since the nineteen forties.
Q. What I meant, Mr. O'Keefe is this: By what mean's did you travel to Europe?

A. We flew. In an airplane.
Q. What was you're date of departure?
A. I left on Sept. eleventh.
Q. With which air line did you fly, do you remember?
A. I don't recall.
Q. Was this your 1st time to fly?
A. In my life time?
Q. Yes sir.
A. No -- I had flown many times with my job.
Q. What kind of work do you do?
A. I don't do any thing, I've been retired now for several years.
Q. Alright. What work did you do before retirement?
A. I was an engineer with Cal-Tex International Oil Company.
Q. What is your educational back ground?
A. I have a BS Degree in structural engineering from Boston Univ.
Q. Was your wife with you on this trip last September?
A. My wife? She was with me; yes.
Q. Where in the plane were your seats?
A. Are asking if they were first-class seats?
Q. No, sir, I am asking in what section of the plane were you seated; For example, in the rear, the middle, the front?
A. Oh, I see. Well I think you could say we were about mid way.
Q. You were approximately in the center section?
A. More or less.
Q. Were you seated by the window in the aisle or in a center seat?
A. I was on the aisle, and my wife was next to me.
Q. Was this the smoking or non-smoking section of the plane?
A. We don't smoke.
Q. You were in the Non-Smoking Section is that right?
A. That's right.
Q. Tell us how the accident occurred?
A. I got up to go to the bath room. And I was walking down the isle to go down their.
Q. And then what happened?
A. This stewardess was pushing a cart full of Soft Drinks and coffee. All of sudden, I can't

tell you why. The cart turned over. The Stewardess sort of lunged forward which pushed the cart at me. The darned thing fell over on me.

Q. What were your injurys?

A. I had a broken bone in the bottom part of my leg and a bunch of bruises.

Q. Was that the extent of your injuries?

A. Some broken glass cut up my arm and face. I was sore all over.

Q. Did you see a dr. about these injurys?

A. Well sure I did.

Q. What was the name of the physician you saw, do you recall?

A. His name was Dr. Bradford.

Q. Where did you see him?

A. I saw him in his office.

Q. Where was his office?

A. I cant recall the address.

Q. Was his office some where in London?

A. That's right. After we landed in London, they took me to see Dr. Bradford.

Q. Who took you?

A. A taxi cab was arranged for me by the airline.

Q. What treatment did you receive their?

A. He set my leg in a cast.

Q. Did this Doctor Bradford do anything else for you?

A. He gave me medicine for pain.

B. The following jury charge contains a variety of errors. Find and correct all errors.

Members Of The Jury, when I have concluded my charge, I will give the case to you for determination and at that time you will take this case and you will render what ever Verdict you in your good and clear conscience and valid judgement appears to you to be the proper verdict or judgment. This trial is conducted under the laws of the state of N. Carolina and it's officials have here sought to show that under the laws of that state the accused Darnell Jarvis Morrison has violated the criminal laws there in. The defendant has pleated not guilty to all 3 counts. I will take all three count's and explain the pertinent Laws for each.

Count No. 1 allages that the defendant on the evening or night of Oct. 14, 1985 stole equipment from the office of the department of transportation. This equipment included the following items, an I.B.M selectric III type writer, two adding machines, two tape-recorders, an electric pencil sharpener, and 4 boxes of computer paper. In order to convinct the defendant of those charges of theft you must be satisfied that the government has proved beyond any reasonable doubt the following elements: that the defendent stole the goods here to fore listed, that the defendant acted wilfuly and knowingly, and with intent to deprive the rightfull owner of these goods, that the good's total value was over one hundred dollars. In order for goods to be stolen they must have been taken unlawfully, it does not have to be proved that the defendant intended to sell these goods, however it must be proved tha possession was taken unlawfully and with intent to deprive the owner of such possession. If you find that the goods were unlawfully removed from said Dept. of Transportation that the se goods were taken with intent to take them into his possession and for his own use whether that use be to sell or to keep then you must find a verdict of guilty. Remember that to steal something means that the defendant took possession of the stolen items having power and control over said items and this was done so unlawfully that is contrary to the laws of this state. Ladies and gentlemen, I will not reiterate the testimony that you have heard in this case I will instead rely on your recollection of what has been said in this court room. Remember that it is the duty of the state to prove the guilt of this and any defendant it is not up to the defendant to prove his inocence.

C. Make corrections in the following passage.

We are here tonight to discuss the proposed new building which if constructed would be built on Gordon Rd. on 5 acres of land, now owned by a Doctor and Missus Ralph Koule of Bennington, Vt. On Oct. fourth, 1986 a letter was sent to the Koule's inquiring about there possible interest in selling that parcel of land, we recod a reply from them on Nov. 11 stating that they would be willing to sell the land for twenty-two thousand five-hundred dollars. If we are interested the letter furter stated we should contact their attorney Mrs. Alison LeBlanc. We have contacted Mrs. LeBlanc to inform her of our possible interest and she has responded with a very general letter.

Under section VI, part B, of our by laws clearly states the procedures where by this Institution can make such land purchases. Please ladies and gentlemen turn in your copies to that section. And you will note that the procedures and guide lines are stated simply & clearly. None of these tenants as far as I can see will be violated by said proposed purchase of land. Does any one have any comment? Or disagreement?

Alright let us continue. Section VII, part E requires that we request bids from contractor's and except the lowest one, provided that the firm offering that low bid is one of fare reputation and solid credentials. This step of course would come farther along in this process and we need not take to much time to discuss that tonight. We're all I'd imagine familiar with the process; nonetheless it must be kept in mind.

Finally, I want to remind every one here that building this proposed business center will effect the number of student's we are able to attract to this institution. We must ask outselfs this question -- are we prepared to handle an increase? How many more students are we talking about? A study will have to be made but this will take sometime but we will simply have to wait until the study is made before we can predict the affects of this proposed center.

Not since the early part of the '70's has this institution under taken such as extensive project. Its one that many want although there will be some opposition. In so far as the cost a study is all ready begun and we will have the results of the cost projections by the middle of next month.

Exercises

A. Using rules that you have learned in previous units, choose "a" or "b" as the correct choice in the following exercise.

1. a. & is a virgule

   b. & is an ampersand

2. a. Defendant's Exhibit No. 5

   b. defendant's Exhibit No. 5

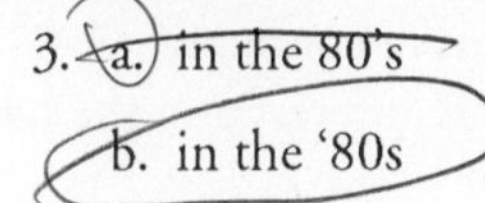

3. a. in the 80's

   b. in the '80s

4. a. Channel Two

   b. Channel 2

5. a. plaster of paris

   b. plaster of Paris

6. a. about 100° Fahrenheit

   b. about 100 degrees Fahrenheit

7. a. Cadillac car

   b. Cadillac Car

8. a. the university of Illinois

   b. the University of Illinois

9. a. his B.S. degree

   b. his B.S. Degree

10. a. the Marines

    b. the marines

11. a. ex-Mayor of Springville

    b. ex-mayor of Springville

12. a. at 10:14 p.m.

    b. at 10:14 P.M.

13. a. 98% accuracy

    b. 98 percent accuracy

14. a. the Catholic church on River Road

    b. the Catholic Church on River Road

15. a. F.B.I.

    b. FBI

16. a. a trip to the Southwest

    b. a trip to the southwest

17. a. the Bible

    b. the bible

18. a. Prof. Smith

    b. Professor Smith

19. a. Day, Hay & May

    b. Day, Hay,& May

20. a. a Caucasian woman

    b. a Caucasian Woman

21. a. in October, 1996

    b. in October 1996

22. a. a U-turn

    b. a u-turn

23. a. on route 16

    b. on Route 16

24. a. a Halloween party

    b. a Halloween Party

25. a 1 Lake Boulevard

    b. One Lake Boulevard

B. When you key this exercise, use the same instructions and guidelines as listed in the Unit 10 exercise.

EXAMINATION CONDUCTED BY MR. LAYY

Q. Clayton will you state your full name for the record please?
A. Clayton Wyatt Rockton.
Q. You are in your 30's.
A. that is correct
Q. You live in what city and state?
A. Beaumont missouri
Q. And the street address is-
A. 708 one-half first Street apartment 8.
Q. Are you married Mr Rockton?
A. Yes sir. My wifes name is Sue Ann Brown-Rockton.
Q. Do you and Sue Ann at this time have any children?
A. No sir.
Q. Are you employed Clayton?
A. Yes. I am emploied at Wayker Construction Company
Q. Does a Mr Wayker own Wayker Construction company?

A. Yes. The owner His name is Dwight Wayker.
Q. Is this Company located in Bowmant?
A. It is along highway 31.
Q. You have worked for Dwight for how many years.
A. 11 years.
Q. your particular job for the Company is an Operator?
A. Yes, sir, that is correct.
Q. On the day of the accident were you operating a peace of equipment for the Company?
A. That is correct sir.
Q. Did the accident happen in the A.M. or the P.M.?
A. It was 10:35 am.

C. As you key the following sentences, you are to include the necessary internal periods, commas, apostrophes,and hyphens. This is a review of what you have learned in Units 1-9.

1. Mr E J Jones Jr is a new realtor in town.
2. Will you close the bedroom door please.
3. Can you come to a 50s party in August?
4. Dan will purchase a T bill with his next paycheck.
5. Ronnie Platz is a first class gentleman.
6. Little Billie Wills has Duchennes disease.
7. Sixty three people attended the lecture.
8. The Christmas parade will start at 9:30 am.
9. Joans exhusband lives in Clearwater Florida.
10. Did you know that Miss Tay has her BS and MS degrees?
11. Do you think Don and Sherry will build an A frame house?
12. Defendants Exhibit No. 4 is a piece of carpet.
13. My neighbor Clint Wood is a member of the US Marine Corps.
14. Anetta will visit Las Vegas Reno and Los Angeles.
15. A trip to Washington DC is scheduled for next spring.
16. Julie Gates an English professor has accepted a position in Oregon.
17. All merchandise in the womens department is on sale this Tuesday.

18. The case of Miland v. Patrick will begin Monday.

19. The answer can be found in Chapter 16 page 6 line 26.

20. I cant find Mary Ruths telephone number.

21. Ann will perform on stage in Atlantic City on September 19 20 21 and 22.

22. Unfortunately she fractured her pelvis when she was skiing in Colorado.

23. The all time record for free throws was set by Mike Spitz.

24. How many Is are in Mississippi?

25. An up to date itinerary is on Mr Blumes desk.

D. Start on line 7 to key this jury charge. Use 1-inch side margins. Double space the material. Make the necessary changes or additions as you key this exercise--punctuation; spelling; one word, two words, hyphenated; etc.

Mr. Foreman and ladies and gentlemen of the jury;

Let me take this opportunity to thank you for spending the passed 2 weeks in my Courtroom. However keep in mind that we are not yet finished with this case.

As a juror you have performed a very important duty for the County and for the State. You should also feel that you personally have performed a very important duty.

As you can sea by looking at the clock on the wall of courtroom a it is almost noon. By the time I finish with my instructions it will be noon. In order for us to move right along at the end of My charge I will have the bailiff escort you jurors to room b hear on the 1st floor of the court house.

Tiffany my court reporter is going to hand Mr. Lane the foreman a pad of paper. I request that each of you right down what you would like to eat for lunch. Tiffany will be going to a fast food business to place the order, It will save time for us to have each of you jurors remain here in the court house. After Tiffany returns to the court house you will be allowed to eat your lunch in room B and to go to the rest room if you need to do so.

If at any time during your deliberations any one of you has a question or needs to go to the rest room just have the foreman Mr. Lane write a note and hand it to the Bailiff.

You jurers are the Judges of the facts and I as the Judge am the judge of the law. You have just herd Mr. Seioy counsel for the Plaintiff and Mr. Jackson council for the defendant give their closing arguments.

Counsel Seioy and counsel Jackson briefly summed up for you a review of the testimony and exhibits that have been presented to this Court. It is your duty to ponder with the leadership of your forman Mr. Lane all the facts and all the evidence that you have witnessed in this Courtroom and either acquit the defendant or find the defendent guilty. After you have done that ladies and gentlemen your decision will be given to the bailiff.

E. On a separate sheet of paper, write down each word that is underlined in this exercise. Write one of the following abbreviations to identify its part of speech: n. for noun; pron. for pronoun; v. for verb; adj. for adjective; adv. for adverb; prep. for preposition; conj. for conjunction; and int. for interjection.

Renovation will begin on the exterior of the Ceely County Courthouse in April or May-- depending on the weather. Lee Painting & Construction Company was unanimously selected by the county board to paint and make minor repairs to the outside of the courthouse. Pakler Roofing Company has been contracted to put on a new roof. The roofing company will be contacted to start the roofing process as soon as the painting company has all of the spray painting completed. Mr. Lee, the owner of Lee Painting & Construction Company, has indicated that, if the weather cooperates, just the spray painting will take four weeks. When it rains or is really windy, that, of course, prolongs the time. A lot of trimming around the windows and doors will take additional time, which is figured in the date of completion in the contract between the county and the company. Lee Painting & Construction Company carries liability insurance. All employees of Mr. Lee are instructed periodically on safety precautions. Also, all of the necessary safeguards for his employees, the public, vehicles, and the building are of the utmost importance to Mr. Lee. For the safety of the public, areas around the courthouse will be blocked off; and rope will also prevent the public from walking right under workers or an area where painting and repairs are being made to the courthouse. At the end of each working day, all equipment will be stored in a fenced area or locked in our trucks and trailers. Oh, if any damage should occur to any vehicle either sitting or passing by due to work performed by the construction company, that individual should report such damage immediately to the foreman or a county official. Lee Painting & Construction Company is a highly reputable company and intends to continue performing services in the future with such a high reputation.

F. In the following passage, make the necessary changes or corrections pertaining to spelling, capitalization, run-on sentences, repeating words, abbreviations, etc. When you type up this exercise, use a 1-inch top and side margins. Double space the material.

The city of Seneca may soon have knew residents and a new business school. A middle aged couple Mr. and mrs. Ray Zeno from the Dallas Dallas area would like to move back to the Seneca area they have several reltives within one hundred miles of Seneca.

Ray and Wilma zeno have been teaching for 20 yrs. and they would like to have there own school. Last July, when they were in in the area on a vacation, they investigated the possibility. They went to the Seneca chamber of Commerce.

Mr. Allen Cox president of the Chamber of Commerce recommended to Mr. and Mrs Zeno to setup an appointment with Mr Ed Dole president of the Seneca Industrial development Committee. The SID Committe is a group of business men in Seneca who try to help a new business locate in the City.

The Real Estate that the Zenos are trying to acquire is located on highway ninety-one and the owners are Doctor and Mrs. Wendall Long and they are going to retire and move to Arizona. Their are twenty acres at the cite which has a too story building on it that is only ten years old. It is a brick building the building has an elevator and it is handicap accessable. There is plenty of parking area around the building too.

The building divided in to offices, had been rented to a cpa, a law firm, a credit Bureau a printing shop, and a beautician. These businesses now have their own buildings. With a few changes class rooms can be set up on both floors of the building

The Dr. and his Wife are asking $100 thousand dollars for the building and the land. Mr. and Mrs. Zeno have talked to the pres. of the Seneca first National Bank about a loan. Noel King president of the bank told Ray and Wilma that the bank would give them a loan for $75,000.00.

They are are scheduled to have one more conferense with the dr. and his wife Mr. & Mrs. Zeno have a down payment of $15,000. They will try to purchase the property by making an offer of $90,000 a business school would be an Asset to the Town and the community.

12
SUGGESTED REFERENCES AND BIBLIOGRAPHY

There are a large number of reference books that cover various specialties, subjects that may arise in the work of a CR. The CR should be familiar with the kinds of reference materials available and be able to make use of them. No one can expect to master the peculiar jargon of every profession; that is why reference materials are so valuable. Wherever the reporter travels, he/she should collect telephone books, city maps, city directories, etc. These sources will be helpful in obtaining spellings, addresses, etc. The following represents a sampling in each category, but only a sampling; there are many more references available.

Suggested References

760

Specialized Documents

Kohler's Dictionary for Accountants, ed. W.W. Cooper, Prentice-Hall.

Jane's Aerospace Dictionary, Bill Gunston, Jane's.

Dictionary of American Slang, Pocket Books, New York.

Dictionary of Architecture and Construction, ed. Cyril M. Harris, McGraw-Hill.

Dictionary of Business and Management, Jerry M. Rosenberg, John Wiley & Sons.

Dictionary of Computers, Data Processing, and Telecommunications, Jerry M. Rosenberg, John Wiley & Sons.

Construction Glossary: An Encyclopedic Reference and Manual, J. Stewart Stein, John Wiley & Sons.

HRC Handbook of Chemistry and Physics: A Ready Reference Book of Chemical and Physical Data, ed. Robert C. Weast, CRS Press, Inc.

McGraw-Hill Dictionary of Earth Sciences, ed. Sybil P. Parker, McGraw-Hill.

The Wiley Engineer's Desk Reference, Sanford I. Heisler, John Wiley & Sons.
McGraw-Hill Dictionary of Engineering, ed. Sybil P. Parker, McGraw-Hill.
Webster's New Geographical Dictionary, O & C Merriam Co.
Concise Dictionary of American History, Thomas C. Cochran and Wayne Andrews, Charles Scribners Sons.
International Maritime Dictionary, Rene de Kerchove, Van Nostrand Reinhold.
Handbook of Physics and Chemistry, ed. Robert C. Weast, Chemical Robber Co.
A Dictionary of Scientific Units, H.G. Jerrard and D.B. McNeill, Chapman and Hall.
The World Almanac and Book of Facts, Doubleday & Co. (published annually).
Columbia Lippincott Gazatteer of the World, Leon E. Seltzer, Columbia University Press.
Complete Dictionary of Abbreviations, Thomas Y. Crowell, New York.
McGraw-Hill Dictionary of Scientific and Technical Terms, McGraw-Hill, New York.
Cambridge Air and Space Dictionary, Cambridge University Press, Cambridge, England.
Dictionary of Naval Abbreviations, compiled and edited by Bill Wedertz, Naval Institute Press, Annapolis, Maryland.
Dictionary of Electronics, Rudolf F. Graf, Howard W. Sams & Co., Indianapolis, Indiana.
Computer Dictionary and Handbook, Charles J. Sippl and Charles P. Sippl, Howard W. Sams & Company, Indianapolis, Indiana.
The Condensed Chemical Dictionary, Gessner G. Hawley, Van Nostrand Reinhold Company, New York.
IEEE Standard Dictionary of Electrical and Electronics Terms, Institute of Electrical and Electronics Engineers, Inc., New York.
Bookman's Glossary, ed. Jean Peters, R.R. Bowker, New York (Terminology of printers, publishing, graphic arts).
Index Medicus, National Library of Medicine, Bethesda, Maryland.

761 Medical References

Blakiston's New Gould Medical Dictionary, The Blakiston Company, Philadelphia, Pennsylvania.
The Reverse Medical Secretary, Richard Franks, Medical Economics Company, New Jersey.
Harbeck's Glossary of Medical Terms, Pacific Coast Publishers and Drug Topics Red Book.

The Pharmacist's Guide To Products And Prices, American Pharmaceutical Association.

Nelson's New Compact Medical Dictionary, Thomas Nelson Inc., Publishers, Nashville, Tennessee.

Webster's Medical Speller (Second Edition; 35,000 Medical words spelled and divided), Merriam-Webster Inc., Springfield, Massachusetts.

The Medical & Health Sciences Word Book (More than 60,000 terms), Houghton Mifflin Company, Boston, Massachusetts.

The Language of Medicine: A Guide for Stenotypists, Elsa Swanson Cooper, Medical Economics Company Book Division, Oradell, New Jersey.

Psychiatric Dictionary, Leland E. Hinsie and Robert Jean Campbell, Oxford University Press.

Physicians' Desk Reference, Jack E. Angel, Medical Economics Co.

The Encyclopedia of Medical Tests, Cathy Pinckney and Edward Pinckney, Facts on File, Inc.

Dorland's Illustrated Medical Dictionary, W.B. Saunders Co.

Stedman's Medical Dictionary: Illustrated, ed. T.L. Stedman, Williams & Wilkins Co.

The Merck Index: An Encyclopedia of Chemicals, Drugs, and Biologicals, ed. Martha Windholz, Merck & Co.

Taber's Cyclopedic Medical Dictionary, ed. Clayton L. Thomas, F.A. Davis Co.

Human Physiology, R.F. Schmidt and O. Thews, Springer-Verlag.

Webster's Medical Desk Dictionary, Merriam-Webster, Springfield, Massachusetts.

AMA Style Book and Editorial Manual, Chicago American Medical Association.

Publication Manual of the American Psychological Association, Washington D.C., American Psychological Association.

762 **Information on Published Materials**

Books in Print: An Author-Title-Series Index to the Publishers' Trade List Annual, R.R. Bowker Co. (published annually in two volumes).

Reader's Guide to Periodical Literature, H.W. Wilson Co.

Cumulative Book Index, H.W. Wilson Co.

British Books in Print, J. Whitaker & Sons, England.

Research in Archives, Philip C. Brooks, University of Chicago Press, Chicago.

British Official Publications, John E. Pemberton, Pergamon Press, Oxford and New York.

Goverment Publications and Their Use, Brookings Institution, Washington, D.C.

Guide to Reference Books, compiled by Eugene P. Sheehy, American Library Association, Chicago, Illinois.

763 **Information on People and Associations**

Dictionary of National Biography, Oxford University Press.

Dictionary of American Biography, Charles Scribners Sons.

Current Biography, H.W. Wilson Co.

Webster's Biographical Dictionary: A Dictionary of Names of Noteworthy Persons With Pronunciations and Concise Biographies, G & C Merriam Co.

Who's Who in America: A Biographical Dictionary of Notable Living Men and Women, A.N. Marquis Co. (revised and reissued biennially).

Official Congressional Directory, U.S. Government Printing Office.

Encyclopedia of Associations, Gale Research Co.

American Men and Women of Science: Physical and Biological Sciences, Jaques Cattell Press, ed. R.R. Bowker, New York.

American Men and Women of Science: Social and Behavioral Sciences, Jaques Cattell Press, ed. R.R. Bowker, New York.

Dictionary of American Scholars, ed. Jaques Cattell Press, R.R. Bowker, New York.

International Who's Who, Europa Publications, London (published annually).

Who's Who: An Annual Biographical Dictionary, St. Martin's Press, New York.

764 **Grammar and Punctuation**

The Careful Writer: A Modern Guide to English Usage, Theodore M. Bernstein, Atheneum.

A Dictionary of Modern English Usage, H.W. Fowler, Clarendon Press.

Conquer the Comma, D. Finley, GCS, Inc.

Help With the Hyphen, D. Finley, GCS, Inc.

Precision With Word Division, D. Finley, OCS, Inc.

Harbrace College Handbook, J.C. Hodges and M.E. Whitten, Harcourt Brace Jovanovich.

An English Guide for Court Reporters, Lillian Morson, Vantage Press.

English for the Shorthand Reporter, National Shorthand Reporters Association.

Writer's Guide and Index to English, Porter G. Perrin, Scott, Foresman & Co.

Practice in English, Elwood L. Prestwood, Houghton Mifflin Co.

Words Into Type, Marjorie E. Skillin, Robert M. Gay, et al., Appleton-Century-Crofts.

Grammar for Shorthand Reporters, Irwin Weiss, National Court Reporters Association.

Punctuation for Shorthand Reporters, Nathaniel Weiss, National Court Reporters Association.

A Manual of Style, The University of Chicago Press.

Errors in English and Ways to Correct Them, Harry Shaw, Barnes & Noble.

A Pocket Guide To Correct English (Second Edition 1990), Michael Temple, Barron's Educational Series, Inc., New York.

Modern American Usage: A Guide by Wilson Follett, Grossett and Dunlap, New York.

The New York Times Manual of Style and Usage: A Desk Book of Guidelines for Writers and Editors, revised and edited by Lewis Jordan, Quadrangle/New York Times Book Co., New York.

The Elements of Style, W. Strunk, Jr. and E.B. White, MacMillan, New York.

Style Manual, U.S. Government Printing Office, Washington, D.C.

On Writing Well: An Informal Guide to Writing Nonfiction, William Zinsser, Harper & Row, New York.

765 General Dictionaries and Word Books

20,000 Words, Louis A. Leslie, Gregg Division/McGraw-Hill.

Webster's New Dictionary of Synonyms, G & C Merriam Co.

The Complete Dictionary of Abbreviations, Robert J. Schwartz, Thomas Y. Crowell Co.

ACRONYMS, Initialisms, and Abbreviations Dictionary, ed. Ellen T. Crowley and Helen E. Sheppard, Gale Research Co.

The Random House Dictionary of the English Language, Random House.

The American Heritage Dictionary of the English Language, American Heritage Publishing Co. and Houghton Mifflin Co.

The American College Dictionary, Random House.

The Word Book II, 40,000, Houghton Mifflin, Boston, Massachusetts.

Webster's Third New International Dictionary of the English Language, Unabridged, G & C Merriam Co.

Webster's New World Dictionary of the American Language, William Collins Publishers.

Webster's Ninth New Collegiate Dictionary, Merriam-Webster.

6,000 Words: A Supplement to Webster's International Dictionary, Merriam-Webster, Springfield, Massachusetts.

Roget's International Thesaurus, Harper & Row, New York.

The Complete Plain Words, Sir Bruce Frasier, Penguin Books, Baltimore, Maryland.
Glossary of Astronomy and Astrophysics, University of Chicago Press.
Concise Dictionary of American History, Thomas C. Cochran and Wayne Andrews, eds., Charles Scribner's Sons, New York.

766 **Legal Terminology**

Black's Law Dictionary, Henry C. Black, West Publishing Co.
Stroud's Judicial Dictionary of Words and Phrases, John S. James, Sweet and Maxwell, Ltd.
Legal Studies, to Wit: Basic Legal Terminology and Transcription, Wanda Walker Roderick, South-Western Publishing Co.
Law Dictionary, Steven H. Gifis, Barron's Educational Series, Inc.
Cochran's Law Lexicon, W.H. Anderson Company, Cincinnati, Ohio.
Legal Terminology, A Programmed Approach, Mary H. Knapp, John Wiley & Sons, Inc., New York.
Webster's Legal Speller (28,000 Legal words spelled and divided), Merriam-Webster Inc., Springfield, Massachusetts.
Legal Words and Phrases: Speed Abbreviations, Joel Larus, Aurico Publishing Company, Boston, Massachusetts.
A Uniform System of Citation, Harvard Law Review Association, Cambridge, Massachusetts.

767 **Atlases and Gazettes**

Hammond's Ambassador World Atlas, C.S. Hammond & Company, Maplewood, New Jersey.
World Atlas, Rand-McNally, New York.
Encyclopedia Britannica World Atlas, Encyclopedia Britannica, Chicago, Illinois.
Columbia Sippincott Gazetteer of the World, ed. Leon E. Seltzer, Columbia University Press, New York.

768 **Encyclopedias**

Encyclopedia Britannica, Encyclopedia Britannica, Inc., Chicago, Illinois.
Columbia-Viking Desk Encyclopedia (two volumes), Viking Press, New York.
Lincoln Library of Essential Information, The Frontier Press, Buffalo, New York.
Grolier Encyclopedia, The Grolier Society, New York.
The International Geographic Encyclopedia and Atlas, Houghton Mifflin Co.

769 Miscellaneous Publications and Books

The Kelley Blue Book—Automobile Market Report, Kelley Blue Book Company, Costa Mesa, California.

Bible

The Encyclopedia of Etiquette, Crown Publishers, New York.

Hotel Red Book, American Hotel Association Directory Corporation, New York.

N.W. Ayers & Sons' Dictionary of Newspapers & Periodicals, N.W. Ayers & Sons, Philadelphia, Pennsylvania.

Robert's Rules of Order, Revised Edition, H.M. Robert, William Morrow & Company, New York.

United States Directory of Post Offices, Publication No. 26, Superintendent of Documents, GPO, Washington, D.C.

Thomas' Register of American Manufacturers, Thomas Publishing Company, New York.

Familiar Quotations, John Bartlett, Little, Brown & Company, Boston Massachusetts.

Roget's International Thesaurus, Harper & Row, New York.

Reporter's Desk References, National Shorthand Reporters Association, Vienna, Virginia.

6,000 Soundalikes, Look-Alikes, And Other Words Often Confused, 1989, National Court Reporters Association.

One Word, Two Words, Hyphenated ? Mary Louise Gilman, 1989, National Court Reporters Association.

Reference Manual For The Office (7th Edition), 1989, House and Sigler, South-Western Publishing Company, Cincinnati, Ohio.

The Gregg Reference Manual (6th Edition), William A. Sabin, 1985, Gregg Division/McGraw-Hill Book Company.

National Five-Digit Zip Code & Post Office Directory, Publication 65, U.S. Postal Service (annual publication).

World Almanac and Book of Facts, Doubleday, New York.

Bibliography

Finley, D. *Conquer the Comma!* Lake Park, Florida: OCS, Inc., 1978.——. *Help With the Hyphen.* Lake Park, Florida: OCS, Inc. 1978. ——. *Precision With Word Division.* Lake Park, Florida: GCS, Inc., 1978.

Freer, Carolee. *Computer Shorthand: Speed Building and Transcription.* New York: John Wiley & Sons, 1984.

French, Christopher W., Eileen A. Powell, and Howard Angione (eds.). *The Associated Press Stylebook and Libel Manual.* Reading, Massachusetts: Addison-Wesley Publishing Co., 1980.

Gordon, Frank S., Thomas M.S. Hemnes, and Charles E. Weinstein. *The Legal Word Book,* 2d ed. Boston: Houghton Mifflin Co., 1982.

Hodges, J.C., and M.E. Whitten. *Harbrace College Handbook,* 9th ed. New York: Harcourt Brace Jovanovich, 1982.

Lidell, Theo C. *Basic Language: Messages and Meanings.* New York: Harper & Row, 1983.

Morson, Lillian. *An English Guide for Court Reporters.* New York: Vantage Press, 1974.

National Court Reporters Association. *English for the Shorthand Reporter.* Vienna, Virginia: National Shorthand Reporters Association, 1975.

Perry, Devern. *College Vocabulary Building,* 7th ed. Cincinnati: South-Western Publishing Co., 1983.

——, and J.E. Silverton. *Word Division Manual,* 3d ed. Cincinnati: South-Western Publishing Co., 1984.

Prestwood, Elwood L., and Bertha Handlan Campbell. *Practice in English.* Boston: Houghton Mifflin Co., 1979.

Sachs, H.J., H.M. Brown, and P.J. Canavan. *Practical English Workbook.* New York: D. Van Nostrand Company, 1978.

Shaw, Harry. *Errors in English and Ways to Correct Them,* 2d ed. New York: Barnes & Noble, 1970.

The University of Chicago Press. *A Manual of Style,* 12th ed. New York: University of Chicago Press, 1969.

Webster's Ninth New Collegiate Dictionary. Springfield, Massachusetts: Merriam-Webster, 1985.

Weiss, Irwin. *Grammar for Shorthand Reporters.* Vienna, Virginia: National Court Reporters Association, 1978.

Weiss, Nathaniel. *Punctuation for Court Reporters.* Vienna, Virginia: National Court Reporters Association, 1971.

INDEX

Numbers refer to paragraph numbers.

B

C

Numbers refer to paragraph numbers.

Numbers refer to paragraph numbers.

O

P

Numbers refer to paragraph numbers.

Q

R

S

T

U

V